ENCYCLOPAEDIA OF INTEREST FREE BANKING: BANKING IN ISLAM

ENCYCLOPAEDIA OF INTEREST FREE BANKING: BANKING IN ISLAM

D.R. Joshi

CYBER TECH PUBLICATIONS
4264/3, Ansari Road, Daryaganj, New Delhi-110002 (India)
Ph.: 011-23244078, 011-43559448 Fax: 011-23280028
E-Mail: cyberpublicationsdelhi@yahoo.com
Website: www.cybertechpublications.com

ENCYCLOPAEDIA OF INTEREST FREE BANKING: BANKING IN ISLAM

D.R. Joshi

First Edition 2010

Published by :

G.S. Rawat for **Cyber Tech Publications**

4264/3, Ansari Road, Daryaganj, New Delhi-110002 (India)

Ph.: 011-23244078, 011-43559448 Fax: 011-23280028

E-Mail: cyberpublicationsdelhi@yahoo.com

Website: www.cybertechpublications.com

Printed at: Asian Offset Printers, Delhi-53

Preface

Islam was the basis of creation of our country and we call it Islamic Republic of Pakistan. But tragically until now writ of un-Islamic laws inherited from foreign rulers has not ceased to run and the writ of Islam runs nowhere in any walk of life in the country. Interest which is strictly forbidden in Quraan and most vehemently condemned by our Prophet Muhammad *s.a.w.s.* has not only persisted in our economy but has also consistently been promoted by our rulers so much so that even those who avoid it cannot escape from afflictions of inflation and unemployment resulting from it. Perhaps ours is the time about which our Prophet Muhammad *s.a.w.s.* predicted "a time will come when all people will consume interest and if somebody will not consume it, its smoke and steam shall reach him".

That prohibition of interest in all its forms old and new is strict, absolute and unambiguous is the unanimous view held throughout by eminent Muslim scholars of the past and present. Not a single Muslim scholar of high calibre has ever disagreed with this view. There is complete agreement among all Islamic sects that interest is *Riba* and that it must be abolished. Only those who do not study Islamic literature on the subject and have not attained any knowledge about the customs and trade practices prevalent in the Arab society in the pre-Islamic days and the changes brought about by Islamic teachings, and who are subdued with Western culture and capitalist system tend to contest the above unanimous view held throughout by the Muslim Ummah.

Baseless contentions of the advocates of interest belied by logic and historical evidence have all been repelled time and again by eminent Muslim scholars and economists. Now the only relevant question in this context which requires an answer is how to eliminate interest from the banking system. A satisfactory answer to this question with illustration of practical methodology is given in this booklet.

Our economy managers do not utter a word about abolishing interest which is held by eminent economists to be the main cause of inflation and unemployment and which has ruined the country's economy to such an extent that even for paying interest on outstanding debts we have to beg for fresh loans and when a fresh loan is doled out to us for meeting a debt commitment it is pronounced to be a proof of recovery of economy whereas it is in fact drowning ever deep into the morass of foreign debt. A news item appeared in the press on 13 July'98 reading "Government says it may have to consider calling a moratorium on debt repayments unless sanctions are lifted. Finance Minister

Sartaj Aziz says sanctions have deprived Pakistan of about $1.5 billion or half the money it requires to service its total debt every year".

Our Prime Minister admitting interest to be an act of war against Allah and His Rasool *s.a.w.s* committed to abolish it in a public speech on 31 March'97. Alas! nothing has so far been done about it and this subject was not even mentioned in our Finance Minister's so called Economic Reform Agenda and Prime Minister's National Agenda for Self-Reliance announced on 11 June'98.

In my previous book 'INTEREST IS RIBA' I explained at length why interest should be abolished. My whole argument and correspondence with advocates of interest reproduced in the book were based on the writings of eminent economists, philosophers and highly learned scholars who had spent lifetimes in intensive studies of Quraan and Sunnah. The advocates of interest with whom I corresponded could not reply my objections to their invalid contentions.

Unfortunately most of the independent economists who write frequently in the press and analyze country's economic situation with precision deal with symptoms of the sick economy but do not address the core disease and real cause of downward slide of our economy nor do they give any solution of the problem. Apparently like our rulers and economy managers they are also so much subdued with Western capitalist system based on interest that they do not ever make any mention of its adverse effects on the economy. If they give serious thought and unbiased consideration to evolve a solution for taking the country out of the economic crisis I am sure they will agree with my submissions and plead for elimination of interest from the economy.

I wish and pray our rulers and economy managers do realize that so long as interest persists perennial inflation and rising unemployment cannot be arrested what to say of bringing any improvement in the shattered economy. I invite those in the government concerned with this matter who disagree with the above view and who insist on sustaining interest in the banking system, to have a meaningful discussion with me on the subject and for this purpose I offer to travel at my own expense at any time and to any place of their choice.

—Author

Contents

1

Introduction

Islamic banking refers to a system of banking or banking activity that is consistent with the principles of Islamic law (*Sharia*) and its practical application through the development of Islamic economics. Sharia prohibits the payment of fees for the renting of money (Riba, usury) for specific terms, as well as investing in businesses that provide goods or services considered contrary to its principles (Haraam, forbidden). While these principles were used as the basis for a flourishing economy in earlier times, it is only in the late 20th century that a number of Islamic banks were formed to apply these principles to private or semi-private commercial institutions within the Muslim community.

HISTORY OF ISLAMIC BANKING

Classical Islamic Banking

During the Islamic Golden Age, early forms of proto-capitalism and free markets were present in the Caliphate, where an early market economy and an early form of mercantilism were developed between the 8th-12th centuries, which some refer to as "Islamic capitalism". A vigorous monetary economy was created on the basis of the expanding levels of circulation of a stable high-value currency (the dinar) and the integration of monetary areas that were previously independent. A number of innovative concepts and techniques were introduced in early Islamic banking, including bills of exchange, the first forms of partnership (*mufawada*) such as limited partnerships (*mudaraba*), and the earliest forms of capital (*al-mal*), capital accumulation (*nama al-mal*), cheques, promissory notes, trusts (see *Waqf*), startup companies, , transactional accounts, loaning, ledgers and assignments. Organizational enterprises similar to corporations independent from the state also existed in the medieval Islamic world, while the agency institution was also introduced. Many of these early capitalist concepts were adopted and further advanced in medieval Europe from the 13th century onwards.

Riba

The definition of *riba* in classical Islamic jurisprudence was "surplus value without counterpart." or "to ensure equivalency in real value" and that "numerical value was immaterial." During this period, gold and silver currencies were the benchmark metals that defined the value of all other materials being traded. Applying interest to the benchmark itself (*ex natura sua*) made no logical sense as its value remained constant relative to all other materials: these metals could be added to but not created (from nothing).Applying interest was acceptable under some circumstances. Currencies that were based on guarantees by a government to honor the stated value (i.e. fiat currency) or based on other materials such as paper or base metals were allowed to have interest applied to them. When base metal currencies were first introduced in the Islamic world, no jurist ever thought that "paying a debt in a higher number of units of this *fiat* money was *riba*" as they were concerned with the real value of money (determined by weight only) rather than the numerical value. For example, it was acceptable for a loan of 1000 gold dinars to be paid back as 1050 dinars of equal aggregate weight (i.e., the value in terms of weight had to be same because all makes of coins did not carry exactly similar weight).

Modern Islamic Banking

The first modern experiment with Islamic banking was undertaken in Egypt under cover without projecting an Islamic image—for fear of being seen as a manifestation of Islamic fundamentalism that was anathema to the political regime. The pioneering effort, led by Ahmad Elnaggar, took the form of a savings bank based on profit-sharing in the Egyptian town of Mit Ghamr in 1963. This experiment lasted until 1967 (Ready 1981), by which time there were nine such banks in the country.

In 1972, the Mit Ghamr Savings project became part of Nasr Social Bank which, till date, is still in business in Egypt. In 1975, the Islamic Development Bank was set-up with the mission to provide funding to projects in the member countries. The first modern commercial Islamic bank, Dubai Islamic Bank, opened its doors in 1975. In the early years, the products offered were basic and strongly founded on conventional banking products, but in the last few years the industry is starting to see strong development in new products and services.

Islamic Banking is growing at a rate of 10-15% per year and with signs of consistent future growth. Islamic banks have more than 300 institutions spread over 51 countries, plus an additional 250 mutual funds that comply with the Islamic principles. The relative stability of Islamic banking institutions in current recession has gained it attention. Even The Vatican said banks should look at the rules of Islamic finance to restore confidence amongst their clients at a time of global economic crisis. The World Islamic Banking Conference, held annually in Bahrain since 1994, is internationally recognized as the largest and most significant gathering of Islamic banking and finance leaders in the world.

Principles

Islamic banking has the same purpose as conventional banking except that it operates in accordance with the rules of Shariah, known as *Fiqh al-Muamalat* (Islamic rules on transactions). The basic principle of Islamic banking is the sharing of profit and loss and the prohibition of *riba* (usury). Amongst the common Islamic concepts used in Islamic banking are profit sharing (*Mudharabah*), safekeeping (*Wadiah*), joint venture (*Musharakah*), cost plus (*Murabahah*), and leasing (*Ijarah*).

In an Islamic mortgage transaction, instead of loaning the buyer money to purchase the item, a bank might buy the item itself from the seller, and re-sell it to the buyer at a profit, while allowing the buyer to pay the bank in installments. However, the fact that it is profit cannot be made explicit and therefore there are no additional penalties for late payment. In order to protect itself against default, the bank asks for strict collateral. The goods or land is registered to the name of the buyer from the start of the transaction. This arrangement is called *Murabaha*. Another approach is *ElJara wa ElqtIna*, which is similar to real estate leasing. Islamic banks handle loans for vehicles in a similar way (selling the vehicle at a higher-than-market price to the debtor and then retaining ownership of the vehicle until the loan is paid).

An innovative approach applied by some banks for home loans, called *Musharaka al-Mutanaqisa*, allows for a floating rate in the form of rental. The bank and borrower forms a partnership entity, both providing capital at an agreed percentage to purchase the property. The partnership entity then rent out the property to the borrower and charges rent. The bank and the borrower will then share the proceed from this rent based on the current equity share of the partnership. At the same time, the borrower in the partnership entity also buys the bank's share on the property at agreed installments until the full equity is transferred to the borrower and the partnership is ended. If default occurs, both the bank and the borrower receives the proceeds from an auction based on the current equity. This method allows for floating rates according to current market rate such as the BLR (base lending rate), especially in a dual-banking system like in Malaysia.

There are several other approaches used in business deals. Islamic banks lend their money to companies by issuing floating rate interest loans. The floating rate of interest is pegged to the company's individual rate of return. Thus the bank's profit on the loan is equal to a certain percentage of the company's profits. Once the principal amount of the loan is repaid, the profit-sharing arrangement is concluded. This practice is called *Musharaka*. Further, *Mudaraba* is venture capital funding of an entrepreneur who provides labor while financing is provided by the bank so that both profit and risk are shared. Such participatory arrangements between capital and labor reflect the Islamic view that the borrower must not bear all the risk/cost of a failure, resulting in a balanced distribution of income and not allowing lender to monopolize the economy.

And finally, Islamic banking is restricted to Islamically acceptable deals, which exclude those involving alcohol, pork, gambling, etc. Thus ethical investing is the only acceptable form of investment, and moral purchasing is encouraged. In theory, Islamic banking is an example of full-reserve banking, with banks achieving a 100% reserve ratio. However, in practice, this is not the case, and no examples of 100 per cent reserve banking are observed. Islamic banks have grown recently in the Muslim world but are a very small share of the global banking system. Micro-lending institutions founded by Muslims, notably Grameen Bank, use conventional lending practices and are popular in some Muslim nations, especially Bangladesh, but some do not consider them true Islamic banking. However, Muhammad Yunus, the founder of Grameen Bank and microfinance banking, and other supporters of microfinance, argue that the lack of collateral and lack of excessive interest in micro-lending is consistent with the Islamic prohibition of usury (riba).

Shariah Advisory Council/Consultant

Islamic banks and banking institutions that offer Islamic banking products and services (IBS banks) are required to establish Shariah advisory committees/consultants to advise them and to ensure that the operations and activities of the bank comply with Shariah principles. On the other hand, there are also those who believe that no form of banking can ever comply with the shariah. In Malaysia, the National Shariah Advisory Council, which additionally set up at Bank Negara Malaysia (BNM), advises BNM on the Shariah aspects of the operations of these institutions and on their products and services. (See: Islamic banking in Malaysia) A number of Sharia advisory firms (like BMB Islamic) have now emerged to offer Sharia advisory services to the institutions offering Islamic financial services.

ISLAMIC FINANCIAL TRANSACTION TERMINOLOGY

Bai' al-Inah (Sale and Buy Back Agreement)

The financier sells an asset to the customer on a deferred-payment basis, and then the asset is immediately repurchased by the financier for cash at a discount. The buying back agreement allows the bank to assume ownership over the asset in order to protect against default without explicitly charging interest in the event of late payments or insolvency. Some scholars believe that this is not compliant with Shariah principles.

Bai' Bithaman Ajil (Deferred Payment Sale)

This concept refers to the sale of goods on a deferred payment basis at a price, which includes a profit margin agreed to by both parties. This is similar to Murabahah, except that the debtor makes only a single installment on the maturity date of the loan. By the application of a discount rate, an Islamic bank can collect the market rate of interest.

Bai muajjal (Credit Sale)

Literally *bai muajjal* means a credit sale. Technically, it is a financing technique adopted by Islamic banks that takes the form of murabaha muajjal. It is a contract in which the bank earns a profit margin on the purchase price and allows the buyer to pay the price of the commodity at a future date in a lump sum or in installments. It has to expressly mention cost of the commodity and the margin of profit is mutually agreed. The price fixed for the commodity in such a transaction can be the same as the spot price or higher or lower than the spot price.

Mudarabah (Profit Sharing)

Mudarabah is an arrangement or agreement between the bank, or a capital provider, and an entrepreneur, whereby the entrepreneur can mobilize the funds of the former for its business activity. The entrepreneur provides expertise, labor and management. Profits made are shared between the bank and the entrepreneur according to predetermined ratio. In case of loss, the bank loses the capital, while the entrepreneur loses his provision of labor. It is this financial risk, according to the Shariah, that justifies the bank's claim to part of the profit. The profit-sharing continues until the loan is repaid. The bank is compensated for the time value of its money in the form of a floating rate that is pegged to the debtor's profits.

Murabahah (Cost Plus)

This concept refers to the sale of goods at a price, which includes a profit margin agreed to by both parties. The purchase and selling price, other costs, and the profit margin must be clearly stated at the time of the sale agreement. The bank is compensated for the time value of its money in the form of the profit margin. This is a fixed-income loan for the purchase of a real asset (such as real estate or a vehicle), with a fixed rate of profit determined by the profit margin. The bank is not compensated for the time value of money outside of the contracted term (i.e., the bank cannot charge additional profit on late payments); however, the asset remains as a mortgage with the bank until the Murabaha is paid in full.

This type of transaction is similar to rent-to-own arrangements for furniture or appliances that are very common in North American stores.

Musawamah

Musawamah is the negotiation of a selling price between two parties without reference by the seller to either costs or asking price. While the seller may or may not have full knowledge of the cost of the item being negotiated, they are under no obligation to reveal these costs as part of the negotiation process. This difference in obligation by the seller is the key distinction between Murabaha and Musawamah with all other rules as described in Murabaha remaining the same. Musawamah is the most common type of trading negotiation seen in Islamic commerce.

Bai salam

Bai salam means a contract in which advance payment is made for goods to be delivered later on. The seller undertakes to supply some specific goods to the buyer at a future date in exchange of an advance price fully paid at the time of contract. It is necessary that the quality of the commodity intended to be purchased is fully specified leaving no ambiguity leading to dispute. The objects of this sale are goods and cannot be gold, silver, or currencies based on these metals. Barring this, Bai Salam covers almost everything that is capable of being definitely described as to quantity, quality, and workmanship.

Basic Features and Conditions of Salam

1. The transaction is considered Salam if the buyer has paid the purchase price to the seller in full at the time of sale. This is necessary so that the buyer can show that they are not entering into debt with a second party in order to eliminate the debt with the first party, an act prohibited under Sharia. The idea of Salam is to provide a mechanism that ensures that the seller has the liquidity they expected from entering into the transaction in the first place. If the price were not paid in full, the basic purpose of the transaction would have been defeated. Muslim jurists are unanimous in their opinion that full payment of the purchase price is key for Salam to exist. Imam Malik is also of the opinion that the seller may defer accepting the funds from the buyer for two or three days, but this delay should not form part of the agreement.
2. Salam can be effected in those commodities only the quality and quantity of which can be specified exactly. The things whose quality or quantity is not determined by specification cannot be sold through the contract of salam. For example, precious stones cannot be sold on the basis of salam, because every piece of precious stones is normally different from the other either in its quality or in its size or weight and their exact specification is not generally possible.
3. Salam cannot be effected on a particular commodity or on a product of a particular field or farm. For example, if the seller undertakes to supply the wheat of a particular field, or the fruit of a particular tree, the salam will not be valid, because there is a possibility that the crop of that particular field or the fruit of that tree is destroyed before delivery, and, given such possibility, the delivery remains uncertain. The same rule is applicable to every commodity the supply of which is not certain.
4. It is necessary that the quality of the commodity (intended to be purchased through salam) is fully specified leaving no ambiguity which may lead to a dispute. All the possible details in this respect must be expressly mentioned.
5. It is also necessary that the quantity of the commodity is agreed upon in unequivocal terms. If the commodity is quantified in weights according to the usage of its traders, its weight must be determined, and if it is quantified through measures, its exact measure should be known. What is normally weighed cannot be quantified in measures and vice versa.

6. The exact date and place of delivery must be specified in the contract.
7. Salam cannot be effected in respect of things which must be delivered at spot. For example, if gold is purchased in exchange of silver, it is necessary, according to Shari'ah, that the delivery of both be simultaneous. Here, salam cannot work. Similarly, if wheat is bartered for barley, the simultaneous delivery of both is necessary for the validity of sale. Therefore the contract of salam in this case is not allowed.

Hibah (Gift)

This is a token given voluntarily by a debtor to a creditor in return for a loan. Hibah usually arises in practice when Islamic banks voluntarily pay their customers a 'gift' on savings account balances, representing a portion of the profit made by using those savings account balances in other activities.

It is important to note that while it appears similar to interest, and may, in effect, have the same outcome, Hibah is a voluntary payment made (or not made) at the bank's discretion, and cannot be 'guaranteed.' However, the opportunity of receiving high Hibah will draw in customers' savings, providing the bank with capital necessary to create its profits; if the ventures are profitable, then some of those profits may be gifted back to its customers as Hibah.

Ijarah

Ijarah means lease, rent or wage. Generally, Ijarah concept means selling benefit or use or service for a fixed price or wage. Under this concept, the Bank makes available to the customer the use of service of assets / equipments such as plant, office automation, motor vehicle for a fixed period and price.

Advantages of Ijarah

Ijarah provides the following advantages to the Lessee:

Ijarah conserves the Lessee' capital since it allows up to 100% financing.

Ijarah gives the Lessee the right to access the equipment on payment of the first installment. This is important as it is the access and use (and not ownership) of equipment that generates income.

Ijarah arrangements aid corporate planning and budgeting by allowing the negotiation of flexible terms.

Ijarah is not considered Debt Financing so it does not appear on the Lessee' Balance Sheet as a Liability. This method of "off-balance-sheet" financing means that it is not included in the Debt Ratios used by bankers to determine financing limits. This allows the Lessee to enter into other lease financing arrangements without impacting his overall debt rating.

All payments towards Ijarah contracts are treated as operating expenses and are therefore fully tax-deductible. Leasing thus offers tax-advantages to for-profit operations.

Many types of equipment (i.e computers) become obsolete before the end of their actual economic life. Ijarah contracts allow the transfer of risk from the Lesse to the Lessor in exchange for a higher lease rate. This higher rate can be viewed as insurance against obsolescence.

If the equipment is used for a relatively short period of time, it may be more profitable to lease than to buy.

If the equipment is used for a short period but has a very poor resale value, leasing avoids having to account for and depreciate the equipment under normal accounting principles.

Ijarah Thumma Al Bai' (Hire Purchase)

Parties enter into contracts that come into effect serially, to form a complete lease/ buyback transaction. The first contract is an *Ijarah* that outlines the terms for leasing or renting over a fixed period, and the second contract is a *Bai* that triggers a sale or purchase once the term of the Ijarah is complete. For example, in a car financing facility, a customer enters into the first contract and leases the car from the owner (bank) at an agreed amount over a specific period. When the lease period expires, the second contract comes into effect, which enables the customer to purchase the car at an agreed to price.

The bank generates a profit by determining in advance the cost of the item, its residual value at the end of the term and the time value or profit margin for the money being invested in purchasing the product to be leased for the intended term. The combining of these three figures becomes the basis for the contract between the Bank and the client for the initial lease contract.

This type of transaction is similar to the contractum trinius, a legal maneuver used by European bankers and merchants during the Middle Ages to sidestep the Church's prohibition on interest bearing loans. In a contractum, two parties would enter into three concurrent and interrelated legal contracts, the net effect being the paying of a fee for the use of money for the term of the loan. The use of concurrent interrelated contracts is also prohibited under Shariah Law.

Ijarah-Wal-Iqtina

A contract under which an *Islamic bank* provides equipment, building, or other assets to the client against an agreed rental together with a unilateral undertaking by the bank or the client that at the end of the lease period, the ownership in the asset would be transferred to the lessee. The undertaking or the promise does not become an integral part of the lease contract to make it conditional. The rentals as well as the purchase price are fixed in such manner that the bank gets back its principal sum along with profit over the period of lease.

Musharakah (Joint Venture)

Musharakah is a relationship between two parties or more, of whom contribute capital to a business, and divide the net profit and loss pro rata.

This is often used in investment projects, letters of credit, and the purchase or real estate or property. In the case of real estate or property, the bank assess an imputed rent and will share it as agreed in advance.

All providers of capital are entitled to participate in management, but not necessarily required to do so. The profit is distributed among the partners in pre-agreed ratios, while the loss is borne by each partner strictly in proportion to respective capital contributions. This concept is distinct from fixed-income investing (i.e. issuance of loans).

Qard Hassan (Good Loan)

This is a loan extended on a goodwill basis, and the debtor is only required to repay the amount borrowed. However, the debtor may, at his or her discretion, pay an extra amount beyond the principal amount of the loan (without promising it) as a token of appreciation to the creditor.

In the case that the debtor does not pay an extra amount to the creditor, this transaction is a true interest-free loan. Some Muslims consider this to be the only type of loan that does not violate the prohibition on riba, since it is the one type of loan that truly does not compensate the creditor for the time value of money.

Sukuk (Islamic Bonds)

Main article: Sukuk

Sukuk is the Arabic name for a financial certificate but can be seen as an Islamic equivalent of bond. However, fixed-income, interest-bearing bonds are not permissible in Islam. Hence, Sukuk are securities that comply with the Islamic law (Shariah) and its investment principles, which prohibit the charging or paying of interest. Financial assets that comply with the Islamic law can be classified in accordance with their tradability and non-tradability in the secondary markets.

Conservative estimates suggest that over US$500 billion of assets are managed according to Islamic investment principles.

Takaful (Islamic Insurance)

Takaful is an alternative form of cover that a Muslim can avail himself against the risk of loss due to misfortunes. Takaful is based on the idea that what is uncertain with respect to an individual may cease to be uncertain with respect to a very large number of similar individuals. Insurance by combining the risks of many people enables each individual to enjoy the advantage provided by the law of large numbers. See Takaful for details.

Wadiah (Safekeeping)

In *Wadiah*, a bank is deemed as a keeper and trustee of funds. A person deposits funds in the bank and the bank guarantees refund of the entire amount of the deposit, or any part of the outstanding amount, when the depositor demands it. The depositor, at the bank's discretion, may be rewarded with *Hibah* (see above) as a form of appreciation for the use of funds by the bank.

Wakalah (Power of Attorney)

This occurs when a person appoints a representative to undertake transactions on his/her behalf, similar to a power of attorney.

Islamic Equity Funds

Islamic investment equity funds market is one of the fastest-growing sectors within the Islamic financial system. Currently, there are approximately 100 Islamic equity funds worldwide. The total assets managed through these funds currently exceed US$5 billion and is growing by 12–15% per annum. With the continuous interest in the Islamic financial system, there are positive signs that more funds will be launched. Some Western majors have just joined the fray or are thinking of launching similar Islamic equity products.

Despite these successes, this market has seen a record of poor marketing as emphasis is on products and not on addressing the needs of investors. Over the last few years, quite a number of funds have closed down.

Most of the funds tend to target high net worth individuals and corporate institutions, with minimum investments ranging from US$50,000 to as high as US$1 million. Target markets for Islamic funds vary, some cater for their local markets, e.g., Malaysia and Gulf-based investment funds. Others clearly target the Middle East and Gulf regions, neglecting local markets and have been accused of failing to serve Muslim communities.

Since the launch of Islamic equity funds in the early 1990s, there has been the establishment of credible equity benchmarks by Dow Jones Islamic market index (Dow Jones Indexes pioneered Islamic investment indexing in 1999) and the FTSE Global Islamic Index Series. The Web site failaka.com monitors the performance of Islamic equity funds and provide a comprehensive list of the Islamic funds worldwide.

Islamic Laws on Trading

The Qur'an prohibits gambling (games of chance involving money) and insuring ones health or property (also a game of chance). The hadith, in addition to prohibiting gambling (games of chance), also prohibits *bayu al-gharar* (trading in risk, where the Arabic word *gharar* is taken to mean "risk" or excessive uncertainty).

The *Hanafi madhab* (legal school) in Islam defines *gharar* as "that whose consequences are hidden." The Shafi legal school defined *gharar* as "that whose nature and consequences are hidden" or "that which admits two possibilities, with the less desirable one being more likely." The Hanbali school defined it as "that whose consequences are unknown" or "that which is undeliverable, whether it exists or not." Ibn Hazm of the Zahiri school wrote "*Gharar* is where the buyer does not know what he bought, or the seller does not know what he sold." The modern scholar of Islam, Professor Mustafa Al-Zarqa, wrote that "Gharar is the sale of probable items whose existence or characteristics are not certain, due to the risky nature that makes the trade similar to gambling." There are a number of *hadith* that forbid trading in *gharar*, often giving specific examples of *gharhar* transactions (e.g., selling the birds in the sky or the fish in the water, the catch of the diver, an unborn calf in its mother's womb etc.). Jurists have sought many complete definitions of the term. They also came up with the concept of *yasir* (minor risk); a financial transaction with a minor risk is deemed to be *halal* (permissible) while trading in non-minor risk (*bayu al-ghasar*) is deemed to be *haram*.

What *gharar* is, exactly, was never fully decided upon by the Muslim jurists. This was mainly due to the complication of having to decide what is and is not a minor risk. Derivatives instruments (such as stock options) have only become common relatively recently. Some Islamic banks do provide brokerage services for stock trading.

Microfinance

Microfinance is a key concern for Muslims states and recently Islamic banks also. Islamic microfinance tools can enhance security of tenure and contribute to transformation of lives of the poor.

Controversy

In Islamabad, Pakistan, on June 16, 2004: Members of leading Islamist political party in Pakistan, the Muttahida Majlis-e-Amal (MMA) party, staged a protest walkout from the National Assembly of Pakistan against what they termed derogatory remarks by a minority member on interest banking:

Taking part in the budget debate, M.P. Bhindara, a minority MNA [Member of the National Assembly]...referred to a decree by an Al-Azhar University's scholar that bank interest was not un-Islamic. He said without interest the country could not get foreign loans and could not achieve the desired progress. A pandemonium broke out in the house over his remarks as a number of MMA members...rose from their seats in protest and tried to respond to Mr Bhindara's observations. However, they were not allowed to speak on a point of order that led to their walkout.... Later, the opposition members were persuaded by a team of ministers...to return to the house...the government team accepted the right of the MMA to respond to the minority member's remarks.... Sahibzada Fazal Karim said the Council of Islamic ideology had decreed that interest in all its forms was *haram* in an Islamic society. Hence, he said, no member had the right to negate this settled issue.

Some Islamic banks generate profits by charging for the time value of money, the common economic definition of Interest (Riba). These institutions are criticized in some quarters of the Muslim community for their lack of strict adherence to Sharia.

The concept of Ijarah is used by some Islamic Banks (the Islami Bank in Bangladesh, for example) to apply to the use of money instead of the more accepted application of supplying goods or services using money as a vehicle. A fixed fee is added to the amount of the loan that must be paid to the bank regardless if the loan generates a return on investment or not. The reasoning is that if the amount owed does not change over time, it is profit and not interest and therefore acceptable under Sharia.

Islamic banks are also criticized by some for not applying the principle of Mudarabah in an acceptable manner. Where Mudarabah stresses the sharing of risk, critics point out that these banks are eager to take part in profit-sharing but they have little tolerance for risk. To some in the Muslim community, these banks may be conforming to the strict legal interpretations of Sharia but avoid recognizing the intent that made the law necessary in the first place. Islamic principles on banking have helped to offer a spiritual awareness to the world of big business, suggesting a relevance to transpersonal business studies.

During the past several decades hundreds of valuable books and research papers have been published on the justness and completeness of Islamic economic system and about two hundred Islamic banks have been established and many web sites have been opened for dealing with Islamic finance. But most unfortunately for the Muslim ummah professional Islamic economists and bankers have not yet come up with any practicable Islamic alternative of interest with the result that in spite of having mobilized billions of dollars of Muslim ummah Islamic banks do not have any system of advancing interest-free loans which should be their main function and therefore for meeting their own short-term needs of liquidity they get loans on interest from conventional banks.

Prohibition of interest in Islam and role of Islamic banks in eliminating interest

[1] The gravest but least addressed problem facing Muslim Ummah today is prevalence of interest-based banking in Muslim world. Quraan orders believers to fear Allah and give up interest, holds giving up of interest to be a sign of fearing Allah and condition of Imaan and warns offenders of war from Allah and His Rasool saws. According to a hadeeth adultery and interest invite Allah's anger. Allama Iqbal severely condemned bank interest holding it to be a tool of exploitation, source of financial miseries and cause of moral degradation. He said that intellect, culture and religion have no meaning until interest-based banking system is demolished. Syed Qutab Shaheed held that Islam and interest cannot co-exist and that obedience of Allah and Rasool saws was inconceivable

in the society in which interest-based system prevails. Quaid-e-Azam in his speech at the time of inauguration of State Bank in 1948 urged to mould economic system of the country on Islamic principles. It is a matter of shame and irony that in spite of what is said above interest-based banking prevails in Muslim world that keeps Muslim Ummah at war with Allah and deprived of His blessings. Consequently, despite having vast areas of land with immense wealth of natural resources, Muslim Ummah remains weak, oppressed and humiliated. Obviously eliminating interest in Muslim world is the first and foremost essential step for Muslim Ummah to gain strength and respectability.

[2] In Islamic Summit Conference held in Lahore in 1974 it was decided to promote socio-economic co-operation among Muslim countries according to Islamic principles. In 1975 Islamic Development Bank (IDB) was established in Jeddah with the purpose "to foster the economic development and social progress of member countries and Muslim communities individually as well as jointly in accordance with the principles of Shariah". The selected paper on interest-free banking presented in the First International Conference on Islamic Economics held in Makkah in February 1976 urged "to introduce a system of interest-free banking not as a supplement to but as a substitute for prevalent system of banking". In the conference communiqué "it was recommended that all Muslim countries should make their laws as well as social and economic institutions conform to the principles of Islam". IDB prize winner in Islamic banking, Dr. Ziauddin Ahmad in his speech in the prize ceremony in 1991 raised the core issue "what concrete steps can be taken to better attune the Islamic Banks for playing a more dynamic role in the attainment of Islamic socio-economic objectives".

[3] Unfortunately Islamic economists and bankers have ignored the above deliberations for finishing interest and achieving Islamic socio-economic objectives. Interest-free banking as substitute for conventional banking has not so far been introduced. However, in the last 31 years more than 200 Islamic Banks have emerged. They have mobilized billions of dollars and are prospering in 70 countries due to Islamic sentiment of their clients. As Islamic banks do not provide interest-free loans, they are supplement to and not substitute for conventional banks and that is why they have produced no dent in interest-based banking and there is no sign of elimination of interest in any Muslim country. In response to Pakistan's urgent request for funds in 1998, IDB and several other Islamic banks could offer only interest-bearing loan at 5% above LIBOR! Islamic banks do not provide loans even to one another. In his book "Introduction to Islamic Finance" M. Taqi Usmani writes:

"The case of Islamic banking cannot be advanced unless a strong system of inter-bank transactions based on Islamic principles is developed. The lack of such a system forces the Islamic banks to turn to the conventional banks for their short-term needs of liquidity which the conventional banks do not provide without either an open or camouflaged interest".

M. Taqi Usmani is Chairman or Member of Shariah Boards of a dozen or more Islamic Banks. His realistic comment and sad instance of 1998 mentioned above highlight the necessity of interest-free lending by Islamic banks.

[4] Loan is indispensable need of mankind. Trade, Industry, Governments and Welfare Organizations very frequently and rich persons occasionally need loans. As Islam caters for all needs of mankind a Hadeeth e Qudsi strongly commends interest-free loan by declaring reward for qard is 18 times implying that Islam wants extensive use of loans in society. Our Prophet saws himself bought edibles on credit and borrowed money for State purposes. Several Sahaba Karam ra took loans for doing business and Imam Abu Haneefa ra did business with borrowed money. It is not understood why Islamic Banks ignore Hadeeth e Qudsi and exclude loans from their operations. It is a gross misconception that ideal Islamic alternative of interest is profit sharing. Islam prohibited interest, permitted Mudarabah and Musharikah which were in vogue in pre-Islamic era and highly commended interest-free loan. Thus interest-free loan is the ideal Islamic alternative of interest. Moreover, as interest is a lending device, its alternative can only be an interest-free lending device just as the only alternative of zina is nikah. Surprisingly present Islamic economists and bankers do not realize that interest cannot be finished without providing interest-free loan facility to loan seekers just as zina cannot be finished without providing nikah facility to all men and women.

[5] If the aim of Islamic banks is not only to make money but also to play effective role in finishing interest, then they must arrange to provide interest-free loans on as large a scale as loans are provided by interest-based banks. It can profitably be done on the basis of an interest-free lending device TMCL (Time Multiple Counter Loan). This novel interest-free Islamic lending device that can perform all functions as are performed by interest in the present system was invented by late Professor Sheikh Mahmood Ahmad applauded in Pakistan Supreme Court judgment of December 23rd 1999 as "our country's most outstanding economist, researcher and leading thinker had devoted considerable part of his life to the study of the theory of interest".

[6] TMCL transaction comprises two simultaneously exchanged interest-free loans between two parties such that the multiple of the amount and period of one loan equals the multiple of the amount and period of the other loan. It facilitates interest-free loans of large sums against counter loans of much smaller sums advanced for proportionately longer periods. For example a trader can get interest-free loan of Rs. 10 million for one year by advancing counter-loan of Rs. 1 million to the bank for ten years. Thus TMCL fulfills the client's need of funds and enables the bank to cover its expenses and earn

profit for its share holders and depositors by long term investment of counter loan amounts. TMCL-based transaction is just and equitable as in this transaction, unlike interest-based transaction, none of the two parties is a definite gainer or loser and each one of them may gain or lose by investing the loan amount borrowed from the other party. As in TMCL transaction both parties do good to each other it conforms with Quraanic precept "hal jaza ul ihsan illa al-ihsan" and the noble teaching of our Holy Prophet saws that a favor done should be reciprocated. Hence putting it into practice will have Allah's blessings and bring prosperity to the people. Briefly following are sufficient proofs of validity of TMCL in Islamic finance and Shariah:-

a. 17 member Panel of Senior Bankers and economic experts in its report of January 28th 1980 advised Council of Islamic Ideology about TMCL: "It has been suggested here in view of its potential usefulness for consideration of the council subject to its permissibility under the Shariah".

b. Council of Islamic Ideology did not find any Shariah objection on TMCL and in its report of June 15th 1980 recommended adoption of TMCL principle by banks to provide loans to account holders for personal and non-productive purposes.

c. TMCL-based interest-free banking plan was presented and explained in detail during the hearing of Riba case by 5 member Supreme Court Shariat Appellate Bench including two Islamic Scholars, M. Taqi Usmani and Dr. Mahmood Ahmad Ghazi. No objection on TMCL was raised by any judge during the hearing. TMCL plan is also described without any adverse comment in the Supreme Court Shariat Appellate Bench unanimous judgment of December 23rd 1999.

d. Extract from Kuwaiti Finance House Fatwa No. 162:-

"Question No. 4: Is it permissible that I take loan of 1000 Dinars for 1 year from you on the condition that I give a loan of 3000 Dollars to you for 1 year?

Reply: It is permissible".

USE OF FAKE MURABAHA BY ISLAMIC BANKS FOR FINANCING AND EARNING DISGUISED INTEREST

Normal sale is based on price known in advance. If price is unknown, sale is, of necessity, based on profit payable together with the expenses to be incurred by the seller in procurement. Upon taking delivery, the buyer pays in cash. Sharia permits such cash sale naming it Bai Murabaha as it is based on profit. Logically genuine Murabaha sale is negotiated only when the price is not known. If in a credit sale transaction the buyer is charged more than the price at which he can buy what he needs against cash payment, then such a sale is fake Murabaha and mark-up on the price is interest.

Bai Murabaha is basically cash sale involving no credit and no finance provider. But Islamic banks use fake Murabaha to provide finance and receive disguised interest in the name of profit in Murabaha sale. What happens is briefly as follows.

The buyer knows the seller and price of the item he needs but lacks ready cash to pay. It is no case for a genuine Murabaha. Islamic bank, under a fake Murabaha agreement with the buyer, provides finance by paying the price to the seller. In agreed time after delivery, the bank receives from the buyer the finance provided by it plus an agreed amount nearly the same as interest on the finance provided by Islamic bank calculated at conventional inter-bank interest rate. Islamic banks profess the additional amount is profit in Murabaha sale. But common sense tells the additional amount is price of time the buyer takes in paying and that is plain interest.

Enclosed herewith is a five page document including extracts from authentic writings on the subject discussed above. Islamic bankers and their sharia advisors must give thoughtful consideration to this discourse and realize that playing tricks with letters of sharia law will damage the cause of eliminating interest and bring disgrace to Islamic banking and to themselves also.

ON-GOING WAR FROM ALLAH AND HIS RASOOL SAWS-THE MOST GRIEVOUS CALAMITY FOR MUSLIM UMMAH

Allah permits profit in business and prohibits interest and orders *"O ye who believe fear Allah and forgo whatever is left of interest if you are believers, and if you do it not then be warned of war from Allah and His Rasool." (Surah Al Baqarah).* Muhammed *saws* said that devouring interest is unpardonable sin and that interest and Zina enrage Allah. Allama Iqbal held bank interest to be a tool of exploitation, source of financial miseries and cause of moral degradation and brutal crimes and said:- "Intellect, culture and religion cannot bear any fruit until interest-based system is demolished". Syed Qutub Shaheed held "interest and Islam cannot co-exist" and "obedience of Allah and Rasool *saws* is unimaginable where interest-based system prevails".

Due to prevalence of interest-based system in all Muslim countries, Muslim *Ummah* as a whole is at war with Allah and earning His wrath. Resultantly, in spite of having very big population and owning vast areas of land with immense natural resources we are weak, despondent and victims of oppression and injustices. For Muslim Ummah to come out of this miserable condition and regain respectability, Muslim countries must get rid of interest as first essential starting step towards recovery. A gist of the acts of commission and omission in promoting and letting interest-based system to persist in Pakistan is as follows.

14th August 1947: In the holy month of *Ramadhan* on the 27th blessed night Allah created Pakistan fulfilling Indian Muslims' desire to own a homeland and live under writ of Islam.

1st July 1948: State Bank of Pakistan opened. In his inaugural speech, Quaid-e-Azam urged to evolve banking practices compatible with Islamic ideals. But against the wishes of the people and directive of the founder of Pakistan, our rulers and economy managers have promoted interest-based banking in flagrant defiance of Islamic injunctions.

12th March 1949: Constituent Assembly of Pakistan passed Objective Resolution affirming that in the state of Pakistan Muslims shall be enabled to order their lives in the individual and collective spheres in accordance with the teachings and requirements of Islam as set out in the Holy Quraan and the Sunnah. Even after more than seven hundred months since the Objective Resolution was adopted, un-Islamic laws inherited from foreign rulers remain in force and the writ of Islam runs nowhere in the country in any walk of life!

14th August 1973: Constitution of Islamic Republic of Pakistan came into force. The Constitution required all existing laws to be brought in conformity with the injunctions of Islam as laid down in the Holy Quraan and Sunnah and no law repugnant to such injunctions to be enacted. Until now no fiscal law involving interest has been brought in conformity with Islamic injunctions.

22nd to 24th February 1974: Islamic Summit Conference held in Lahore resolved to promote social and economic co-operation among Muslim countries.

20th October 1975: Islamic Development Bank (IDB) formally opened in Jeddah with the purpose "to foster the economic development and social progress of member countries and Muslim communities individually as well as jointly in accordance with the principles of shariah".

21st to 26th February 1976 (21st to 26th Safar 1396H): The first International Conference on Islamic Economics held at Makkah Mukarramah attended by two hundred economists and *Ulama* from all parts of the world. The selected paper on 'Some Conceptual and Practical Aspects of Interest-Free Banking' read in the conference held "interest in all its forms is prohibited by the Holy Quraan" and that "the Muslim society in an Islamic state is genuinely interested in eliminating Riba and sincerely desires to introduce a system of *interest-free banking, not as supplement to, but as a substitute for the prevalent system of banking*". In the conference communiqué "It was recommended that all Muslim countries should make their laws as well as Social and Economic Institutions conform to the principles of the *shariah*". Muslim rulers have so far ignored the conference recommendations and interest still remains lawful and interest-based banking dominates in all Muslim countries. Islamic economists who participated in the conference, excepting one, have so far not cared to produce interest-free banking model for replacing the existing system. Contrary to the conference deliberations, Islamic banks have emerged as supplement to interest-based banks and that is why about 300 Islamic banks prospering in 70 countries have not produced any dent in conventional banking.

5th July 1977: General Zia imposed Martial Law and suspended 1973 Constitution in which it was mandated to transform all laws to conform to Quraan and Sunnah within a period of ten years i.e. by 14th August 1983.

29th September 1977: Council of Islamic Ideology (CII) was given the task to prepare blueprint of interest-free economic system.

November 1977: CII appointed a 15-member Panel of Experts in Economics and Banking to assist in remodeling Economic and Financial systems conforming to the Holy Quraan and Sunnah. Two senior officials of State Bank of Pakistan Research Department were also associated with the work of the Panel.

10th February 1979: Time limit of 3 years set for eliminating interest from the economy.

28th January 1980: The Panel finalized its report and submitted it to CII in February 1980 with the note: "*No serious attempt has been made so far in any Muslim country to get rid of interest.*

Muslim thought also has remained nearly dormant in the field of money and banking for centuries so that there is very little in the available literature on which the Panel could draw in its work related to an interest-free economic and financial system".

This note demonstrates (i) Muslim rulers' lack of will to eliminate interest (ii) Lack of will and ability of contemporary Islamic economists and bankers to produce interest-free banking model for replacing conventional banking system. Professor Sheikh Mahmud Ahmad, a member of the Panel who had participated in the 1976 International Conference, devised and presented before the Panel members an interest-free banking model based on a novel interest-free lending device TMCL (Time Multiple Counter Loan). All Panel members were convinced that TMCL was potentially useful in eliminating interest and in their report TMCL was endorsed in the following words "It has been suggested here in view of its potential usefulness for consideration of the Council subject to its permissibility under the Shariah".

15th June 1980: CII finalized its report and submitted it to the Government on 25th June 1980. Following contents of the report show that instead of producing a blueprint of interest-free economic system CII made only general recommendations many of which were for maintaining and not eliminating interest:-

i. "Ideally the real alternatives to interest under our Islamic economic system are profit/ loss sharing or qard-i-hasan i.e. loaning without additional charge over and above the principal amount. Although the recommendations are based largely on the principle of profit/loss sharing, yet some of the recommendations lean on other methods in view of the difficulties faced in the practical application of the profit/loss sharing system in its pure form on account of the prevalent standards of morality in the society. **These alternative methods are, however, no more than a second best solution** from the viewpoint of an ideal Islamic economic system". It is not understood why CII avoided the best solution and did not make recommendations based on TMCL principle of interest-free loan endorsed by the panel of experts in economics and banking.

ii. "The operations of foreign branches of Pakistani banks, foreign currency deposits held with commercial banks in Pakistan and certain other transactions of banks with banks abroad **would have to continue on the basis of interest".**

iii. "Government borrowing from external sources **will have to be continued, for the time being on the basis of interest".**

iv. "Interest-bearing foreign loans channeled by the Government to these bodies **would, however, need to be continued on the existing basis"**.

v. "PICIC's foreign currency borrowings **may continue to be on interest-basis** until a viable alternative conforming to shariah is available".

vi. "Borrowings from International agencies **may continue to be interest-bearing** until alternative arrangements compatible with shariah become available".

vii. "State Bank's transactions with International Financial institutions and foreign aid agencies **would have to be continued on the basis of interest** until a viable solution is evolved in consultation with the parties concerned".

viii. "The interest-bearing foreign loans channeled by the Federal Government to the Provincial Governments **may, however, continue on the basis of interest** till a viable alternative compatible with shariah is found in respect of borrowings from abroad".

ix. "Elimination of interest from transactions relating to international trade and aid, which poses the most difficult problems, should be covered in the third phase".

Despite holding interest-free loan to be ideally real alternative to interest and finding no defect in TMCL, Council of Islamic Ideology approved very limited use of TMCL principle by banks for giving loans to their account holders only for personal and non-productive purposes. Ignoring the unanimous view on TMCL of the 17-member panel of experts in Economics and Banking and without stating what was wrong in eliminating interest by way of adopting TMCL as permanent alternative of interest, CII arbitrarily held "It would not be correct to use this (TMCL) method by way of a permanent alternative system to the interest-based system". Had CII not given this short single sentence un-argued and unsubstantiated wrong verdict, Pakistan and subsequently other Muslim countries would have got rid of interest long ago.

26th June 1980: Federal Shariat Court (FSC) constituted but financial matters including Riba were excluded from its jurisdiction until 25th June 1983.

19th May 1983: Restriction on jurisdiction of FSC extended up to 25th June 1984.

26th April 1984: Restriction on jurisdiction of FSC extended up to 25th June 1985.

2nd March 1985: Restriction on jurisdiction of FSC extended up to 25th June 1990.

10th February 1986: Professor Khurshid Ahmad in his speech in the Senate said "Today we have with us a clear outline plan showing how a new system can be structured. If it is in our power we will finish interest in 24 hours. Has not the time come for us to at least have cease-fire in the war with Allah?" During about 5 years' MMA Rule in NWFP with Professor Khurshid Ahmad as Financial advisor there was no cease-fire in the war with Allah!

17th August 1988: General Zia was killed in air crash. After his demise there came no further extension in the date of restoration of FSC jurisdiction regarding financial matters.

26th June 1990: Jurisdiction of FSC restored to examine fiscal laws.

7h February to 24th October 1991: FSC heard petitions challenging provisions of laws relating to interest.

14th November 1991: FSC delivered judgment deciding provisions of the laws relating to interest to be repugnant to the injunctions of Islam to take effect on 1st July 1992.

12th January 1992: The Agricultural Development Bank of Pakistan filed appeal in the Supreme Court Shariat Appellant Bench against the judgment of FSC.

1st July 1997: Government submitted an application to FSC seeking a workable solution to prevent the country from becoming international defaulter and allow functioning of the banking system complying with Islamic injunctions.

28th May 1998: Pakistan detonated nuclear device and became Atomic Power. In subsequent financial crisis, against Pakistan's urgent need of funds, *Islamic Development Bank together with several other Islamic banks offered a loan at interest rate 5% above LIBOR! This shows Islamicity of so called Islamic banks.*

13th February 1999: Government submitted an application to FSC to lay down and declare the principles of Islam on the basis of which the existing banking system can be remodeled so as to bring it in conformity with the requirements of Islam.

22nd February 1999: Supreme Court Shariat Appellate Bench comprising Justice Khalil-ur-Rehman (Chairman), Justice Munir A. Sheikh, Justice Vajeehuddin Ahmad, and two Shariah scholars justice Muhammad Taqi Usmani and Justice Dr. Mahmud Ahmad Ghazi, started hearing appeals against FSC's judgment of 14th November 1991. Government applied to withdraw its appeal on the plea that the Government wanted to implement the judgment and FSC had been requested to give guidance as to how the system can be remodeled so as to bring it in conformity with Islamic injunctions. Government's request to withdraw its appeal was rejected and Chairman urged the need to identify Riba and its alternative and said that it was the problem for the entire Muslim Ummah and not only for Pakistan.

22nd February to 6th July 1999: During hearing of the appeals by Supreme Court (SAB) many Islamic scholars, economists and bankers and the writer contented that interest in all its forms is Riba prohibited in Quraan and substantiated this view with ample supporting material from Quraan and Sunnah. The writer presented in the court TMCL-based interest-free baking plan for replacing conventional banking immediately without any disruption. The writer presented his book 'Interest-Free Banking' in the court officially and also individually to each judge. The book describes working of TMCL-based interest-free banking system and shows how its implementation will reduce prices and unemployment. The book also shows with supporting calculations how domestic and foreign debts can be cleared after adoption of this system. It was well received and no judge raised any objection on TMCL plan. Nobody else presented any interest-free banking plan for replacing conventional banking.

Dr. Sayyid Tahir, Director General of International Institute of Islamic Economics (IIIE), International Islamic University Islamabad placed on the court record publication titled IIIE's Blueprint of Islamic Financial system including strategy for elimination of Riba. Like CII Report this so called blueprint also does not include interest-free banking model for replacing the existing system. In this publication frivolous objections on TMCL-based interest-free banking model were raised in the following words: *"Time Multiple Counter Loan (TMCL). This transaction requires a bank to give an interest-free loan in return for a similar counter-loan to the bank so that the product of the sum lent and the associated time period is the same at both ends of the exchange – as, for example, Rs. 100,000 for one year in return for a counter-loan of Rs. 10,000 for 10 years or Rs. 12,500 for 8 years. One may argue that the TMCL instrument offers an ingenious solution to the problems of riba, gharar and having two mutually exclusive conditions in one contract. But its viability is questionable for several reasons. Some of these are as follows. Counter-loans would be "liability" of the banks. Therefore, while the sum generated might be used to meet their operating expenses, it would not be distributable as profits among their shareholders or depositors who provide funds on partnership basis. This will compel the banks to turn to trading, leasing and other profitable options. It is also possible that clients may use loans from banks, whether directly or indirectly, to give the counter-loans. This, in turn, casts further doubts on the usefulness of the TMCL option. Last but not the least, a resource to TMCL is also not advisable because ensuing credit expansion is likely to fuel inflation".*

Obviously the above cursory remarks on TMCL have been made without properly understanding the working of the model and without taking into account the following important points. The sum generated by counter-loans will be invested in long-term profitable businesses. The profits earned by the banks will be shared with the depositors in investment accounts. There is no harm in the banks turning to *shariah*-compliant trading modes. Every loan will be advanced against collateral and will have to be returned on due date.

There is no reason why any sensible person will use the loan from bank to give counter-loans for further loans instead of utilizing it in meeting his business requirements. Credit expansion will be controlled by raising or lowering the time multiple ratio in TMCL just as it is controlled in the present system by raising or lowering interest rate. The Blueprint also includes a baseless misleading contention that banks should not be expected to enter into pure lending operations. Loan is indispensable need of mankind and interest prevails only because it meets the needs of all sectors of society for loans. It is not understood why mainstream Islamic economists do not realize that interest cannot be eliminated unless and until interest-free loan facility is made available to loan seekers. It is also not understood why Islamic bankers and their *sharia* advisors persistently ignore *hadeeth qudsi* declaring reward for *qard* to be 18 times implying that Islam wants widespread use of loans in society.

Professor Khurshid Ahmad, without giving any plan or calculations said: "It would take a year to completely transform the domestic debt into the new system, while two to three years in respect of international agreements".

23rd December 1999: Supreme Court (SAB) passed unanimous judgment holding interest to be Riba prohibited in Quraan and ordered the Government to constitute a fully empowered commission to carry out, control and supervise transformation of the existing financial system to the one conforming to shariah by 30th June 2001. The order related to elimi ation of interest from Domestic transactions only. As regards foreign transactions the order states: "serious efforts shall be started by the Federal Government to relieve the nation from the burden of foreign debts as soon as possible and to renegotiate the existing loans. Serious efforts shall also be made to structure the future borrowings, if necessary, on the basis of Islamic modes of financing".

Supreme Court order has two serious flaws. Firstly it covers elimination of Riba from domestic transactions only whereas Quraanic prohibition applies to all transactions, domestic and foreign both. Secondly, it permits interest to persist in domestic transactions for more than eighteen months whereas shariah does not authorize anybody to permit violation of Divine command for even shortest span of time. TMCL-based interest-free banking plan is described in the Supreme Court judgment without any adverse comment. It is not understood why Supreme Court did not order immediate elimination of interest from both domestic and foreign transactions by way of implementing TMCL-based interest-free banking plan.

There are some worth noting and commenting upon misconceptions and errors in the concurring judgment written by Mr. Justice M. Taqi Usmani. Relevant extracts from the judgment and comments thereupon are as follows:

"159. In order to limit the use of loans, the shariah has permitted to borrow money only in cases of dire need and has discouraged the practice of incurring debts for living beyond one's means or to grow one's wealth". This contention is not supported by any material from Quraan or Sunnah and the fact is exactly opposite to what is stated. A *hadeeth qudsi* declares reward for *qard* is eighteen times, implying that Islam wants widespread use of loans in society. Shariah does not discourage the practice of incurring debts to grow one's wealth. Several Sahabah Karam *ra* and Imam Abu Haneefa *ra* borrowed money for doing business.

"159. The well-known event that the Holy Prophet (peace be upon him) refused to offer the funeral prayer of a person who died indebted was, in fact to establish the principle that incurring debt should not be taken as a natural or ordinary phenomenon of life". What is quoted about this event is only half truth; the half truth omitted is that the Holy Prophet *saws* led the funeral prayer after the debt was cleared. It proves that the refusal was to establish incumbency to clear debts and not to discourage incurring debt. As loan is an indispensable need of mankind and Islam caters for all genuine needs of mankind, it is natural that Islam commends lending (of course interest-free) and condemns default in repayment of loan. It is not understood why only a part of an event was quoted and a wrong misleading conclusion drawn therefrom.

"199. The experience accumulated by Islamic banks in general, and the Islamic Development Bank in particular, as well as attempts made in a number of Muslim countries to apply an Islamic Financial system, indicate that the application of such an Islamic system by any Muslim country, at the national level is feasible". This statement does not present true picture of current Islamic banking. True Islamic financial system is not reflected in the operations of present Islamic banks which ignore *hadeeth qudsi* and do not advance interest-free loans. Present Islamic banks themselves are not rid of interest and most of their earnings come from interest-like fixed returns. In his own book 'Introduction to Islamic Finance' M. Taqi Usmani writes "The case of Islamic banking cannot be advanced unless a strong system of inter-bank transactions based on Islamic principles is developed. The lack of such a system forces the Islamic banks to turn to the conventional banks for their short-term needs of liquidity which the conventional banks do not provide without either an open or camouflaged interest". It is highly regrettable that Justice M.Taqi Usmani commended application of so called Islamic banking soiled with element of interest and ignored TMCL plan whereby Pakistan could have got rid of interest immediately.

"204. The basic and foremost characteristic of Islamic financing is that, instead of a fixed rate of interest, it is based on profit and loss sharing". The contention that Islamic financing is based on PLS is not supported by any quotation from Quraan and Sunnah. As present financing is based on interest which is a lending device, Islamic financing must naturally be based on interest-free lending device like TMCL. Interest-bearing loans and PLS were in vogue in pre-Islamic days. Islam prohibited interest, permitted PLS to continue and commended Interest-free loan. Hence Interest-free loan can logically be said to be the basis of Islamic finance and not PLS which is only permitted and not commended.

"229. The upshot of this discussion is that the Doctrine of necessity cannot be applied to protect the present interest-based system for ever or for an indefinite period. However, this doctrine can be availed of for allowing a reasonable time to the Government necessarily required to the switch-over to an interest-free Islamic financial system". This contention is untenable on two grounds. (i) Allah knows when, where and what is necessary for His creatures and has allowed concession where necessary like eating pork for saving life and postponing fasting during illness and travel. Allah has not allowed any such concession in respect of interest nor has He authorized anybody to permit delay in implementing His command using dubious doctrine of necessity. The unanimous judgment written by Mr. Justice Khalil-ur-Rehman states: "The *Ahkam* of Riba are no different from the *Ahkam* of, for example, *salah* (prayer) and *saum* (fasting). The *Ahkam* for none of these were prescribed with the dawn of Islam. *However, once ordained, the relevant Ahkam were enforced at once"*. (ii) Immediate switch-over to interest-free banking is possible by implementing TMCL-based interest-free banking plan.

23rd January 2000: As per Supreme Court (SAB) order of 23rd December 1999, Federal Government constituted 11 member fully empowered Commission for transformation of the financial system on Islamic principles, headed by I.A.Hanafi (Chairman) a former Governor of State Bank of Pakistan, with Faheem Khan of Islamic Development Bank to act as member/ secretary of the Commission and *Mufti* Rafi Usmani as *sharia* Scholar.

After rejoicing upon Supreme Court's judgment of 23rd Dec 99 and congratulating each other Islamic economists and proponents of Islamic system did nothing to get the judgment implemented and to save it from annulment. But advocates of interest started campaign to prove impracticality of interest-free banking and implementation of the judgment.

12th February 2000: Publication in daily 'DAWN' of an article 'Riba: some unanswered questions' written by an influential bureaucrat Dr. Akdas Ali Kazmi, Joint Chief Economist, Planning Commission. He raised following challenging questions about Islamic banking to prove that Supreme Court order to eliminate interest could not be implemented:-

i. Is there any single bank in the Islamic or non-Islamic world which is truly run on an interest-free basis?

ii. Can a central bank conduct its monetary policy without the norm of interest?

iii. Are not the practices of Islamic banks a queer blend of interest-based modes of finance carrying a façade of Islamic names?

iv. What are exactly the Islamic compliant instruments of finance? What is the number of such instruments? Can these instruments meet the myriad and diverse needs of modern trade, finance and banking?

v. When and where have these instruments been applied and with what degree of success?

vi. Does the Islamic Development Bank as the model Islamic Bank operate on interest-free basis? If that's the case why did it offer to extend a loan to the Government of Pakistan after Nuclear detonation at an interest rate of 5% above LIBOR?

vii. By what mechanism can Islamic banks undertake financial intermediation which is the primary function of all commercial banks throughout the world?

TMCL can perform all functions as efficiently as are performed by interest in modern banking. Following are fit answers to the above quoted challenging questions:-

i. Use of TMCL for interest-free lending and earning from sharia compliant profit yielding modes will turn present Islamic banks into true Islamic interest-free banks.

ii. Central bank will be able to conduct its monetary policy by varying Time Multiple ratio in TMCL as it does in the present system by varying interest rate.

iii. Malpractices of Islamic banks will cease when they start giving interest-free loans on TMCL basis and earning profits through genuine *sharia*-compliant modes.

iv. Islamic compliant instruments of finance are interest-free loan, *Mudarbah* and *Musharakah*. These instruments can fully meet the myriad and diverse needs of modern trade, finance and banking.

v. Islamic banks have yet to apply these instruments fully and when they do so they will surely meet with great success.

vi. Islamic banks can operate on interest-free basis by adopting TMCL for advancing interest-free loans.

vii. TMCL is interest-free lending device whereby Islamic banks can undertake financial intermediation and perform all commercial banks' functions.

21st February 2000: UBL filed petition for review of the order and judgment dated 23rd December 1999 passed by Shariat Appellate Bench of the Supreme Court of Pakistan.

8th March 2000: Seminar 'Towards Islamic Banking – Experiences and Challenges' organized by the Institute of Policy Studies run by Prof. Khurshid Ahmad in Islamabad.

In his inaugural address Governor State Bank of Pakistan, Dr. Ishrat Husain, urged Islamic scholars to make practical suggestions for ensuring transition to Riba-free financial system is smooth and compatible with the Islamic principle of equitable distribution of income and wealth from rich to poor. Quoting the 1996 Directory of Islamic banks, he observed "these institutions provided only 26% of their credit to manufacturing and agriculture. All the rest was advanced for short-term trading ventures". He said Pakistan needed a system of economic management different from the current exploitative system. He assured the audience including Islamic scholars from within Pakistan and outside that *the Government was in the earnest about the transformation of existing system into Riba-free one.* He requested them to provide practical solutions to a number of problems which face the country in connection with the implementation of Supreme Court (SAB) judgment as well as those already observed in other countries e.g. *1)* the rates of return offered by the Islamic banks under the profit & loss system is much lower than that offered by the banks on fixed rate basis *2)* How can the Riba-free system be made commensurate with the Islamic tenets of justice and equity? *3)*The problem of moral hazard quite pervasive in connection with the operations of Islamic banks in Iran where the proportion of investments has dropped to 13% since the introduction of Islamic banking. *4)* The documents now available show that the *Islamic banks have increasingly fallen on fixed return modes of financing* such as Morabaha and leasing. This constituted a high 80% of total financing by these institutions leaving only 20% to PLS. He also asked for the scholars' guidance about the problem of deficit financing. In order to make up the resource gap, the Government borrows from banks and the small savings schemes against fixed rates of return. What would be the substitute of these institutions in a Riba-free dispensation? he asked. He wondered as to what the role of SBP would be in a Riba-free financial system, particularly as it conducts its operations in the market from time to time which necessitate commitments on the fixed rates of return.

Speaking at the concluding session of the seminar Finance Minister Shaukat Aziz hailed the Supreme Court's judgment against Riba as landmark and declared that it would be implemented in letter and spirit to introduce interest-free banking system in the country. He said "Pakistan is the only country in the Muslim world which is going to have an interest-free banking". He called upon the scholars and financial and legal experts to help the Government implement the decision against Riba. He assured the participants of the seminar that the Government will implement the SC judgment. He also said "It is our requirement to eliminate Riba and have an Islamic mode of banking".

IPS Chairman Prof. Khurshid Ahmed urged Finance Minister to use his influence in implementing the Supreme Court judgment. He did not present any interest-free banking plan nor did he address the difficulties in the way of implementing Supreme Court judgment pointed out by State Bank Governor. Malpractices of Islamic banks mentioned by State Bank Governor remained unattended by Prof. Khurshid Ahmed. He ignored the fact that satisfactory answers to all the problems and questions raised in the conference lie in implementing TMCL-based interest-free banking system.

13th to 15th August 2000: Fourth International Conference on Islamic Economics and Banking held in Loughborough University organized jointly by Islamic Development Bank and Islamic Foundation UK. In a question/answer session the writer asked as to why TMCL was not used for interest-free lending to get Islamic banks and Muslim Ummah rid of interest. Dr. Nejatullah Siddiqui chairing the session answered every other question from the audience but did not say a word about the writer's question! The writer personally requested about 150 participants in the Conference including Prof. Khurshid Ahmed to take notice of Dr. Kazmi's article and to strive to remove shortcomings in Islamic banks and produce an interest-free banking model or endorse TMCL-based interest-free banking model for replacing existing system.

22nd August 2000: Following is an extract from the writer's fax sent from London to Professor Khurshid Ahmad in Markfield. "For achieving the objective of eliminating interest as a first basic starting step towards realization of the final goal of establishing Islamic Economic order it is incumbent on Islamic economists to give adequate answers to the challenging questions posed by advocates of interest like Dr. Akdas Ali Kazmi. This can be done only by advocating adoption of Islamic loaning instrument neutral to moral hazard which can perform all financial intermediation functions performed by interest in the modern banking system. Otherwise there is a risk that, God forbid, all efforts made for achieving the long cherished verdict of the apex court on interest may come to naught. For advancing my mission I intend to stay in England for 2-3 weeks more. For evolving a common strategy to frustrate the efforts of advocates of interest in Pakistan, it would be highly beneficial to have a thorough discussion on the vital subject. If you kindly agree, I shall be only too glad to come to Markfield for this purpose". Professor Khurshid Ahmad did not respond!

2nd October 2000: From amongst those personally contacted during the conference only IDB President responded. Photocopy of IDB letter addressed to the writer is attached (Annex 1). In more than seven years since this letter was received, Islamic banks have not moved an inch towards true Islamic interest-free banking!

8th January 2001: In an article 'ISLAMIC BANK, a misnomer' published in daily 'DAWN', Dr. Akdas Ali Kazmi asserted that interest-free banking is not feasible and contended: "The reports of various commissions set up from time to time in the past to evolve an interest-free economic and banking framework have not provided any meaningful or practical guidance in this crucial matter". As shown above satisfactory answers to the contentions of the advocates of interest are available only in TMCL plan which is being persistently ignored by Islamic economists and bankers and that is why they keep mum and do not refute the claims of the advocates of interest.

9th January 2001: Federal Religious Affairs Minister Dr. Mahmud Ahmad Ghazi announced that the *Government will put a permanent end to the giving and taking of interest from July 2001*. The Government did not abide by this commitment!

21st January 2001: In the special report of 'The News' daily appears a statement of Professor Khurshid Ahmad from which an extract reads: "The success of interest-free economic system depends on its implementation. The question is not the viability of the system but the modes of bringing it into effect. The Government seems non-serious in bringing the system into effect. Since the decision in December 1999 no real steps have been taken for the transition. *We need a definite plan for the switch-over but nothing has been done as yet.* The failure then should not be blamed on the Islamic model, but on the inept implementation". Explaining the interest-free economic system he said "the system was far superior and the most growth and justice oriented in the world.

"Economists from around the world agree that this is a very viable and superior system if implemented correctly. Islam just does not support the idea of a fixed pre-determined return on capital and proposes returns that are according to the market situation. The idea is of profit sharing. Islamic banks are working this way and are attracting huge amount of money. In fact Islamic banks have capital shares of more than $10 billion and deposits of more than $200 billion. Our economy is heading towards complete destruction in the prevalent interest-based system. The Government needs to change the system into an Islamic one with full conviction. Right now it is showing no will at all".

In the same special report appears a statement of another prominent Islamic Economist Dr. Shahid Hassan Siddiqui. He said "At present over 200 banks and financial institutions are operating under the banner of Islamic banking but for 80% of their financing they are resorting to *Murabaha* or like modes which are interest-based. These banks cannot provide a model for other banks to follow".

Prof. Khurshid Ahmed is dead right in criticizing the government and saying that a definite plan is needed for a switch-over but the question arises as to why he himself has not produced the needed plan although he had said in the Senate on 10th February 1986: "Today we have with us a clear outline plan showing how a new system can be structured". Following questions also need to be answered by him.

i. Why did he not present a definite switch-over plan in the Supreme Court (SAB) when he was condemning interest-based system and was asked by the court as to what was the alternative of interest-based system?

ii. Why did he not present a definite switch-over plan to the State Bank Governor and Finance Minister during the seminar on 8th Mar 2000 in the inaugural address of which State Bank Governor invited practical suggestions for implementing judgment of 23rd Dec 1999?

iii. UBL filed a review petition in the Supreme Court (SAB) first for extension in the period for implementing the judgment of 23rd Dec 1999 and then for setting aside the judgment. What held him back from presenting a definite switch-over plan to refute the claim that no interest-free banking plan was available?

iv. What did he practically do to get the judgment of 23rd Dec 1999 implemented and to save it from being annulled on 24th June 2002?

v. What is he doing to win the Riba case pending for readjudication in the Federal Shariat court since it was remanded vide Supreme Court (SAB) judgment of 24th June 2002?

vi. What held him back in implementing interest-free banking system in NWFP during about 5 years' MMA rule while he was financial advisor of NWFP Government?

vii. What makes him praise Islamic banks while for 80% of their financing they resort to *Murabaha* or like modes which are interest-based?

viii. What holds him back from endorsing TMCL-based interest-free banking plan especially when no other switch-over plan to interest-free banking is available?

19th March 2001: Member/Secretary CTFS addressed a letter to the writer, photocopy of which is attached (Annex 2). It shows rubber stamp conduct of CTFS members as they did not apply their own minds to the crucial problem and were swayed by a wrong verdict.

31st March 2001: The writer requested CTFS members in a letter:

i. Not to be swayed by a wrong arbitrary observation and give serious consideration to the most crucial national issue.

ii. To give sound reasons for disagreeing with the writer's submissions and give the writer an opportunity to meet CTFS members, individually or collectively for discussion.

iii. Not to reject TMCL-based interest-free banking plan without devising another method whereby banking system can be got rid of interest by 30th June 2001.

CTFS members neither responded to the writer's repeated requests nor accomplished their assigned duty to produce and implement interest-free banking system in the country!

11th April 2001: Supreme Court (SAB) comprising Justice Sheikh Riyaz Ahmad (Chairman); Justice Munir A.Sheikh; Justice Syed Deedar Husein Shah and Justice M.Taqi Usmani issued notices to the Attorney General and 35 other respondents in the UBL petition seeking review of the Riba judgment of 23rd Dec 1999.

5th May 2001: Governor State Bank of Pakistan Dr. Ishrat Husain said that due to some technical constraints complete elimination of Riba from the economy was not possible immediately after July 2001 as per directives of the Supreme Court. He said the country was in a serious financial crisis. He also said: "if any experiment of enforcing a whole new system would be carried out, it was feared that the attempt would lead to collapse of the system. The implementation of the new system was a big challenge and arrangements would be made from July to implement it. Whatever problems arose in the process, they would be brought into the notice of the apex court. An Islamic Transition Commission had been constituted and its recommendations would be incorporated in the new system. A task force to eliminate borrowing had also been formed. There was no perfect Islamic system enforced in any Islamic country".

Dr. Ishrat Husain overlooked the fact that TMCL plan for immediate switch-over to interest-free banking was available and described in the Supreme Court judgment. Later on he launched in Lahore late Prof. Sheikh Mehmud Ahmed's book 'Man and Money' on TMCL concept. It is a gross misconception that complete elimination of interest from the economy is not possible immediately. It is beyond imagination that Allah would give warning of war for not doing the impossible. Allah's orders are all beneficial for mankind and enforceable at all times and in all circumstances.

14th June 2001: Justice Sheikh Riyaz Ahmad (Chairman); Justice Munir A.Sheikh; Justice Syed Deedar Husein Shah and Justice M.Taqi Usmani heard UBL review petition. UBL filed an application seeking suspension of the judgment of 23rd Dec 1999 till 31st Dec 2005. The Federal Government also sought the extension to 31st Dec 2005. The Attorney General stated that "The Government was sincere in the implementation of the judgment but was facing practical difficulties as *there was no model of interest-free banking*. For implementation of the judgment two task forces and a Transformation Commission have taken place and a draft ordinance had been framed".

Proponents of Islamic order and Islamic economists having big name in Pakistan neither refuted the Attorney General's statement nor cared to counter UBL petition by presenting an interest-free banking model. Supporters of interest-free banking led by Ismail Qureshi opposed UBL request without presenting an interest-free banking model for replacing existing system. Justice Munir asked whether they had given thought to the scenario what would happen to people in the absence of an alternative banking instrument. Mr. Ismail Qureshi asked the court not to suspend the operation no matter what were the consequences!

The court allowed time for implementing the judgment till 30th June 2002. The period for eliminating interest was extended by one year only because Ismail Qureshi representing Jamaat-e-Islami could not present in the court an interest-free banking model for replacing conventional banking and Honorable judges did not realize that they were not authorized to permit any delay in implementing a Divine command.

5th September 2001: Shariat review petition filed by Qazi Husain Ahmad in Supreme Court (SAB) against the order dated 14th June 2001 extending the date for elimination of interest to 30th June 2002.

6th, 7th, 13th, 14th & 17th to 22nd June 2002: Supreme Court (SAB) comprising Chief Justice Sheikh Riyaz Ahmad, Justice Munir A.Sheikh, Justice Qazi Muhammad Farooq, Dr. Khalid Mahmood and Dr. Rashid Ahmad Jullunduri heard review petitions from the Supreme Court judgment of 23rd Dec 1999. Counsel for the Government said that transformation of entire financial system is not practicable and that Federal Government was committed to allow the Riba-free banking as a parallel banking system in the country and had already allowed setting of Al-Meezan Bank.

Affidavit filed on behalf of the Ministry of Finance reads: "The Government of Pakistan has made best possible efforts under article 190 and article 203D(3)(a) of the Constitution of the Islamic Republic of Pakistan, 1973 to find ways and means to implement the directives contained in paragraphs 7, 8 & 9 of the order of 23rd December 1999 of Honorable Supreme Court of Pakistan (SAB) but has found that implementation of the said directives is not practical or feasible and if attempted will pose high degree of risk to the economic stability and security of Pakistan".

Another affidavit filed by the Deputy Governor of State Bank of Pakistan reads: "Having taken a series of steps to promote Islamic banking in para 21 above and considering all other practical problems associated with the complete transformation of the financial system discussed herein, it is State Bank of Pakistan's considered judgment that a parallel approach will be in the best interest of the country. This means that Islamic banking is introduced as a parallel system of which a beginning has already been made, it is provided a level playing field vis-à-vis the existing conventional banks and its further growth and development is supported by Government and State Bank of Pakistan through appropriate actions. This approach will eliminate the risk of major costs/damage to the economy, give a fair chance to Islamic banks to develop along side the conventional banks, and will provide a choice to the people of Pakistan and the foreigners doing business in/with Pakistan to use either of the two systems".

Above quoted affidavits show that Finance Minister and State Bank Governor did not mean what they said on 8th Mar 2001 in their addresses in seminar in Islamabad.

Their actions and stance in the court showed that they wanted to protect interest-based system and avoid elimination of interest. Present Islamic banks have not played and cannot play any role in eliminating interest. Islamic banks started emerging in mid seventies of the last century and now about 300 Islamic banks are prospering in 70 countries and yet they have not produced any dent in conventional banking. If these banks were doing real Islamic banking interest would have by now vanished from Muslim countries as per Quranic verse 17:81 "When the right comes the wrong vanishes".

Presentation in the court of an interest-free banking model capable of effectively and immediately replacing interest-based banking was absolutely necessary for effective rebuttal of the claims of the advocates of interest and saving the judgment of 23rd Dec 1999 from annulment. Unfortunately Advocate Ismail Qureshi who was defending the judgment had not been provided by his client an interest-free banking model for presenting in the court and as such he could not effectively defend the judgment and lost the case.

24th June 2002: As could reasonably be expected in the absence of an effective defence of the judgment of 23rd Dec 1999, it was set aside by Supreme Court (SAB) and Federal Shariat Court judgment of 14th Nov 1991 remitted to Federal Shariat Court for determination afresh. Responsibility for the annulment of the judgment of 23rd Dec 1999 and continuation of interest-based banking in the country lies largely on the shoulders of the following personalities and institutions:-

i. Our rulers, Finance Ministers and State Bank Governors promoting interest-based system in violation of Islamic injunctions, Allama Iqbal's teachings, Quaid-e-Azam's directives and the Constitution of Islamic Republic of Pakistan.

ii. Islamic economists, Directors in Islamic Research Institutes and proponents of Islamic order who turned deaf ears to repeated requests to refute the claims of the advocates of interest and present interest-free banking model for replacing interest-based banking be it the one devised by themselves or TMCL-based model. They did nothing to save the judgment of 23rd Dec 1999 from annulment on 24th June 2002.

iii. Judges of Supreme Court Shariat Appellate Bench including Sharia scholar M.Taqi Usmani for not ordering immediate elimination of interest by way of implementing TMCL-based interest-free banking plan and permitting interest to persist in foreign transactions for indefinite period and for 18 months in domestic transactions whereas Allah's laws are for implementation at all times and in all circumstances. Allah has not authorized anybody howsoever high in status or learning, to permit delay in implementing any of His commands.

iv. CTFS failed in its duty to install interest-free banking system. The commission members including Mufti Rafi Usmani by default did not themselves produce any interest-free banking plan and by design (only God knows why) summarily and totally unjustifiably rejected the viable interest-free banking plan presented by the writer that could easily replace the existing system without any disruption.

v. Council of Islamic Ideology which without finding any fault and giving no reason whatsoever gave the erroneous verdict that it was not correct to use TMCL method by way of a permanent alternative system to the interest-based system. Rejecting TMCL method without offering another permanent alternative system irreparably damaged the cause of elimination of interest. If CII had not committed this blunder in its report of 15th June 1980, Pakistan and subsequently other Muslim countries could have got rid of interest long ago.

vi. The owners and *Shariah* advisors including M.Taqi Usmani, of so-called Islamic banks who ignore *hadeeth qudsi*, avoid interest-free lending and borrow on interest. They avoid financing in risk-bearing Islamic profit-sharing modes and concentrate on doubtful risk-free interest-like fixed-return earning modes. Shaikh Saleh Abdullah Kamel, a pioneer in Islamic banking and founder of Al-Baraka Islamic Bank has recently said on BBC TV channel that 90% of what presently Islamic banks are doing is wrong. Islamic banks can get themselves and Muslim *ummah* rid of interest by providing interest-free loan facility to genuine loan seekers for rightful purposes and limiting earnings from profit sharing and other doubtless Islamic modes.

24th October 2002: Federal Shariat Court directed advocate Ismail Qureshi defending judgment of 23rd Dec 1999 to advise the court the objections on the basis of which Riba case was remanded and also his replies to the objections.

14th June 2004: Advocate Ismail Qureshi filed in the Federal Shariat Court a statement highlighting (i) the objections on the basis of which Riba case was remanded and (ii) replies to the highlighted objections. The objections dealt with in his statement are limited to those covered in paras 12 to 16 of the remand order. The statement neither refuted the contents of the affidavits of the Ministry of Finance and State Bank nor included any interest-free banking model for replacing the existing system. As interest is a means to meet the needs of all sectors of society for all types of loans, it can be finished only by providing interest-free loan facility to loan seekers. If the proponents of Islamic order do really want to see interest eliminated then they must arrange to present in the court their own or TMCL-based interest-free banking model for replacing the existing system.

Our prophet Muhammed *saws* said "Those who do not care about the affairs of Muslims are not from amongst us". Hence every Muslim must strive to do utmost to get Muslim countries rid of interest including pressurizing Muslim rulers, bankers and economy managers for switching-over to interest-free banking without delay. The writer offers his services free of charge to work for anybody willing to advance the cause of finishing interest and / or to implement TMCL-based interest-free banking. Description of working and benefits of this system is available on web site given below. Comments and queries on this discourse will be gratefully received and appropriately responded.

SOME BITTER TRUTHS ABOUT INACTION OF ISLAMIC ECONOMISTS AND WRONG DOINGS OF ISLAMIC BANKS AND THEIR SHARIAH ADVISORS

Interest prohibited in Quraan is a definite gain for the lender with no risk of loss to him. Gain in trade permitted in Quraan is governed by the Islamic principle *Alkharaj bi aldhmaan* i.e. no risk no gain. As everything else in the universe, market conditions go on changing and as such definite gain in trade is impossible without risk of loss. Definite gain with no risk of loss is obtainable only as interest in money lending business.

Money lending at interest and profit sharing modes of financing were in vogue in pre-Islamic days. Islam prohibited interest and permitted profit sharing to continue. As profit sharing cannot meet the financing needs of all sectors of society and loan is indispensable need of mankind Islam highly commends interest-free lending. A *hadeeth qudsi* declares reward for *qard* is 18 times implying that *Islam wants widespread use of interest-free loans in society*. It is either by default or by design that this *hadeeth* does not find any place in the writings of Islamic economists and Shariah advisors of so-called Islamic banks.

Interest-based banking, though prohibited in Islam, prevails in the Muslim world only because it meets the indispensable needs of all sectors of society for loans. Hence the only way to eliminate interest is to arrange supply of interest-free loans on a big scale in abidance of the above mentioned *hadeeth*. Advice to eliminate interest without providing interest-free loan facility to loan seekers is as absurd as advice to finish illiteracy without providing schooling facility to every child. It is a gross misconception that interest can be eliminated by way of profit sharing as this mode cannot meet the financing needs of millions of privately owned enterprises keen on protecting their independence and ownership structure.

Late professor Shaikh Mahmud Ahmad was applauded in Supreme Court Shariat Appellate Bench. Judgment of 23rd Dec 1999 in Riba case as "*Our country's most outstanding economist, researcher and leading thinker* who had devoted considerable part of his life to the study of the theory of interest". He presented an interest-free banking model based on *his novel concept of TMCL (Time Multiple Counter Loan)*. This commercially viable interest-free banking model can provide all modern banking services including interest-free loans on a wide scale and as such it can replace interest-based banking system imminently without any disruption and pull Muslim Ummah out of the miserable state of war with Allah and His Rasool saws. Full Information on the working and benefits of this model is available on web site given below.

Supreme Court judgment of 23rd Dec 1999 ordered elimination of interest and replacement of interest-based banking system with interest-free banking system by 30th June 2001. The advocates of interest-based system started claiming that interest-free banking was not feasible and that Islamic banking was *heela* banking. Islamic economists holding high positions in Islamic Research and teaching institutions were requested many times to refute the above claims by presenting in the Supreme Court an interest-free banking model be it the one devised by themselves or readily available TMCL-based model. They did not respond. In the absence of any refutation of their claims advocates of interest-based system succeeded in getting the Supreme Court order set aside on 24th June 2002. Thus due to inaction of Islamic economists having big name the golden chance for Pakistan to get rid of interest was lost. Nearly six years have passed since the Riba case is pending in Federal Shariat Court for re-adjudication and renowned Islamic Economists including King Faisal award and IDB prize winners continue to remain unconcerned about the fate of the case!

International Institute of Islamic Economics – International Islamic University Islamabad published 'The Blueprint of Islamic Financial system including strategy for Elimination of Interest'. Dr. Sayyid Tahir Director General IIIE claimed *"This Blueprint offers a comprehensive treatise on the Islamic Financial System"*. This Blueprint negates the above quoted *hadeeth qudsi* by giving patently wrong advice *"It is also recognized that banks should not be expected to enter into pure lending operations"*. The Blueprint does not give any definite plan for eliminating interest and raises baseless objections on TMCL plan which is the only practicable plan available at present for replacing the existing system. Serious errors in the Blueprint were brought to the personal attention of Dr.Sayyid Tahir. He did not respond.

Dr. M. Umer Chapra in his book 'Towards a just Monetary System' wrote *"the method of Time Multiple Counter Loan could be adopted for small scale financing particularly within the framework of co-operative institutions. For commercial banks it would be of limited capability"*. He did not give any reason in his book for the limited capability of TMCL. Upon being asked as to why he considered TMCL would be of limited capability for commercial banks he replied "I have given my view, take it or leave it"!

Upon being pressed for a detailed discussion on use of TMCL for eliminating interest Dr. Mabid Ali Al Jarhi Director IDB Islamic Research and Training Institute advised the writer in a letter *"Presently IRTI is not in a position to hold any discussion meeting, symposium, seminar or conference on the subject of TMCL as suggested by you"*!

Islamic Banks started emerging in seventies of the last century with the avowed objective of getting Muslim communities and countries rid of interest. But these banks are virtually doing nothing to get Muslim Ummah rid of interest. They exclude interest-free lending from their operations and for meeting their own short-term needs of liquidity they take loans on interest from conventional banks and earn interest on their excess liquidity. They invest mostly in fake Murabaha and make interest-like definite gains with no risk of loss. In 'Elimination of Riba from the Economy' Prof. Khurshid Ahmad writes *'But in order to make themselves eligible to a return on their operations, the banks are compelled to play tricks with the letters of the law. They actually do not buy, do not possess, nor actually sell and deliver the goods; but the transaction is assumed to have taken place. By signing a number of documents of purchase, sale and transfer they might fulfill a legal requirement but it is by violating the spirit of prohibition".*

Sharia Advisors employed by Islamic banks dare not criticize wrong doings of Islamic banks. They approve of whatever Islamic Banks do and also speak highly of their performance. Some of them even tell half truths to justify what Islamic banks are doing. M. Taqi Usmani presides over Shariah Supervisory Board of Meezan Bank. Some extracts from his concurring judgment of 23rd Dec 1999 in Riba case and comments thereupon are as follows:-

"159. In order to limit the use of loans, the Shariah has permitted to borrow money only in cases of dire need and has discouraged the practice of incurring debts for living beyond one's means or to grow one's wealth". This contention is not supported by any material from Quraan or Sunnah and the fact is exactly opposite to what is stated. A *hadeeth qudsi* declares reward for *qard* is eighteen times, implying that Islam wants widespread use of loans in society. Shariah does not discourage the practice of incurring debts to grow one's wealth. Several Sahabah Karam *ra* and Imam Abu Haneefa *ra* borrowed money for doing business.

"159. The well-known event that the Holy Prophet (peace be upon him) refused to offer the funeral prayer of a person who died indebted was, in fact to establish the principle that incurring debt should not be taken as a natural or ordinary phenomenon of life". What is quoted about this event is only half truth; the half truth omitted is that the Holy Prophet *saws* led the funeral prayer after the debt was cleared. It proves that the refusal was to establish incumbency to clear debts and not to discourage incurring debt. As loan is an indispensable need of mankind and Islam caters for all genuine needs of mankind, it is natural that Islam commends lending (of course interest-free) and condemns default in repayment of loan. It is not understood why only a part of an event was quoted and a wrong misleading conclusion drawn therefrom.

"199. The experience accumulated by Islamic banks in general, and the Islamic Development Bank in particular, as well as attempts made in a number of Muslim countries to apply an Islamic Financial system, indicate that the application of such an Islamic system by any Muslim country, at the national level is feasible". This statement does not present true picture of current Islamic banking. True Islamic financial system is not reflected in the operations of present Islamic banks which ignore *hadeeth qudsi* and do not advance interest-free loans. Present Islamic banks themselves are not rid of interest and most of their earnings come from interest-like fixed returns. In his own book 'Introduction to Islamic Finance' M. Taqi Usmani writes "*The case of Islamic banking cannot be advanced unless a strong system of inter-bank transactions based on Islamic principles is developed. The lack of such a system forces the Islamic banks to turn to the conventional banks for their short-term needs of liquidity which the conventional banks do not provide without either an open or camouflaged interest*". It is highly regrettable that Justice M.Taqi Usmani commended application of so called Islamic banking soiled with element of interest and ignored TMCL plan whereby Pakistan could have got rid of interest immediately.

"204. The basic and foremost characteristic of Islamic financing is that, instead of a fixed rate of interest, it is based on profit and loss sharing". The contention that Islamic financing is based on PLS is not supported by any quotation from Quraan and Sunnah. As present financing is based on interest which is a lending device, Islamic financing must naturally be based on interest-free lending device like TMCL. Interest-bearing loans and PLS were in vogue in pre-Islamic days. Islam prohibited interest, permitted PLS to continue and commended Interest-free loan. Hence Interest-free loan can logically be said to be the basis of Islamic finance and not PLS which is only permitted and not commended.

"229. The upshot of this discussion is that the Doctrine of necessity cannot be applied to protect the present interest-based system for ever or for an indefinite peiiod. However, this doctrine can be availed of for allowing a reasonable time to the Government necessarily required to the switch-over to an interest-free Islamic financial system". This contention is untenable on two grounds. (i) Allah knows when, where and what is necessary for His creatures and has allowed concession where necessary like eating pork for saving life and postponing fasting during illness and travel. Allah has not allowed any such concession in respect of interest nor has He authorized anybody to permit delay in implementing His command using dubious doctrine of necessity. The unanimous judgment written by Mr. Justice Khalil-ur-Rehman states: "The *Ahkam* of Riba are no different from the *Ahkam* of, for example, *salah* (prayer) and *saum* (fasting). The *Ahkam* for none of these were prescribed with the dawn of Islam. However, once ordained, the relevant *Ahkam* were enforced at once". (ii) Immediate switch-over to interest-free banking is possible by implementing TMCL-based interest-free banking plan.

Islamic Economists, Bankers and Shariah advisors are requested to give serious consideration to this discourse and produce a well defined commercially viable interest-free banking plan better than the TMCL plan or endorse the later for replacing the interest-based banking system to get Muslim Ummah rid of the curse of interest and earn Allah's blessings.

FOR URGENT ATTENTION OF THE PARTICIPANTS IN 7TH INTERNATIONAL CONFERENCE ON ISLAMIC ECONOMICS

Going by the past experience it can be said that during this conference loud claims will be made that great advances have been made in Islamic economics and banking where as there is yet no sign of any action having been taken on the deliberations of First Conference on Islamic Economics held 32 years ago. If Islamic economists holding responsible positions in prestigious institutes like IDB, IRTI, Islamic Foundation UK and IIIE Islamabad, had fulfilled their official, moral and religious duty 'a system of interest-free banking, not as a supplement to but as a substitute for the prevalent system of banking' would have replaced interest-based banking and interest would have been banned in Muslim countries long ago. Interest remains lawful and interest-based banking prevails in Muslim countries unabated. Many so-called Islamic banks are prospering on Islamic sentiment of their Muslim clients. They defy Islamic principle *Al-Kharaj bi-al-dhamaan* and earn disguised interest in the form of fixed returns from risk-free fake Murabaha transactions. They exclude pure loans from banking operations and for meeting their own short-term needs of liquidity they take loans on interest and also earn interest on their excess liquidity.

The writer took up the matter of shortcomings and defects in Islamic banking personally with IDB president during 4th Conference on Islamic Economics in August 2000. IDB letter of 2nd October 2000 advised the writer *"Referring to the documents submitted to H.E. The president of Islamic development Bank (IDB) about your observation on the Islamic Banking movement, we appreciate very much your good efforts and insights. The Islamic Banks' office of IDB will try to do its best to communicate to the Islamic Banks the shortcomings that you had mentioned in your document."* Islamic banks have not so far moved an inch towards achieving their avowed objective of getting Muslim Ummah rid of interest.

Participants of this conference are requested to give serious consideration to the contents of the attached 6 page document 'Top Priority issue that must be tackled by 7th International Conference on Islamic Economics' and do whatever they can to get Muslim Ummah rid of interest without delay noting that Muhammad *saws* said that those who do not care about the affairs of Muslims are not from amongst us.

DELIBERATIONS OF 7TH INTERNATIONAL CONFERENCE ON ISLAMIC ECONOMICS

Just as Islamic Ideology is based on extinction of *shirk* Islamic Economics is based on extinction of interest. But distinguished speakers on Islamic Economics did not even mention the need of eliminating interest from Muslim world plagued with interest-based system.

According to the deliberations of First such Conference held in 1976 interest must have vanished and banned in Muslim countries long ago. Contrary to those deliberations interest-based banking is flourishing and interest remains lawful in Muslim countries. About 300 so-called Islamic banks and financial institutions have emerged which are supplement to and not substitute of interest-based banks. They do not give loans and at times borrow money on interest and also earn interest on excess liquidity. They are making good money through fake Murabaha transactions. Their Shariah advisors hold whatever they do to be Shariah-compliant! Shaikh Saleh Abdullah Kamel a pioneer in Islamic banking and founder of Al-Baraka Islamic Bank has recently said on BBC TV channel that 90% of present Islamic banking is wrong. It is not understood why Islamic economists do not realise that interest cannot be eliminated without providing interest-free loan facility to loan seekers just as illiteracy cannot be eliminated without providing schooling facility to every child. In extremely short time allowed in two sessions of the conference I brought the following points to the attention of the elite gathering to which nobody responded:-

"Interest-bearing loans and profit-sharing were the financing modes that prevailed in pre-Islamic days. Islam prohibited interest and permitted profit-sharing to continue. As loan is indispensable need of mankind and profit-sharing cannot meet the needs of all sectors of society for loans Islam highly commended interest-free lending by way of a *hadeeth qudsi* declaring reward for *qard* is eighteen times implying that Islam wants widespread use of interest-free loans in society. Borrowing money by Muhammad *saws* and investing borrowed money in business by several sahaba karam *ra* and Imam Abu Haneefa *ra* prove that interest-free debt-based system is desirable in Islam. Regrettably contemporary Islamic economists ignore these facts and say profit-sharing is ideal Islamic alternative of interest and denounce debt-based system even if it is interest-free. It is like condemning *nikah* alongwith *zina*! Late Prof. Shaikh Mahmud Ahmad was perhaps the only participant who took seriously the deliberations of the First Conference on Islamic Economics held in 1976. Accordingly he strove for finding a substitute of interest-based banking and produced a commercially viable interest-free banking model based on his novel concept of Time Multiple Counter Loan – TMCL. This model can provide all modern banking services and interest-free loans on wide scale and as such it can easily replace conventional banking without any disruption. Information on working details of this model and its benefits for Muslim Ummah is available on my website: www.realislamicbanking.com It is the moral and professional duty of Islamic economists and bankers to either devise a better alternative or support and adopt TMCL model for replacing conventional banking."

Recipients of this discourse are requested to ponder on it and the attached 2 page Word document on 'Basic Principles and Methodology for True Islamic Banking' and comment on them.

BASIC PRINCIPLES AND METHODOLOGY FOR TRUE ISLAMIC BANKING

Islamic bank must conduct business strictly complying in letter and spirit with Islamic principles laid down in Quraan and Hadeeth and fulfill the following requirements in its own and Muslim Ummah's interest:-

Total abstention from interest. No open or disguised interest shall ever be paid or charged by the bank. All transactions shall be interest-free, transparent and above doubt with no promise or understanding separate from the main contract.

The bank shall earn profits only from investing in PLS and permissible trading modes noting that gain in trade permitted in Quraan is governed by the principle *Al-Kharaaj bi Al-dhamaan* meaning that profit is tied with risk of loss i.e. no risk no gain. Risk here means market risk and not the risk of loss due to some accident or failure in payment. As market conditions constantly change definite gain without risk of loss is impossible from genuine trading. Definite gain with no risk of loss is obtainable only from lending money at interest. The bank shall strictly avoid interest - like profit earning in the form of predetermined return on investment.

Islamic bank shall advance interest-free loans. Quraan lays down that lender's claim is limited to the principal amount of loan and as such the bank shall not receive from the borrower any amount on any pretext like service charge, in excess of the principal amount of loan. Loan is indispensable need of mankind and interest-free loans are not available on commercial scale. Interest-based banking prevails in Muslim countries only because it fulfills the needs of all sectors of the society for loans. As Islam caters for all legitimate needs of mankind, Islamic bank worthy of its name must provide interest-free loans for permissible purposes including business. Muhammad *saws* himself bought food items on credit and borrowed for state purposes. Also several Sahaba Karaam *ra* and Imam Abu Haneefah *ra* borrowed money for doing business. Hence it is terribly wrong to hold borrowing to be undesirable. What is condemnable and unpardonable is non-repayment of loan. Islam prohibits interest and *zina* and commends interest-free lending and *nikah*. Accordingly interest-laden debt-based economy is condemnable, but condemning interest-free debt-based economy is as wrong as condemning *nikah* along with *zina*.

Providing interest-free loan facility to loan seekers by Islamic bank is absolutely necessary for eliminating interest and pulling Muslim Ummah out of the miserable state of war with Allah. Profit sharing and lending at interest were the prevalent financing modes in pre-Islamic days. Islam prohibited interest and permitted profit sharing to continue. Profit sharing cannot meet the financing needs of all sectors of the society especially the financing needs of very large sector of the economy comprising millions of privately owned enterprises keen on protecting their independence and ownership structure. Accordingly Islam highly commended interest-free lending by way of a *hadeeth qudsi* declaring reward for *qard* is eighteen times, implying that Islam wants widespread use of interest-free loans in society. It is quite wrong to hold profit sharing to be ideal Islamic alternative of interest as it is only permitted and not commended whereas interest-free lending is highly commended. Hence interest-free lending can be held to be ideal Islamic alternative of interest and not profit sharing. It is a gross misconception that interest can be eliminated by using profit sharing for financing. Interest cannot be eliminated without providing interest-free loan facility to loan seekers just as illiteracy cannot be eliminated without providing schooling facility to every child.

A true Islamic banking model based on the above stated principles was produced by Late Professor Shaikh Mahmud Ahmad applauded in Supreme Court Shariat Appellate Bench unanimous judgment of 23rd Dec 1999 in Riba case as "our country's most outstanding economist, researcher and leading thinker who had devoted considerable part of his life to the study of the theory of interest". He conceived of a novel interest-free lending device named TMCL (Time Multiple Counter Loan). TMCL-based interest-free banking model devised by him is commercially viable and is capable of providing Islamically all modern banking services and also interest-free loans on as large a scale as interest-bearing loans are provided by conventional banks. This model was unanimously held to be potentially useful by a 17-member panel of senior economists and bankers appointed by Council of Islamic Ideology (CII)) to produce interest-free economic system. In its report of 15th June 1980 to the government CII recommended use of TMCL principle by banks for giving interest-free loans to account holders for personal and non-productive purposes. Supreme Court Shariat Appellate Bench that heard the famous Riba case in 1999 comprised of 5 judges including two renowned Islamic Scholars, Mufti M. Taqi Usmani and Dr. Mahmud Ahmad Ghazi.

The writer presented in the Supreme Court TMCL banking model as Islamic substitute of interest-based banking and argued in its favour. It was well received by all the judges and it is narrated in the Supreme Court Unanimous judgment of 23rd December 1999 without any adverse comment.

HOW ISLAMIC BANKS CAN GET THEMSELVES AND MUSLIM COUNTRIES RID OF INTEREST

It is ironic mistake of Islamic banks not to lend money that is universally recognized main bank function. Islam prohibits interest but highly commends interest-free loan. *Hadeeth qudsi* declares *reward for qard is 18 times*, implying that Islam wants widespread use of interest-free loans in society, Muhammad *saws* took loans for state purpose. Some *Sahabah ra* and also Imam Abu Haneefa *ra* borrowed money for investing in business. Hence it is utterly wrong for Islamic economists to dissent pure loans and for Islamic banks to avoid interest-free lending. Loans bring idle surplus money in circulation and boost the economy. Abundant supply of bank loans, though interest-based, to enterprises brought tremendous economic development in the West.

Islamic banks started emerging in seventies of the last century with the declared aim to get Muslim societies rid of interest. About three hundred Islamic banks are now prospering in seventy countries but so far they have not got even themselves rid of interest, nor have they produced any dent in interest-based banking prevailing in Muslim countries. Islamic banks do not give loans even to one another and in times of need Islamic banks and governments of Muslim countries take loans on interest. Against Pakistan's urgent request for funds in 1998 after nuclear explosion Islamic Development Bank and several other Islamic banks jointly offered a loan on interest and that too at a rate 5% above LIBOR!

M. Taqi Usmani is chairman or member of Sharia Advisory Boards of a dozen or more Islamic banks. In 'introduction to Islamic Finance' on the dire need of Islamic banks for a system of interest-free lending he writes "*The case of Islamic banking cannot be advanced unless a strong system of inter-bank transactions based on Islamic principles is developed. The lack of such a system forces the Islamic banks to turn to the conventional banks for their short-term needs of liquidity which the conventional banks do not provide without either an open or camouflaged interest."*

Loan is indispensable need of mankind and at present interest-based banking meets this need of all sectors of society. That is why interest-based banking, though exploitative and prohibited in Islam, prevails in Muslim and non-Muslim world. If apart from making money Islamic banks also want to get themselves and Muslim countries rid of interest then they must give interest-free loans to loan seekers for genuine business, social welfare and personal needs. IDB-IRTI Research Paper no 29 and Sept 2002 issue of the Journal 'Islamic Economic Studies' highlight the need and importance of interest-free loans as follows:

*In order to effectively replace interest the Islamic economy needs a comprehensive financing mechanism defined as a mechanism which provides*monetary financial accommodation to enterprises but remains neutral with respect to their longer run ownership structure" Obviously the needed mechanism defined here is interest-free loan as it can meet all financing needs of enterprises keen on protecting their independence and ownership structure.

"Dayn financing plays an important role in Islamic financial system" 'Dayn' includes loan and other liabilities.

For giving interest-free loans Islamic banks can use commercially viable novel interest-free lending device TMCL (Time Multiple Counter Loan) invented by late Prof. Sheikh Mahmud Ahmed applauded in Supreme Court Shariat Appellate Bench judgment of 23rd Dec 1999 in Riba case as" our country's most outstanding economist, researcher and leading thinker who had devoted considerable part of his life to the study of the theory of interest".

TMCL transaction comprises two simultaneously exchanged interest-free loans between two parties such that the multiple of the amount and period of one loan equals the multiple of the amount and period of the other loan. It facilitates loans of large sums against counter-loans of much smaller sums for proportionately longer periods. For example, a trader can get a loan of RS 10.M for one year by advancing a counter-loan of RS 1.M to the bank for ten years. As per agreement the trader returns Rs 10.M to the bank in one year and the bank returns Rs 1.M to the trader after 10 years.

The bank earns by investing counter-loan money in long-term profitable shariah-compliant modes. Thus TMCL enables the borrower to get interest-free finance and also enables the bank to earn profit and play effective role in eliminating interest. Unlike interest-based loan, in TMCL transaction none of the two parties is a definite gainer or loser and each of them may gain or lose by investing the money borrowed from the other party. As in TMCL transaction both parties do good to each other it conforms with Quraanic precept hal jaza-ul-ihsan illa-alihsan and teaching in hadeeth that a favour done should be reciprocated.

The five member Supreme Court Shariat Appellate Bench that heard Riba case included two sharia expert judges M.Taqi Usmani and Dr. Mahmud Ahmed Ghazi. The writer presented in the Court TMCL plan for immediate elimination of interest and also submitted his book on TMCL-based interest-free banking officially in the court and also individually to each judge. It was well received in the court and no judge raised any objection on TMCL. The plan is also described with no adverse comment in the Supreme Court unanimous judgment of 23rd Dec1999.

In its report of 15 June 1980 Council of Islamic Ideology held profit-sharing and interest-free loan as ideally real alternatives of interest and recommended use of TMCL principle by banks for giving loans to account holders for personal and non-productive purposes. Kuwaiti Finance House fatwa no: 264 quoted in a book co-authored by Dr. Abdul Sattar Abu Ghudda and Dr. Ahmed Mohiuddin Ahmad and also Dallah Albaraka group unified Sharia panel Fatwa 11/6 clearly indicate permissibility of TMCL in Sharia. Thus compliance of TMCL with Sharia is proved beyond any doubt.

At present TMCL is the only known commercially viable financing device that can effectively and imminently eliminate interest and also fulfill the intent of the above mentioned hadeeth qudsi. Hence use of TMCL for giving interest-free loans is bound to be blissful for Islamic Banks.

Muhammad saws said" Those who do not care about the affairs of Muslims are not from amongst us" Hence every Muslim must strive utmost to get Muslim Countries rid of interest.

2

Prohibition of Interest in Islam

Quraan gives the following order and warning to believers:-

"O ye who believe fear Allah, and give up the Riba that remains outstanding if ye are believers indeed and if ye do it not, be warned of war from Allah and His Rasool s.a.w.s. and if ye repent, for ye will be your capital sums (only). Deal not unjustly, and ye shall not be dealt with unjustly" (2:278, 279)

Upon revelation of the above Quraanic verse, our Prophet Muhammad *s.a.w.s.* invalidated all interest earnings which were due for payment on outstanding debts. At the same time he asked the Christian tribes in Najran also to give up interest and warned them that peace treaty with them would be canceled if they did not give up interest. Our Prophet *s.a.w.s* said that consuming one Dirham of interest is worse than committing the sin of adultery thirty-six times.

The above quotations from Quraan and Sunnah make it absolutely clear, leaving no iota of doubt, that:-

1. All believers (rich and poor) must fear Allah and give up *Riba.*
2. True belief and *Riba* cannot co-exist.
3. Clinging to *Riba* is an act of war against Allah and His Rasool *s.a.w.s.*
4. Any amount (big or small) in excess of the original amount of loan (advanced for any purpose-consumption, trade, industry or agriculture) charged from any one (rich or poor) is *Riba.*
5. Charging of *Riba* by any one and from any one is unjust.
6. Interest charged on all loans including those advanced by banks is *Riba* forbidden in Quraan.
7. Interest paid by banks on deposits is also *Riba* forbidden in Quraan, as the deposits are loans to the banks which the banks have to return to the depositors.

Allah has declared in Quraan:-

"This day have I perfected your religion for you, completed my favour upon you and have chosen for you Islam as your religion" (5:3).

The above declaration makes it quite clear that Quraanic commands are all final, comprehensive and valid for all times. Therefore it is a folly to contend that Quraanic Prohibition does not apply to banking interest on the pretext that at the time of advent of Islam only consumption loans were in vogue which is belied by historical evidence. The above contention of advocates of interest amounts to denial of Quraanic Declaration and deserves to be condemned by all Muslims.

Federal Shariat court in its momentous unanimous fully documented judgment given on 14 November'91 held modern interest in all its forms to be *Riba* and ordered the government to eliminate interest from the fiscal system of the country by 30 June'92.

The government filed in the Supreme Court an appeal on flimsy grounds, which is still pending and the government is unfortunately continuing the interest-based system in contravention of the Quraanic injunctions, which is bringing the country's economy closer and closer to complete collapse.

SYMPTOMS OF INTEREST-BASED AILING ECONOMY

Following extracts from analyses of country's economic situation by independent economists and commentators and finally the frank admission by our Finance Minister himself provides sufficient proof of the failure of interest-based economy. Strangely enough our rulers and economy managers still remain unmoved to reverse the fatal policy of promoting interest and to get rid of the malady which has driven the country into the present disastrous situation.

1. M. Ziauddin-DAWN Economic & Business Review June 29-July 5, 1998 :-

The freeze was put in order actually to cover up the utter failure of the government to manage its foreign exchange budgets which had been burdened with a massive short-term debt over the last sixteen months...Why has the stock exchange crashed? Why has the foreign exchange sector gone into a tailspin?. Why are the banks asking for the margins against L/Cs of our businessmen? Why are we looking for swaps at 2-3% over Libor ? The reason is simple. Pakistan's economy has been in a tailspin since November,1996 when former President Leghari dismissed the then government accusing it of mismanaging the economy. From that point onwards the economy has fallen into a bottomless pit. The economic managers of Farooq Leghari made a mess of things. And when Nawaz Sharif came in with his own managers, things began to go from bad to worse. The government did not freeze the foreign currency accounts on May 28 because it was afraid of capital flight following the nuclear test. The government is using the cover of the Nuclear explosion and the assumed threat to Pakistan's economy from the almost non-existent sanctions to mobilize charity from Pakistanis here and abroad as well as from friendly governments to dole out foreign exchange to cover the widening gap between the resources available and the resources to make the two ends meet in the next twelve months.

2. Sultan Ahmad-DAWN Economic & Business Review June 29-July 5,1998 :-

Overseas Pakistanis have good reasons to be wary of making large funds available to the government even at this stage. They are too unhappy with the manner their foreign currency deposits of $2.1 billion (according to our Finance Minister) in our banks out of the total deposits of $11 billion were frozen immediately after the nuclear explosions of May 28. They hold that too arbitrary and unilateral and a blunt breach of contract with them. The government now wants them to make generous donations instead of deposits as it feels it would not be able to return the funds received as interest-bearing deposits in the short or medium term because of its total external debt of $32 billion even after the freezing of the $11 billion deposits of resident and non-resident Pakistanis in our banks... But the people within the country and abroad fear that if the volume of the new foreign exchange deposits in these accounts rise substantially, the government may grab hold of their deposits again and use them to meet its own emergent needs. So the government has not been able to sell this parallel banking scheme to the resident or overseas Pakistanis...

The educated Pakistanis working abroad on the other hand keep their money abroad, make investment, and acquire apartments. And they are sending very little home. Some of them had sent a part of their savings for foreign exchange deposits in our banks as Pakistan offered attractive interest, and the earnings were free of tax and *zakat* and the source of funds was beyond question... The government is in a real quandary with only a billion dollar reserve, and a reported $500 million to be paid before June 30 to service the overdue short term loans... The state bank of Pakistan documents show that among the $12.848 billion foreign exchange liabilities before freezing the dollar deposits, is a deposit of $450 million made in the State Bank of Pakistan by the U.A.E government and another deposit of $350 million made by China in the State Bank and various foreign exchange bonds of Pakistan. Foreign banks which had provided short term loans at high interest rates are now reported to be unwilling to roll over the loans which had reached their maturity. Foreign banks have now been invited to bring in even half a million dollars as swap funds paid for in Rupees in exchange instead of the $5 million they were asked to bring in and increase their lending volume. But the lowering of the credit rating of Pakistan in the foreign exchange sector by international agencies stands in the way.

3. Report-DAWN Economic & Business Review June 29-July 5, 1998 :-

The State Bank devalued the Rupee by Rs1.97 or 4.4% to a dollar at the fag-end of the week apparently in a bid to boost export to the level of $10 billion set in the new trade policy. The spot buying and selling rates were revised upwards to Rs46.00 and Rs46.46 to a Dollar but in kerb trading it weakened to Rs51.00 and Rs51.51, creating a big wedge of Rs5.00 between the official and the open market rates.

4. M. B. Naqvi-DAWN Economic & Business Review June 29-July 5, 1998 :-

Islamabad, despite these facts, has gone on relying entirely on Pakistan's economy turning the corner and picking up steam as a result of a massive inflow of foreign funds. Mr. Sartaj Aziz has done well to warn that just as East-Asian tigers paid a heavy price for total reliance on capital and for giving it maximum scope without any let or hindrance or control, Pakistanis should be warned against it. Well and truly said, Mr.Aziz, but the persons to be warned are sitting in Islamabad around him and he himself is among them. It is he who is responsible for the policy being pursued which, one has described as foolish within parenthesis, it is for Islamabad's mandarins to take heed and do something about it. The fact of the matter is that Pakistan need particularly strong alarm bells. The reason is that Pakistan economy is and has been in trouble. We have far too many external liabilities for which there are not enough countervailing assets particularly in foreign exchange. We have the short term liabilities which require any thing up to $2 billion and some say even $2.5 billion per year to service. The liability of repayment of the main external official debt is around $2 billion per year. The total size of the country's economy is very small particularly in comparison with the external liabilities; the latter amount to nearly 45% of the GDP. Our total liabilities all told is assessed at some where between $40 to 50 billion whereas our GDP is whisker above $50 billion. The long and short of it is that if massive foreign investments come in despite these conditions what we shall have is a bubble economy. Please remember that the local industries can have only small weight in the economy and their weight in the bourses or stock exchanges would remain particularly small because FDI and the hot money holders will dominate the capital market. What can we do about it is the question. And well may Mr.Sartaj Aziz ponder over it more than an average Pakistani need to ponder.

5. Dr. Mahnaz Fatima-DAWN Economic & Business Review June 29 - July 5, 1998:-

Pakistan's industrial history is therefore, more a history of fiscal concessions and / or incentives, concessionary / subsidised financing at least until the extension of the recent market reforms to the banking sector, and exchange rate adjustments. Such a long history of industrial pampering should have enabled the industry to grow out of its infancy. By now it should have been competing vigorously in the international markets. Short term profits maximization of a handful has been the primary goal of most businesses / industries in the country. Thus the need for more concessions, more protections, more incentives, and more exchange rate adjustments. Unless this vicious circle is broken through a cooperative effort of decision makers at both the micro and macro levels, industrial activity will continue to be seen as a function of fiscal policy alone. And export growth will continue to be regarded primarily a function of frequent exchange rate adjustment which it should not be. The finance ministry has grown powerful but remains not so effective in the alignment of economic objectives. It needs to share power and responsibility with other ministries and departments. By considering action on the above lines with a view to removing structural weaknesses, Pakistan should try to achieve sustainable growth rather than looking constantly towards the World Bank / IMF / ADB to keep us afloat. It will however, need a will-power as strong as the one that remained consistently behind the country's nuclear program.

6. Syed Asad Ali Shah-DAWN Economic & Business Review July 6-12,1998 :-

Pakistan is facing the worst financial and economic turmoil in its 50-year history, as the country continues its slide toward economic, social and political chaos. The alarming deterioration in the economic and financial conditions of the country will escalate even more the immense hardships for its people in the days ahead. Already, the economic downturn and lack of industrial and commercial activity has started to take a toll in terms of rising unemployment, social unrest and upsurge in violence and crime.... Thus the per capita income of the country has been drastically reduced from $490 in 1996 to less than $400... The government has already defaulted on its commitments to resident and non-resident Pakistanis by freezing their foreign currency accounts. The country is heading towards a default on its external debt service obligations, as it faces an unbridgeable gap of over $5.5 billion in its balance of payments. What is needed is to adopt a pragmatic approach for developing a viable strategy to rescue Pakistan from its dire predicament. For this we have to accept that the country stands insolvent, and it needs some kind of a moratorium on its debt obligations along with some kind of a bale-out package. The sooner we start working on a realistic rescue strategy, the lesser will be the pain and duration of the remedial process.

7. M. Ziauddin-DAWN Economic & Business Review July 6 - 12, 1998 :-

Pakistan's annual budgets have been collapsing consistently within four months of their announcement since 1995. Every October since October 1995 successive governments have had to devalue the currency upsetting the budgetary estimates announced in July. But this time, the budget for the current year collapsed even before it came into effect as after having passed the budgetary proposals for 1998-99 on June 26, 1998, the government went and devalued the currency on June 27, three days before July 1, 1998 the first day of the new budget. Clearly, almost all the estimates of the 1998-99 budget, especially those that concern imports, and repayments of foreign debt have gone haywire because of the official devaluation on June 27, 1998. The massive gap between the official and the market rate of the dollar also indicates that the government will have to adjust the rupee yet again before long, causing further erosion of the budgetary estimates. Now we are left with $900 million to meet our daily import bills and other payments the bulk of which would be amortization dues on September 30, 1998. There is no likelihood in the immediate future of exports growing at the desired rate. And on the other hand, unless the overseas Pakistani workers regain confidence in the official economic managers of the country, they are not going to remit their hard-earned foreign exchange through the official banking channels which would virtually deprive Pakistan of its legitimate dues amounting to about $1.5 billion a year. They have started sending their money through the *hundi*. This is a highly disturbing scenario. One can make any number of paper suggestions to wish this scenario to vanish. But unless the government comes up with some nationally acceptable and widely welcome economic policies and soon, the scenario is likely to become a reality in six months time.

8. Ather Zaidi-DAWN Economic & Business Review July 6 - 12, 1998 :-

As already stated debt servicing requirements next year would increase by 16% at constant prices as against the stipulated increase of 6% in the GDP and 14% increase in the tax revenue. If we assume that the debt service liability of the government would continue to follow the same trend, it only means that the debt liability of the government would be increasing at a rate higher than the revenue earnings and we would never be able to emerge from the debt trap. This is a very dismal picture but unfortunately this is what the data reflects. In the present scenario, the debt burden as well as the cost of debt servicing will go on increasing in a geometric progression, and would soon be beyond our capacity to pay back. Apart from the rhetorics of the budget speech, the budget document has no relevance to the realities of the situation, and as such makes hardly any move towards self-reliance. As a matter of fact, the government plans to borrow more in absolute terms in the next year to meet its budget deficit than it would be borrowing in the current year.

9. Sultan Ahmed-DAWN Economic & Business Review July 6 - 12, 1998 :-

The government which presumed it had liquidated its major foreign currency burden by repudiating its commitment to repay the $11 billion deposits of private individuals and institutions in our banks in Dollars immediately after the nuclear explosions of May 28, now finds it has created another major problem in the process: fast outflow of funds after conversion into Rupees to foreign safe havens through the *Havala* chain. Mr.Shaukat Tareen the president of Habib Bank has spoken about drying up of the capital markets, while banks and financial institutes are suffering from liquidity problems. Along with that there is pressure on home remittances as overseas Pakistanis have become wary of sending foreign exchange home.

And since our foreign exchange reserves have come down and now stand at $913 million, as stated by the State Bank Governor Dr. Muhammad Yaqub, even if those who have large foreign exchange deposits want to believe the government for patriotic reasons, they find the government does not have the capability to honour its domestic foreign currency commitments even after restoring the foreign currency accounts as he did on Tuesday, following pressure from Pakistanis in Kuwait. So the government's viable options are too small and too tough as in the case of all those heavily indebted countries. And ghastly stories of vast misuse of public funds by the rulers over the years have left the people with little enthusiasm for helping the government. In such a context, the government should be more realistic and less breezily optimistic and come up with the right contingency plan. Having built an unhealthy economic system and a plutocracy in the name of democracy, they cannot expect the people to make heavy sacrifices while the rulers and the owning class will not or do not seem to be doing that. Let the government hence formulate the right policy, pursue that consistently and take the people along with real good governance as its centre piece.

10. DAWN - July 17,1998 :-

PAKISTAN MAY STOP PAYING DEBTS: SARTAJ

Washington, July 16 : Finance Minister Sartaj Aziz said in an interview published here on Thursday that Pakistan was running out of money and might stop paying its debts. He told the *Washington Times* that the flow of money from the lenders from the world over had dried up since the sanctions were imposed last month. The US State Department, however, disagrees with his claims and in several comments made in the last few days senior officials have argued that economic situation in Pakistan was not caused by the impact of the sanctions but because of the government failure to implement the much-needed structural reforms in the past 18 months. Mr. Aziz said : "our reserves are really low. If we don't get new money then obviously we are unable to pay our debt servicing".

11. Irfan Husain-DAWN 18 July, 1998 :-

As Pakistan teeters on the brink of default we have to face the fact that the problem was brewing much earlier than the nuclear tests and the resultant sanctions. Decades of living beyond our means have brought us to this present pass: year after year, a succession of governments have spent more than the revenue they collected, and imported more than we exported. To make ends meet, we have borrowed heavily from internal and external sources. Now we can no longer service our external loans. What are the consequences of the impending default? First and foremost, nobody will lend us a penny unless it is at exorbitant interest rates. No foreign exporter will accept letters of credit from our banks, and will demand cash up front. The Rupee will collapse against the Dollar, and inflation will ravage what is left of the economy. Essential imports will be slow to a trickle, and industry will come to a grinding halt for want of spare parts and raw material. The stock market, already at its lowest ever level, can no longer be considered a vehicle for capital formation: any new offering in the foreseeable future is doomed to sink without a trace.

12. Shaheen Sehbai-DAWN 23 July, 1998 :-

The officials said Pakistan's economy was in deep trouble and was fragile and the fear was that it could get worse. The root cause of this situation was not US sanctions but gross economic mismanagement by Pakistani rulers.

CAUSE OF DETERIORATING PLIGHT OF ECONOMY

For the past many years our successive governments have been spending lavishly on luxuries and very little on the most needed technological development. In the Federal Budget expenditure of Rs495.7 billion for the year 1998-99 only Rs0.14 billion are allocated for Science and Technology.

Living beyond our means and importing goods worth more than export earnings produce gaps between expenditure and revenues and between import and export bills. For bridging the gap between expenditure and revenues, interest bearing savings schemes are floated and excess money is printed which gives rise to inflation. For bridging the gap between import and export bills, foreign currency interest bearing loans are obtained in the name of foreign aid. Interest costs of borrowings widen the gaps between expenditure and revenues and between export and import bills. For bridging of these ever widening gaps the quantum of interest bearing loans obtained every year has consistently been increasing with the consequent rise in the debt burden and expenditure on debt servicing.

Due to the perpetual increase in the quantum of loans and ever increasing interest costs on accumulated debts, the debt burden has grown so much that foreign exchange reserves with the government are not sufficient even to meet foreign currency debt servicing charges, let alone the possibility of retiring any fraction of the debt. Our Finance Minister has said "Pakistan is running out of money and might stop paying its debts". National Agenda for Self-Reliance has been thrown overboard and the government is begging for dollars from outside. Foreign currency accounts were frozen in a frantic confidence shaking move which has caused irreparable damage to the country's faltering economy. Instead of reverting to Allah and seeking Islamic solution of the problem, our rulers acted upon their own wisdom and tumbled throwing the country in unprecedented economic catastrophe.

Allah warns in Quraan:-

"*Whosoever violates My Commands verily for him livelihood will become distressful*" (20:124).

REMEDY FOR DETERIORATING PLIGHT OF ECONOMY

Instead of seeking a remedy for the problem the government looks towards foreign lenders for further interest-bearing loans which aggravate the problem by adding to the debt burden and help the government in postponing the eventual default only for a while.

Professional economists having no vested interests are expressing urgency of reducing interest rate for some economic recovery. In June 1997, the Finance Minister Mr.Sartaj Aziz himself declared that economic revival and 7% industrial growth could be achieved only by reducing interest rate from 22% to 12%. It is not understood why Mr.Sartaj Aziz did not order reduction in interest rate for achieving economic revival and industrial growth so desperately needed by the country. It is also not understood why he did not aim at a larger reduction in interest rate for achieving quicker revival of the economy and growth rate higher than 7%.

Mr.Shahid Kardar in a valuable article published in 'DAWN' of 12 September'97 has stated inter alia "... These efforts have to be supplemented with a reduction in the rates of interest that industry is being called upon to pay in these recessionary conditions. ... The formidable amount required for servicing the debt built up over the years is the root cause of the current fiscal crisis.

Debt servicing, both domestic and external, has become prohibitively expensive... . No amount of growth in revenues will be adequate to service the huge stock of debt... the current levels of interest rates payable by the government on its borrowings is a critical factor in its inability to have enough from its revenues to fund developmental activities. Since savings in government-sponsored schemes are offering interest rates of 16% to 19% the more practicable proposition for pruning the size of deficit would be for the government to lower the yields on its securities and savings schemes. ...Industrial revival is being thwarted by the high rates of interest. These rates which are higher than the returns being earned on productive investments, are merely deepening the recession and increasing financial distress... The double squeeze of high interest rates and a highly depressed economy is straining the corporate sector's profitability and steadily driving even the better managed companies into a very tight corner... There is every reason to fear that even the few healthy banks and companies that are still there may find it difficult to survive in these difficult times... THE ONLY CHANCE OF SOME RECOVERY AND OF GETTING THE ECONOMY MOVING LIES IN CUTTING INTEREST RATES... DOMESTIC INTEREST RATES ARE FAR TOO HIGH EVEN TO KEEP THE REAL ECONOMY AFLOAT, LET ALONE GET IT ON TO A SUSTAINABLE GROWTH LEVEL".

The above assertions make it clear that professional economists who have grown up and lived with interest-based system recommend reduction in interest rate for some recovery of the economy. They do not recommend elimination of interest for full recovery of the economy probably because they are not conversant with any viable banking instrument which can replace interest. If they are anxious to alienate themselves from interest and sincerely look for a substitute of interest, as Shaikh Mahmud Ahmad *r.a.* did, they would surely find that interest can beneficially be replaced by TMCL-Time Multiple Counter Loan - based on Islamic concept of *Qard hasan.*

The only remedy for deteriorating plight of our economy and the only way to bring prosperity to the country and to take it out of the debt trap is elimination of interest and its substitution by TMCL.

Allah says in Quraan "*verily never will Allah change the condition of a people until they change what is in themselves*" (13:10). Therefore for saving the economy from complete collapse and the country from disaster, it is absolutely essential that we revert to Allah, repent on the past sins and ask for His pardon, and abolish interest in abidance of His Command. Allah says in Quraan "*Whosoever follows My guidance will not lose his way nor fall into misery*" (20:123).

PRACTICABLE WAY TO ABOLISH INTEREST

Allah is All-Knowing and whatever He has ordained is feasible and good for humanity and whatever He has forbidden is harmful for humanity and is not indispensable. No good can ever be achieved without implementing Allah's Will and Allah's wrath cannot be averted while persistently indulging in what He has forbidden. Any one believing in Quraan should have no hesitation in implementing Quraanic precepts. However, if our rulers somehow misapprehend insurmountable difficulties in their way to abolish interest, they should take inspiration and courage from the Quraanic verse "*To Him who believes in Allah and the last day and for those who fear Allah He (ever) prepares a way out. And He provides for him from (sources) he never could imagine. And if anyone puts his trust in Allah sufficient is Allah for him*"(65:2,3).

If our rulers fear Allah and confide in His Words and resolve to finish the on-going war against Allah and His Rasool *s.a.w.s* and if logic is allowed to prevail upon prejudice against change we will soon find interest-free banking system working in the country satisfactorily and economy recovering fast.

Government is required only to decide and declare that interest will cease to be legal in six months and after six months it will become criminal offence according to the country's law as it is according to the Divine Law. Even for those who are earning interest on their savings the above decision will be far less shocking and of much less consequence than the declaration of emergency and freezing of foreign currency accounts. This decision of the government to abolish main cause of inflation and unemployment will be highly applauded in the country and all people, excepting infinitesimal minority of vested interests, will welcome the first practical step towards vindicating our allegiance to Islam and ideology of Pakistan.

Logical sequel to the government's decision to abolish interest will be that bankers will immediately set out to evolve interest-free banking system for which fortunately there is no need to start ab-initio because present banking system can be easily converted into interest-free system by inducting a new instrument conceived by Shaikh Mahmud Ahmad *r.a.* which he named Time Multiple Counter Loan -TMCL as substitute for interest. TMCL is a workable substitute for interest but shorn of its exploitative content.

Immediately after the government's above mentioned declaration, banks will stop paying and receiving interest and entering into interest-based deals and commence transforming current interest-based transactions into TMCL-based transactions. Such transformations may involve some complications but there is sufficient talent available in the country and the same bankers who have developed and are successfully running the present system can surely convert the present system into TMCL-based interest-free system within six months or even earlier. Where there is a will there is a way. TMCL concept and TMCL-based interest-free banking and gains to accrue therefrom are elaborated in the following chapters.

PRINCIPLE OF INTEREST-FREE BANKING

Every loan is composed of two elements, one is the amount of loan and the other is the period for which the loan is advanced. Multiple of these two elements is defined as the loan value. Loan of five thousand Rupees advanced for two years has loan value of 5000x2=10,000 Rupee-years. Similarly loan of one thousand Rupees advanced for ten years has also loan value of 1000x10=10,000 Rupee-years. If two parties exchange loans of different amounts but of same loan value the transaction is equitable and interest-free as each party receives and pays back whatever it gives and takes in loan. Such transaction facilitates obtaining interest-free loan of large amount by any entrepreneur against advancing loan of much smaller amount for proportionately longer period which is named as Time Multiple Counter Loan - TMCL.

Main function of conventional banks to provide loans of large amounts for industry, agriculture and trade can be performed by granting interest-free loans of large amounts in exchange of TMCL of much smaller amounts but of equal loan values advanced by the borrowers to the bank. For example if an entrepreneur needs a loan of two million Rupees for a period of one year he can get this loan free of interest on TMCL basis by advancing two hundred thousand Rupees to the bank for a period of ten years. In this transaction the borrower gets ten multiples of the amount of money he advances to the bank and the period in which he gets his money back is also ten multiples of the period in which he has to return the loan to the bank. Thus interest can be eliminated from the existing banking system easily through the substitution of interest by TMCL. In the following chapter is given brief description of functioning of TMCL-based interest-free banking system in providing the same services and facilities as are available in the existing interest-based banking system.

TMCL concept is in fact institutionalization of Islamic principle of *Qard hasan* which is defined as "a loan with the only stipulation to return the loaned sum in the future without any increase". It is compatible with the Quraanic precept "*Hal Jaza-ul-Ihsan illul Ihsan*" and also with the noble teaching of our Prophet Muhammad *s.a.w.s* that "*any one to whom a favour is done should reward* it", because the two parties exchanging loans of equal loan values do the same good to each other. Therefore, banking system based on TMCL concept is sure to have Allah's blessings and as such it shall succeed and bring prosperity to the country.

OPERATION OF INTEREST-FREE BANKING SYSTEM

According to the Divine Law interest is a criminal offence of such a magnitude that it amounts to rebellion against Allah and His Rasool *s.a.w.s.* Rebellion cannot be tolerated for even one moment and there is no concept of a declared crime being permitted to be phased out in stages or continued for even one day. It is the duty of the government to stop crime and punish criminals, but it is nobody's duty to tell criminals how not to commit crimes like murder, robbery, stealing, adultery etc. No criminals are allowed anywhere to get away with committing crime on the plea that they did not know how to stop committing crime. It is the bounden duty of the government and the financial institutions to ensure that all interest-based transactions are immediately stopped. Immediate execution of this duty in abidance of Quraanic precept is bound to result in immense good for all. It is for the criminals to decide what to do after giving up criminal activity and in the context of interest it is for the bankers to decide how the banking system should be run without interest. However, there is widespread misconception that modern banking system cannot function without interest. For removing the above misconception, following workable proposal is presented for operation of banking system without interest.

For immediate implementation of the Quraanic precept to give up interest there is no necessity to devise a new banking model. What is required to be done by conventional banks is to stop entering into new interest-based contracts, stop paying and charging of interest, and commence providing finance on TMCL basis and start negotiations for converting outstanding interest-based transactions into TMCL-based transactions.

There may be some teething problems which should be resolved as and when they arise. The proposal should not be set aside only due to some envisaged difficulty or problem. If somebody in authority rejects the proposal then he should present a better proposal, but on no account the interest-based system should be allowed to continue as it works against the best interest of the people and flagrantly violates Quraanic injunction.

Existing banks will continue to function as at present but with the basic difference that no interest will be paid to any one and no interest will be charged from any one. In all transactions where credit is involved interest will be replaced by TMCL. Borrowers will be advanced interest-free loans against counter loans of same loan values. Services not involving any credit will be provided against appropriate fees and charges. Main banking functions will be performed with some variations as described below:-

RECEIPT OF DEPOSITS

Banks will continue to receive deposits in customers' accounts and issue cheque books to account holders as at present, but will not pay any interest on deposits.

In spite of non-payment of interest people will perforce continue to deposit their savings in banks as there is no alternative available to them to keep their money in safe custody with facility of making payments by cheques. Discontinuation of payment of interest may displease some depositors but nobody need be sorry for them, firstly because interest is strictly prohibited in Islam, secondly because abolition of interest will alleviate financial miseries of millions of poor people who are deprived of even basic necessities of life and they deserve sympathy far more than those who are earning enough to live well and save, and thirdly because they will also benefit from the general prosperity in the country resulting from elimination of interest from the economy.

Even if some depositors angered by non-payment of interest withdraw their deposits from banks, their money will come back to the banking system through somebody else's account as and when they spend it or invest it or give it away as a gift or in charity. In these days only banks are the resting places for money. The days are gone when people were keeping their money under pillows. Banks may also offer their shares to the depositors who will have the option to convert their deposits into equity and have a share in the profit earnings of the bank.

As shown above there will be no dearth of capital available to the banks. On the contrary with elimination of interest deposits are likely to increase considerably. Keynes, the most eminent economist of the century argued that lower the rate of interest, the higher the level of investment, therefore higher the level of employment, therefore higher the level of incomes, therefore higher the level of savings. His contention was that highest level of savings can be obtained at the lowest level of interest.

Empirical proof supports the above contentions of Keynes. According to world bank statistics gross domestic savings in Pakistan were 13% in 1965 when interest rate was 9% and the savings fell to 5% in 1985 when interest rate had risen to 18%. If logic and empirical evidence have any validity, there is not an iota of doubt that highest possible savings must occur at zero rate of interest. Thus it can be safely concluded that with elimination of interest savings and consequently bank deposits will rise considerably and loaning capacity of banks will increase which will raise levels of investment and employment.

ADVANCEMENT OF LOANS

Higher level of deposits will raise lending capacity of banks. Borrowers will be required to provide collateral as at present. Banks will advance interest-free loans against counter loans of equal loan values. Amount of counter loan may be any percentage of the principal loan amount, negotiable between the bank and the borrower or the monetary authority may fix this percentage and make it obligatory for all loans to be advanced by banks. It is however suggested to be fixed at 10% at the initiation of the interest-free system.

Any entrepreneur borrowing one million Rupees for one year will advance to the bank a counter loan of one hundred thousand Rupees for ten years. If the borrower is unable to return the loan in one year he may get the period extended by giving additional counter loan of appropriate loan value. For example, the period can be extended for another three months if the borrower deposits twenty five thousand Rupees with the bank for ten years or agree to receive back his counter loan amount of one hundred thousand Rupees after twelve and a half years instead of ten years.

In case of default the bank as in the present system can recover the loan from collateral through legal action. In case of inordinate delay in recovery the bank may compensate itself by retaining the borrower's counter loan amount for an appropriate additional period.

CREDIT AVAILABILITY AND LIMITATION TO CONTROL INFLATION

As is shown in the chapter 'economic and financial benefits of interest-free banking' of this booklet, banks in interest-free system will obtain capacity of infinite advancement of loans. Since expansionism is necessary to provide employment to all, the new system will encourage productive expansionism. Credit will be made available against all requests for productive loans whether pertaining to industry, agriculture or trade. In spite of the capacity of infinite advancement of loans in the interest-free system, to exclude consumptional expansionism which has been operative throughout the world ever since the end of World War II, and inflicting virtually unending inflation on it, all non-productive loans whether related to consumptional or speculative or even government budget deficit covering purposes will be denied.

As maximizing of profit earning is the only motive behind the interest-based capitalist economic system, the banks in this system advance all kinds of loans even for consumptional and speculative purposes. The only criteria before the banks in this system is the borrower's financial standing and capability to pay back the capital sum loaned along with the amount of interest accrued. They are not concerned where the loaned sum is invested even if it is utilized in drug or smuggling trade. Advancement of loans for non-productive purposes in this system gives rise to consumptional expansionism which results in unending inflation. Moreover the need for consumptional loans in the capitalist system is largely dictated by the incapacity of purchasing power to keep pace with the productive capability of the system. Leakage of purchasing power occurs primarily due to the element of interest in the cost of production, with identical impulses extending from interest to rent and profit levels. This cumulative exploitation makes labourers incapable of purchasing goods which they themselves produce.

As interest-free system has an ideological base aiming at providing maximum good to maximum number of people, credit will be made available against all requests for loans for productive purposes and requests for loans for non-productive purposes will be denied. Only in exceptional cases consumptional loans will be granted for welfare purposes.

GOVERNMENT BORROWINGS

In the interest-free system, as is shown in the chapter 'economic and financial benefits of interest-free banking' of this booklet, budget deficit will not only vanish but surplus money will also be available for debt retirement and developmental and welfare projects. However if need be, for capital intensive projects in public sector, the government will obtain loans from the money market as at present but such loans will be contracted on counter loan basis and not on interest.

PROCUREMENT OF FUNDS FOR WAR EFFORT

In the existing interest-based capitalist system the money which the government borrows for war effort has to be returned with accumulated interest.

Both men and money are needed to prosecute a war. Distorted sense of values and cultural perversity produced by interest are reflected in the fact that whereas men can be conscripted and get killed in defending the country but the money blooms and prospers. Instead of urging the people to advance *Qarz-e-hasan* for the noble cause of defending the country they are allured to buy Defence Certificates because of higher rate of interest (fraudulently called profit)!

In the interest-free system government will borrow for war effort from the money market on counter loan basis and due to ideological base of the economic system people will come forward in large numbers and make substantial voluntary contributions and donate heavily for war effort which is not likely if the government continues to pursue the policy of sustaining and promoting interest. Experience of National Debt Retirement Scheme in which 85% of the amount came in the interest-based section is sufficient proof of the fact that the policy of sustaining interest in the country has produced amongst the people aversion to serve national cause.

ENCASHMENT OF PREMATURE COMMERCIAL AND TREASURY BILLS

Banks will encash premature bills and bonds as at present but at face value without any charge or discount against an appropriate counter loan advanced by the owner of the bill or bond on TMCL basis. For example if the owner of a bill of ten thousand Rupees wants to encash it thirty days before maturity the bank will pay him ten thousand Rupees against a counter loan having loan value of 10,000x30=300,000 Rupee-days which may be one thousand Rupees for three hundred days or five hundred Rupees for six hundred days etc.

ISSUANCE OF LETTERS OF CREDIT, BANK DRAFTS AND GUARANTEES

Banks will issue letters of credit, drafts, etc. as at present against service charge and where any advance payment by the bank is involved the transaction will be based on TMCL, which means that the customer will not pay any interest but will advance to the bank counter loan of appropriate loan value commensurate with the amount of credit and period involved.

LIQUIDITY ARRANGEMENT

As in the interest-based system, in the interest-free system also every loan amount will come back to the banking system through derivative deposits long before the borrowers return their loans. The banks can lend out these derivative deposits as well and obtain capacity of infinite advancement of loans. In the interest free system statutory bank reserve, together with its affliction of artificial injection of scarcity in the supply of capital will be done away with.

For obtaining liquidity banks will deposit twenty percent of each counter loan amount with the Central Bank against which the Central Bank on the basis of ten percent TMCL will allow banks to draw two hundred percent of counter loan amounts for one year. This will provide twenty percent liquidity to the banking sector. Additional 2% liquidity will be obtained by retaining 20% of counter loan money as till money.

For example, let total deposit in a bank be Rupees ten million all of which is loaned out against receipt of counter loans amounting to Rupees one million. Twenty percent of Rupees one million will be deposited with the Central Bank for ten years against which the bank will be able to draw two hundred percent of Rupees one million (= Rupees two million) for one year. This will provide twenty percent liquidity to the banking sector. Additional two percent liquidity will be obtained by retention of twenty percent of total counter loan amount as till money which will raise the liquidity of the banking sector to 22 percent. Thus in interest-free system 22 percent liquidity will be obtained without diminishing infinite capacity of banks to advance loans. Samuelson records the argument of bankers that legal reserves of as little as ten percent - some of us would say five percent - are all that prudence requires. So far as till money is concerned according to Samuelson "perhaps less than two percent normally seems needed in the form of cash". Hence 22 percent liquidity and 2 percent till money should be regarded more than adequate. However if the monetary authority so desires these can be lowered or raised by varying counter loan and till money percentages.

PROFIT EARNING BY INTEREST-FREE BANKS

As shown in the previous clause on liquidity arrangement, from the total counter loan money received by the banks twenty percent will go to the Central Bank and twenty percent will be held as till money. The remaining sixty percent of the total counter loan money will be available to the banks for profitable investment for which the banks can assume the role of investment banks in the most direct sense. The obvious openings are stock exchange, real estate, investment in new ventures consistent with national priorities and objectives and participating on profit and loss sharing basis in industrial and commercial undertakings owners of which are not keen on concealing from the banks their real incomes for tax evading purposes.

FINANCING AIMED AT DISTRIBUTIVE JUSTICE

In addition to providing interest-free debt-finance for industrial and agricultural development, TMCL- based banks unlike the present Islamic banks dominated by fixed-return modes especially *Murabahah* which do not make any contribution towards distributive justice but adversely affect the people due to increase in prices of goods as is done through interest-based loans, TMCL-based banks will concentrate on profit- sharing modes which are real Shariah compliant financing modes and contribute to distributive justice and welfare of people.

The banks will give option to its account holders to decide as to whether they would keep their money in demand deposits or in investment deposits or split their money into demand deposit and investment deposit. Demand deposits will be invested by the bank but the depositors will have no claim on the profits earned by the bank, and refund of full amounts of deposits will be guaranteed by the bank. Investment deposits will also be invested by the banks and the profit and loss both will be shared on prorata basis between the bank and the account holders. Details can be worked out as to how the profit and loss should be calculated and divided between account holders and the bank. However, in the start, it is suggested that investment account holders may be paid annually of half-yearly profits calculated on daily product basis. The banks will be free to earn profits by all *Shariah* compliant means including whole-sale trading and imports and exports.

SPIRITUAL AND IDEOLOGICAL BENEFITS OF INTEREST-FREE BANKING

The basis of creation of Pakistan was Islam which demands total submission to the Will of Allah. It is irreligious, hypocritical and treacherous to claim allegiance to Islam and ideology of Pakistan and to continue to cling to the evil of interest which is not only an act of disobedience but is also an act of war against Allah and His Rasool *s.a.w.s.* Clinging to the worst of all sins is the main cause of our spiritual degradation and our drifting away from the right path. Abolition of interest will be the first step towards vindicating our allegiance to Islam and ideology of Pakistan. After finishing the on-going war against Allah and His Rasool *s.a.w.s* we can commence our journey to every Muslim's cherished goal of attaining the pleasure of Allah and His Rasool *s.a.w.s.* and good in this world and deliverance and eternal happiness hereafter.

MORAL AND SOCIAL BENEFITS OF INTEREST-FREE BANKING

Interest produces in men unending greed for amassing wealth and it drives them into the morass of selfish motives for obtaining material gains through immoral and criminal means inflicting financial and social miseries upon innocent people and that is why Quraan says "*those who devour interest will not stand except as stands one whom Satan by his touch hath driven to madness. That is because they say trade is like interest*" (2:275).

Allama Iqbal *r.a.* the greatest Muslim thinker of the century, while living in Europe closely studied western culture and institutions and warned Muslims against blind imitation of the west. He held modern bank interest to be an instrument of exploitation, means of affliction and torture, and cause of moral degradation and extinction of affection and fraternity towards fellow human beings. Translation of some of his verses vehemently condemning interest is given below: -

In architectural beauty, shine and candor

Bank buildings excel churches

In appearance it is trade, in reality it is gamble

Interest of one brings destruction to millions

what is the end product of interest ? miseries !

It deprives man of the pleasure of Qard hasan

Interest renders life gloomy, heart rigid as brick and stone

It turns man into beast without teeth and claws.

Not only Muslim exegetes and jurists but also eminent thinkers of high intellect and learning outside the pale of Islam from Aristotle to Bertrand Russel condemned interest as a social evil.

Aristotle wrote "the most hated sort and with the greatest reason, is interest which makes a gain out of money itself, and not from the natural object of it, for money was intended to be used in exchange but not to increase at interest. Of all modes of getting wealth, this is the most unnatural". Bertrand Russel wrote in 'HISTORY OF WESTERN PHILOSOPHY' "usury means all lending money at interest, not only as now, lending at exorbitant rate. Throughout the middle ages the law of nature was held to condemn usury i.e. lending money at interest".

Interest is now so much ingrained in our society that with the exception of an extremely small minority all earn bank interest on their savings and avoid advancing loans to their needy friends because for them money takes precedence over moral obligation to help others. Those who prefer to earn interest and forgo satisfaction and pleasure derived from meeting others' needs, in Iqbal's words, are those who are deprived of the feeling of pleasure obtainable from *Qard hasan* which means advancing of loans without earning any material gain.

With extinction of interest the urge of earning interest on savings will perforce fade away and the biggest obstacle in the way of fulfilling the moral and social duty to help the needy with *Qard hasan* will vanish. Those who are fortunate enough to be able to save from their honest earnings will tend to help the needy with *Qard hasan* and earn moral satisfaction in this world and reward hereafter. This attitude in helping the needy will give impetus to the human instinct of sympathy and affection for fellow beings and will pave the way to establish Islamic social welfare order in the country.

ECONOMIC AND FINANCIAL BENEFITS OF INTEREST-FREE BANKING

Economic and Financial gains to accrue from interest-free banking are many, of which several conspicuous ones are as follows:-

Prices of Consumer Goods Will Fall

In the present system industrialists borrow large sums of money on interest from banks. Interest on the borrowed money paid by the industrialists to the banks is charged to the cost of manufacture. Ex-factory prices of manufactured goods include interest and also an element of profit on the amount of interest. Stockists, distributors, whole-salers and even some retailers also take loans on interest for investing in their business. At each stage of transfer of goods interest charge is added to the cost of goods. Ultimately the consumer bears the entire burden of the interest-charge together with addition of profit element also on the interest charge at each stage of the transfer of goods.

In the interest-free system there will be no interest charge at any stage. Therefore, other cost factors and profits remaining the same, consumer price level of manufactured goods in interest-free system will be much lower than that in interest-based system. Similarly extinction of interest from business and trade will lower prices of non-manufactured goods and other necessities of life also. Our Prophet Muhammad *s.a.w.s.* said that Allah imposes dearness of necessities of life upon the society in which interest gains prevalence. Keynes said the same thing in different words by laying down that direct relationship between interest and prices is one of the most completely established empirical facts within the whole field of quantitative economics. Experience in Pakistan also shows that with continuous rise in interest rate and its spread, prices have consistently risen and they reach new heights every year. Without abolishing interest, consistent rise in prices cannot be checked.

Construction Costs and House Rents Will Fall

With the steep rise in interest rate and its spread in the country the cost of construction and house rents, as for other necessities of life, have also risen tremendously. In major cities of the country houses of moderate size and standard costing about Rs100,000 were rented at about Rs500 per month in 1965 when interest rate was 9% now cost more than Rs500,000 and fetch rent of about Rs2,500 per month when interest rate is about 20%. Apparently construction costs and house rents and prices in general have risen in geometric progression along with the rise in interest rate.

Overall effect of tremendous rise in construction costs and consequent extremely high house rents beyond the reach of most wage earners is that fewer people are building houses for renting out and housing shortage is becoming acute day by day. The reason is that people having surplus money easily earn without doing anything about 15% interest by depositing their money in schemes enticing them in various ways like the possibility of becoming *crorepati*!

With extinction of interest, surplus money will naturally find its way into healthy investment activities including house building, which will cost much less due to fall in prices of construction materials. Availability of more houses will result in provision of living accommodation to more people and at reasonable rents within reach of honest living earners.

Savings and Bank Deposits Will Increase

Lower prices of goods and reduction in house rents will result in less expenditure and more savings which will of course come to the banks in the form of deposits in customers' accounts. Thus in interest-free system bank deposits will boost.

Banks Will Obtain Capacity of Infinite Advancement of Loans

Interest and statutory bank reserve are the two principal and essential instruments of interest-based banking system. In the capitalist exploitative system capital is held to be the main driving force for all economic activity and interest is charged as price of capital. As no price can justifiably be charged for anything which is bountiful, artificial scarcity is injected in the supply of capital by statutory reserve. As in interest-free banking no interest is charged as price of capital, there is no necessity of creating any artificial scarcity of capital and as such statutory bank reserve is also done away with. In the interest-free system loaning capacity of banks will rise firstly due to increase in deposits and secondly to a very much higher level due to deletion of statutory bank reserve which injects artificial scarcity in the supply of capital. Black-marketers hoard and create artificial shortage of goods and then exploit the consumers by charging unduly much higher prices on the pretext of scarcity in supply of goods. In interest-based capitalist system, interest is charged as price of capital and it is argued that its payment is necessary to attract capital which is scarce, although capital in fact is bountiful and scarcity in its supply is artificially injected into the capital market by statutory bank reserve. Keynes in his famous 'GENERAL THEORY' wrote: "Whilst there may be intrinsic reasons for the scarcity of land, there is no intrinsic reason for the scarcity of capital. Thus we might aim in practice at an increase in the volume of capital until it ceases to be scarce so that the functionless investor will no longer receive a bonus". In this quotation obviously bonus refers to interest and functionless investor refers to lender of money at interest. Following is elaborated the role of statutory bank reserve in creating artificial scarcity in supply of capital. In the present system with statutory bank reserve of 35% loaning capacity of bank is limited to 2.86 multiples of total bank deposits. If statutory bank reserve is reduced to 20%, loaning capacity of banks will rise to five multiples of total deposits. If it is reduced to 1%, the loaning capacity of banks will rise to 100 multiples of bank deposits. Thus in the present system the banks are constrained to limit their advances of loans to maximum amount arrived at by dividing the total deposit by the percentage of statutory bank reserve.

In the interest-free system no interest will be paid as price of capital, therefore there will be no necessity for creating artificial scarcity in the supply of capital. No doubt statutory bank reserve is useful in providing liquidity to the banking sector in the present system. In the interest-free system as already shown in the chapter 'operation of interest-free banking system' liquidity will be arranged without any statutory bank reserve. Thus there will be no constraint like statutory bank reserve on advancing of loans by banks and consequently the banks in interest-free system will obtain capacity of infinite advancement of loans.

Employment Opportunities Will Rise and Everybody Willing to Work Will Get Employment

With capacity of infinite advancement of loans, there will be no dearth of capital in interest-free banking system and credit will be available for all productive industrial and agricultural projects including labour and capital intensive ventures. Entrepreneurs will get credit for all new projects and also for revitalizing and modernizing existing slack industrial units. With the required capital being available entrepreneurs will go ahead with their production plans which will provide employment to presently unemployed millions and nobody willing to work will remain unemployed. Only those who are not willing to work will remain unemployed and such people are not likely to exceed 0.5% of the able bodied. So it can be concluded that elimination of interest will lead to virtual extinction of unemployment.

Industrial and Agricultural Production Will Be Boosted

Availability of capital in plenty in interest-free system, together with all the other three elements of production namely skill, labour, and materials already available in plenty in the country, will give boost to industrial and agricultural production. Self-sufficiency in food will soon be achieved and in foreseeable future surplus food will also be available for export. In the industrial sector product costs will be reduced considerably due to elimination of interest from the cost of production. The cost reduction in production will generate considerable export potential and also expand the area of import substitution which will result in considerable reduction in import bill.

Budget Deficit Will Vanish And Domestic Debt Retirement Capability Will Be Generated

With boost in production and extinction of unemployment, income levels will rise and budgetary receipts will increase. Due to extinction of interest, budgetary expenditure will reduce considerably. Increase in budgetary receipts and substantial reduction in expenditure will produce surplus budget which would enable the government to retire domestic debt which is ever rising higher and higher under the present system. Following examples support the above contention.

According to State Bank of Pakistan's annual report for the year 1986-87 the consolidated budgetary receipts for that year were Rs99.55 billion, the total expenditure was Rs155.98 billion and the total deficit was Rs53.65 billion after excluding Rs2.78 billion available as surplus of autonomous bodies. The revenue receipts formed 16.5 percent of gross domestic product. Pakistan economic survey 1984-85 gives the figure of 4% for unemployment but adds that under-employment accounts for one-fourth of the employed persons. This means that besides 4% who were unemployed 24% were under-employed. Taking 24% under-employment to be equal to 12% unemployment, the total unemployment comes to 16% for the year 1984-85. Same figure of unemployment can safely be assumed to hold for the year 1986-87 for which budgetary receipt and deficit are given above. As already discussed, inception of interest-free banking will reduce unemployment to 0.5%, therefore in the year 1986-87, interest-free banking could have cured 15.5% of unemployment.

Increase in GNP resulting from 15.5% reduction in unemployment can be measured by "Okun's" law enunciated by professor Arthur M.Okun. According to 'Okun's' law each percentage point reduction in unemployment lifts GNP by 3.2 percent. This means that introduction of interest-free banking in the year 1986-87 would have increased the GNP by 15.5x3.2=49.6 percent. With the same taxation level this would have raised budgetary receipts by Rs99.55 X 0.496 = Rs49.37 billion. On the expenditure side interest-free banking would have provided saving of Rs15.32 billion which is the amount government of Pakistan paid as interest on domestic debt in that year. Thus gain from interest-free banking in the year 1986-87 would have been Rs49.37 billion increase in budgetary receipts and Rs15.32 billion reduction in budgetary expenditure.

These together would have converted the budget deficit of Rs53.65 billion into surplus of Rs11.04 billion in the Federal budget for the year 1986-87.

In the budget announced for the financial year 1998-99 total expenditure is given as Rs606.3 billion and total income is given as Rs593.7 billion including external assistance of Rs142.0 billion and bank borrowings of Rs43.0 billion which would in fact be debt burdens and not real income. Thus the budget deficit in fact would be Rs197.6 billion and not Rs12.6 billion. Net revenue receipts are estimated at Rs367.1 billion. In the economic survey for the year 1997-98 unemployment percentage is given as 5.37 and the employed also include all those who are employed only part-time for even one hour per working day. It means that out of every group of 10,000 persons 537 are fully unemployed. From the remaining 9463 persons it can optimistically be assumed that 50% that is 4732 are fully employed, 25% that is 2366 are half-time employed (i.e. half-time unemployed) and 25% that is 2366 are 3 quarter time employed (i.e. quarter time unemployed). 2366 half-time unemployed means 50% of 2366 = 1183 fully unemployed. 2366 one quarter time unemployed means 25% of 2366 = 591 fully unemployed. Thus from a group of 10,000 persons fully unemployed are 537 + 1183 + 591 = 2311 = 23.11%.

In the prevailing circumstances of golden hand-shakes unemployment is likely to rise but assuming it to remain at the same level as last year the curable unemployment to be brought about by interest-free banking would be 23.11% - 0.5% (incurable) = 22.61%. Applying Okun's law to the financial year 1998-99 increase in budgetary receipts due to inception of interest-free banking will be Rs22.61 X .032 X 367.1 = Rs265.6 billion. On the expenditure side interest free system will provide saving of Rs164.6 billion which is the amount of interest payable on domestic debt. Thus increase of Rs265.6 billion in budgetary receipts and reduction of Rs164.6 billion in expenditure will convert the deficit of Rs197.6 billion into budget surplus of Rs232.6 billion.

It should be quite clear from the above calculations that with the inception of interest-free banking it will become possible to commence retiring the domestic debt which can then be totally cleared within a few years and after that surplus in the budget can be used in social welfare and development projects. Such a happy situation of our economy cannot be visualized so long as the curse of interest persists in our banking system.

Balance Of Payments Will Tilt In Our Favour And Foreign Debt Retirement Capability Will Be Generated

Self sufficiency in food combined with high export potential and reduced import bill will substantially improve the country's balance of payment position. Export earnings during the year 1997-98 were around $8.5 billion. "Exports must foot the annual import bill of $10.0 billion" this is the main objective of the new trade policy and " the devaluation aims at supplementing the National effort to boost exports to the level of $10 billion". Owing to reduction in cost of production in the interest-free system, all exportable goods manufactured in the country could be sold at competitive prices in the foreign markets. With the reduction in unemployment, production of exportable goods will also rise in the same proportion as GNP. Applying Okun's law to production of exportable goods and taking into account the present foreign exchange earning from exports, increase in foreign exchange earning in the interest-free system will be $8.5 X 22.61 X .032 = $6.15 billion. The increase of $6.15 billion in foreign exchange earning will convert the current negative balance of $1.5 billion into surplus of $4.65 billion without having to devalue our currency. Thus inception of interest-free banking will boost foreign exchange earning which will generate foreign debt retirement capability and the country will soon be able to come out of the foreign debt trap.

Foreign debt liability has consistently been rising for the past several decades and if we continue to cling to the same interest-based system the same snowball trend in debt increase will continue and nothing will be able to stop our economy from drowning ever deep into the morass of foreign debt. Therefore, for protecting national liberty and honour, it is imperative that the interest-based system which has laden the country with unbearable burden of foreign debt should be done away with and replaced by interest-free TMCL-based banking system and the earlier it is done better it will be for the nation.

Corruption in Granting Loans Will be Eliminated and Total Loss in Case of Bankruptcy and Wilful Default Will be Averted

As in interest-free banking system every loan will be granted against a counter loan, discretion and consequent corruption involved in granting loans to favourites on special concessionary terms will be eliminated. Any rescheduling required will also be done on the basis of counter loan. In rare cases of bankruptcy and wilful default the bankers will recover the prime loan from collateral as at present. Inordinate delays involved in recovery will be compensated by retention of the borrower's counter loan money for a proportionately extended period.

LESSONS FROM HISTORY

Lessons from history are difficult to learn and it is particularly so in our environment in which prevalence of interest has produced immense greed for worldly riches which has quelled passion for good governance and sense of justice in most of our ruling elite. Allah says "*despair not of the mercy of Allah*" (39:53). Therefore some examples worth following are quoted below from the past and contemporary history in the hope that our rulers will be moved to abide by Allah's Commands and divert state revenues from ruling elite's luxuries and splendour to people's needs and progress and provide good governance which demands respect and protection for the law-abiding citizens and punishment for criminals and law-breakers. Accountability of everyone without any exception is the basis of Islamic justice in which no body is authorized to grant any immunity to law-breakers. Thieves and robbers should not be allowed to enjoy their loot. All assets and bank accounts of tax evaders and loan defaulters should be confiscated to recover unpaid taxes and loans. All wealthy people irrespective of their political affiliation must be compelled to declare their sources of wealth, and ill-gotten wealth should be confiscated and the culprits duly punished, otherwise justice and fair play cannot take root in the society.

Our Prophet Muhammad *s.a.w.s.* completely revolutionized social and economic order such that the rulers became poor and servants of people and the ruled got good governance and prosperity. Lamartin, a French historian, writes "After the fall of Makkah, more than one million square miles of land lay at his feet. Lord of Arabia, he mended his own shoes... swept the hearth, kindled the fire and attended to other offices of the family. The entire town of Madina, where he lived grew wealthy in the later days of his life, everywhere there was gold and silver in plenty and yet in those days of prosperity, many weeks would elapse without a fire being kindled in the hearth of the King of Arabia, his food being dates and water..."

First *khalifah raashid* Abu Bakar *r.t.a.* drew from *bait-ul-maal* only what was essential for sustaining family of an ordinary wage earner. One day his wife prepared a sweet dish. He inquired as to wherefrom she got the money for the sweet dish. She told him that she had saved some money from the daily allowance she was getting from him. He said they could very well live without sweet dishes and from that day onwards he reduced the daily allowance which he was drawing from *bait-ul-maal.* And before dying he disposed off his property and deposited in *bait-ul-maal* the entire amount which he had received as sustenance allowance for his household.

Second *khalifah raashid* Umer bin Khattab *r.t.a.* was questioned in public as to wherefrom he got his long shirt whereas others of much smaller stature could hardly make their shirts from the cloth falling to their share. His son was present in the public and he explained that he had given his share of cloth to his father and that is how he got his long shirt made. Once somebody suggested to him that he should eat bread made from wheat instead of barley. He replied he would do so only when he was sure that every one in the ummah could afford to eat wheat-bread.

Khalifah Umer bin AbdulAziz *r.a* upon taking the reins of rule decided to abandon lavish living and donated all his wealth to *bait-ul-maal* and asked her wife to do the same if she wanted to continue to live with him. She agreed and donated all her jewelry and valuables to *bait-ul-maal.*

Al-Ezz ibn Abdussalam lived at the time when the Islamic state in Baghdad was approaching its end. The Tartar invasion was gathering pace. They ransacked Baghdad and destroyed the central authority of the Muslim state. They soon over ran Syria and were driving South aiming to reach Egypt. At that time, the new ruler took over in Egypt. He was called Quotuz. Quotuz felt that he needed the support of the scholar. When he consulted him the scholar made it clear that it was the ruler's duty to mobilize all the forces he could and plan for stopping the Tartars' advance. Otherwise the Muslim nation would be destroyed. He promised him all the support he could give, provided that he abided by Islamic Law and maintained Islamic principles.

When the question of equipping the army was raised by the ruler the scholar said that all possible resources should be tapped for this purpose. Quotuz mentioned that new taxes had to be imposed. The scholar told him that before he could do that he had to make sure of tapping of certain, more readily available resources, which could generate considerable amount of money without causing any hardship to people. The princes had to relinquish all their privileges and donate all the gold, jewelry and other possessions they had, which they gained from the state over the years. When they had relinquished all that and stood at the same level with the rest of the population, then taxes could be imposed.

It was not right that small group of people could have all that wealth in their coffers and in the shape of jewelry for their women, while new taxes are imposed on the people, resulting in more hardship for the majority of the population.

Quotuz protested that such a ruling would be very hard to implement. The princes were bound to revolt and he might very well be killed in the process. Al-Ezz ibn Abdussalam insisted that he had to stand firm on this point, otherwise he could not expect victory to be granted by God if he were keen to please the princes at the expense of the people. That was an attitude which could not win God's pleasure. Victory could only be gained with God's help, which would not be forthcoming if His law is not implemented. Moreover if the princes relinquished their privilege, first, the people would be ready to accept new taxes if they would be found necessary at a later stage.

Quotuz's sincerity won the day. He realized that he must implement that ruling. At the same time he was certain that he could not declare that ruling to the princes and expect them to carry it out voluntarily. He saw his way to have the ruling implemented before he declared it to the princes. In other words he presented them with a fait accompli. They could do nothing to stop it. When the people of Egypt realized what had happened, they were so pleased. They volunteered in large numbers to join the army and Egypt was converted into a huge army camp. When preparations were completed, Quotuz marched at the head of his army to southern Palestine where he met the Tartars at the decisive battle of Ein Jaloot. The dedication of the ruler, the princes and the people made sure of victory. It is no exaggeration to say that victory was engineered by the great scholar, the Sultan of all scholars, Al-Ezz ibn Abdussalam.

Quaid-e-Azam *r.a.* was taking very little food during his last days in Ziarat. Mohtaramah Fatima Jinnah thought that perhaps he would eat more if the food was prepared by his old favourite cook. So the government made arrangements to bring that particular cook to Ziarat. When Quaid-e-Azam came to know of his arrival he said he would pay from his personal pocket all expenses for his travel and stay in Ziarat because it was a matter of his personal taste and the government was not supposed to cater for personal wishes of Governor General.

Shaheed-e-Millat Nawabzada Liaquat Ali Khan the first Prime Minister of Pakistan had in his bank balance Rs1200 when he was killed and that was all the money he had. He left in India urban and rural properties worth tens of millions of Rupees, but he did not get any evacuee property allotted in his name nor he made any asset or property. During his lifetime he did not allow any thing to be allotted or any permit to be given to any member of his family. Whatever little compensation his descendants received could be received only after his death.

Sardar Abdur-Rab Nishter, Governor of Punjab got his sons admitted in Urdu medium Central Model High School in Lahore. He did not allow the government transport to be used for taking his children to school. They used bicycles for going to school and coming back to Governor House.

Mr. Lee Kaun, the great leader of Singapore built his country out of scratch and transformed it into one of the cleanest, most disciplined, most advanced and most prosperous countries of the world. He once said :-

"When I became the Prime Minister of my country I had an opportunity to make myself rich and to let my country be poor or make my country rich and keep myself poor. I am proud that I selected the later option".

The Japanese Prime Minister, Mr. Ryutaro Hashimoto resigned with a statement that "every thing was due to my lack of abilities".

Olaf Pame was the Prime Minister of Sweden, which is one of the most prosperous countries of the world having per capita income of well over forty times the per capita income in our country. He was gunned down by a maniac when after using a public subway (not motorcade) he was walking back to his apartment (not palace) on a thoroughfare with his wife and without any body guards.

Prime Minister Tony Blair and his family themselves carried their belongings when moving into 10 Downing Street.

Shaikh Rasheed Ahmad, a commoner by birth and profession but a minister in Federal Cabinet, wrote in his thought provoking book *Farzand-e-Pakistan* inter alia "Our trade deficit is in billions of Rupees, our currency was devalued, value of Dollar has reached from eight Rupees to near 16.75 rupees. Our debts are increasing and some people say with great pride that we are given loans because our policy and development programs are being very well executed. I understand that for us as a nation it is a matter of shame that we go with begging bowl from country to country asking for charity and upon getting a dole we acclaim that it is in recognition of our performance! It is misfortune of our country that those who play important role in the country's economy, though their sympathy is with us and they live with us, their thinking and attitude and conduct are such that they snatch away all from the poor and give away to the capitalists. The World Bank officials in their own vested interest exert influence on our economy and no body cares that our every new born child is burdened with debt of fourteen hundred Rupees. I was my self quite satisfied that I had not concealed anything from income-tax authorities and probably that is why in spite of running a modest business of silk my annual income-tax was more than that of Asif Zardari, Benazir Bhutto and all the members of the National Assembly of Pakistan".

The words of Shaikh Rasheed are as true today as they were when he wrote his book while in jail during Benazir Bhutto's rule. The only difference is that Dollar to Rupee ratio has risen to 46 (official rate) and 56 (open market rate) and debt burden on every newly born child has risen from fourteen hundred Rupees to twenty one thousand Rupees (at official rate).

NECESSITY FOR ISLAMIC BANKS TO ADOPT TMCL FOR DEBT FINANCING

During the past several decades many Islamic Banks have been established in various parts of the world by those who are Islamically motivated to promote interest-free banking. They are doing a great service by providing finance to interest-averse Muslims through *Shariah* compliant transactions like *Murabahah, Ijarah*, *Mudarabah*, and *Musharakah*. However they have concentrated mainly on *Murabahah* which is risk-free mode of sale based on cost plus fixed profit and which was never meant to be used for financing as it is being practiced by Islamic banks. Although this mode of sale is permitted in Islam, its widespread use for financing produces adverse economic effects just like interest because both increase the cost of goods to the detriment of consumers and society. Following are a few excerpts from a recent publication 'Challenges Facing Islamic Banking' issued by Islamic Development Bank Islamic Research and Training Institute Jeddah First Edition 1419H (1998) :-

"While Islamic Banks use *Mudarabah* on the resource mobilization side, they use a number of Shariah compliant financial instruments on the asset side. It is generally observed that the modes of finance used by Islamic Banks are dominated by fixed-return modes especially *Murabahah* .... In order to provide some empirical evidence on this issue data was compiled for the period 1994-1996.... As far as the use of various modes of finance is concerned *Murabahah* accounts for 70 percent of total financing. *Ijarah* accounts for another 5 percent. Thus the fixed-return modes account for 75 percent of total financing. The unspecified 'others' category takes another 11 percent. The profit-sharing modes account for less than 14 percent financing. In case of financing by sectors trading gets the biggest proportion i.e. 42 percent. The second largest sector is real estate which accounts for 13 percent. Agriculture claims only 2 percent and industry 12 percent of the financing ... This calls for rethinking the role of Islamic Banks in economic development against the hopes which had been raised in the past regarding their ability to finance agriculture and industry".

Present Islamic banks are Islamic only in a limited sense as they use *Shariah* compliant financial instruments in their public dealings. But ironically, for their short-term needs of liquidity they turn to conventional banks for interest-based loans. In his recent book 'Introduction to Islamic Finance' Hon.Justice Muhammad Taqi Usmani writes :-

"The case of Islamic banking cannot be advanced unless a strong system of inter-bank transactions based on Islamic principles is developed. The lack of such a system forces the Islamic banks to turn to the conventional banks for their short-term needs of liquidity which the conventional banks do not provide without either an open or camouflaged interest".

TMCL is a true Islamic substitute of interest as it can perform all transparent and legal functions in Islamic manner which interest performs in conventional banking system including interest-free inter-bank transactions. Therefore, instead of seeking interest-based loans from conventional banks, Islamic banks should adopt TMCL as debt-financing instrument which would facilitate setting up of institutional arrangement of lender of the last resort. This will not only save Islamic banks from the glaringly sinful act of obtaining loans on interest from conventional banks, but will also enable them to provide finance to cost-conscious enterprises and also to those loan seekers who are averse to external interference. In this way Islamic banks can obtain the status of full fledged banks with capability to compete with conventional banks in international financial market.

The need for adoption of TMCL for debt-financing by Islamic banks is also underscored in the following excerpts from the above mentioned Islamic Development Bank publication:-

"Islamic banks, like all other commercial banks are required to keep some of their deposits with central banks. Central banks usually pay interest o those deposits which Islamic banks cannot accept. An alternative is needed to ensure that Islamic banks get a fair return on their deposits with the central banks".

"Central banks function as lenders of last resort to commercial banks providing loans at times of liquidity crunch. Although most of Islamic banks function under the supervision of central bank, they cannot legitimately benefit from such a facility because such funds are usually provided on the basis of interest. It is understandable that such assistance cannot be free of cost. However, there is a need to devise and implement an interest-free framework for such assistance".

"In countries where the central bank conducts open market operations, Islamic banks are not able to participate in these operations because of interest-based nature of the securities bought and sold. Thus Islamic banks are constrained by the fact that financial assets that could be liquidated quickly are not available to them. This introduces some rigidity in the asset structure of Islamic banks".

"While Islamic banks and investment funds have so far mobilized huge financial resources, a large part of these resources have found its way into Western financial markets. Likewise, the same thing happened with resources mobilized with conventional banks. There is no Islamic (or for that matter, conventional indigenous) financial institution which has been able to channel savings from Western countries into Muslim countries in spite of the great demand for such resources in the latter countries. This is another challenge for Islamic banks with very important implications for Muslim countries".

"Every system has its institutional requirements. Islamic banks alone cannot cater for all of their institutional requirements which is supposed to provide alternative ways and means for meeting the needs of venture capital, consumer finance, short-term capital, long-term capital etc. A number of mutually supporting institutions / arrangements are needed to perform various functions. These include security markets, investment banks, and equity institutions such as mutual funds, pension plans etc. Even within the commercial banking arena, a number of supporting institutional arrangements, such as lender of the last resort, insurance and re-insurance facilities , inter-bank markets etc. need to be established". "Building a proper institutional set-up is perhaps the most serious challenge for Islamic finance. To face this challenge a functional approach towards building this set-up should be adopted. The functions being performed by various institutions in the conventional framework should be examined and attempts should be made to establish institutions that can perform those functions in an Islamic way".

"Islamic banks have succeeded in mobilizing large amounts of funds. However, it will require much more strenuous efforts to maintain a reasonable rate of growth in future. There are several reasons for that. Firstly, it must be realized that much of the deposits now with the Islamic banks came not due to the attraction of higher returns or better services but because of religious commitment of the clients. Many of them were keeping their savings in conventional banks without taking any interest on them and many others were keeping them in private safes. For all such persons, a modest return or even no return from Islamic banks, was acceptable. Most of this money has already found its way into the coffers of Islamic banks. Therefore this source has been almost dried up. Secondly, so far Islamic banks had a fairly large degree of 'monopoly' over the financial resources of Islamically motivated public. This situation is changing fast. Islamic banks are now facing ever-increasing competition. An important development in Islamic banking in the last few years has been the entry of some conventional banks including some major multinational Western banks in that market".

Islamic Development Bank was established in 1975 with the purpose to foster the economic development and social progress of member countries and Muslim communities individually as well as jointly in accordance with the principles of *Shariah*. But against Pakistan's urgent request for funds in financial crises of 1998, Islamic Development Bank together with the Islamic banking community of more that one hundred profitably operating Islamic banks could make an offer no better than a consolidated loan on interest at a rate of 5 percent above LIBOR !

With the inception of TMCL as an instrument for debt financing, Islamic banks can easily establish a central organization which can operate as lender of the last resort for all Islamic banks and Governments. In times of need Islamic banks and Governments will take loans free of interest on TMCL basis from this organization which in due course will have large funds of foreign exchange and Islamic banks and Governments will not have to deposit their surplus funds in Western banks.

INEXPLICABLE BIAS AGAINST TMCL

Many a time in history logic failed to prevail upon prejudice against change and new fruitful and logically superior ideas were summarily rejected without any justification. Galileo, the founder of modern experimental science was condemned for upholding perfectly valid Copernican theory of motion of heavenly bodies which was later accepted and utilized in bringing tremendous technological development.

A perfectly valid proposal to use TMCL as debt financing instrument which could have long ago eliminated interest from the banking system, taken our country out of the foreign debt-trap, and brought prosperity to the suffering millions was summarily rejected in June 1980 without any justification. The crucial judgment which was to have most serious consequence upon the national economy was delivered without any discussion and without pointing out any defect in TMCL, in one sentence reading "*It would, however, not be correct to use this method by way of a permanent alternative system to the interest-based system*". And the remedy prescribed in preference to TMCL included the following recommendations:-

(*i*) For Domestic Transactions: "*Interest may be eliminated from the economic system in a phased manner*", "*during the period of about 1 year and 8 months the rest of the measures for elimination of interest from the domestic transactions should be taken in three clearly defined phases with specific time schedule*".

(*ii*) For Foreign Transactions: "*Borrowings from International agencies may continue to be interest-bearing until alternative arrangements compatible with Shariah become available*"!

The above recommendations were clearly a license for the government to continue to remain at war with Allah and His Rasool *s.a.w.s.* for at least 20 months at the home economic front and for an indefinite period at the foreign economic front. More than 18 years have already passed since the above recommendations were made and still there is no sign of a cease-fire in the on-going war with Allah and His Rasool *s.a.w.s.* We do not know for how many more years this war will continue and our nation will continue to suffer with the evil fate of disobedience of Allah and His Rasool *s.a.w.s*, only because majority of Pakistani economists and bankers appointed by the Council of Islamic Ideology, for designing an interest-free economic system, did not find any substitute of interest for inception in the modern banking system, and also did not accept a perfectly valid proposal submitted by Shaikh Mahmud Ahmad for inception of TMCL as substitute of interest in the banking system which could have been put into practice immediately.

The sad story of the continuos ill fate of our economy runs as follows. The Council of Islamic Ideology was entrusted by the government of Pakistan with the task of preparing a blue-print of interest-free economic system. The CII in turn appointed a panel of economists and bankers for examining technical aspects and recommending ways and means for eliminating interest. The panel included Shaikh Mahmud Ahamd who was an ideologically dedicated Islamic scholar having deep knowledge of Islamic tenets and also of modern economic system. He pleaded for inception of TMCL as an ideal alternative to replace interest in the banking system. Unfortunately the panel did not accept his pleadings although TMCL could facilitate immediate switch-over of interest-based banking system to interest-free banking system. As TMCL was a practical debt-financing instrument the panel could not find any technical defect in it and could not reject it on any technical ground. However, in its recommendations submitted to the CII in February 1980, the panel unjustifiably expressed a doubt about compatibility of TMCL with *Shariah*, although the panel was required and was competent to examine only technical aspects and not *Fiqhi* aspects.

Shaikh Mahmud Ahmad submitted his dissenting note to the Council of Islamic Ideology in March 1980, but in vain. The CII submitted its report in June 1980. Following are some excerpts from the report based largely on the recommendations of the majority of economists and bankers on the panel excluding Shaikh Mahmud Ahmad :-

> *"Ideally the real alternatives to interest under an Islamic economic system are profit/loss sharing or qard hasan i.e. loaning without additional charge over and above the principal amount. Although the recommendations are based on the principle of profit/loss sharing, yet some of the recommendations lean on other methods in view of the difficulties faced in the practical application of the profit/loss sharing system in its pure form on account of the prevalent standards of morality in the society. These alternative methods are, however no more than a second best solution from the viewpoint of an ideal Islamic economic system. This is because of the fact that although these alternative methods are free of the interest element in the form in which they are specifically laid down in this Report, there is a danger that this could eventually be misused as a means for opening a back-door for interest along with its attendant evils. They should, therefore, be applied to the minimum extent that may be unavoidably necessary, and that their use as general techniques as financing must never be allowed. In this connection, a basic policy decision may be taken to the effect that with the passage of time the operational field of PLS and qard hasan should gradually be expanded while that of the other alternatives reduced. At the same time efforts must be stepped up to bring about a substantial improvement in the standards of honesty in the society and to remove illiteracy, because both dishonesty and illiteracy militate against the success of the new system."*

> *'Time Multiple Counter Loans - Under this method a bank may give by way of interest-free loan a multiple of interest-free deposit by a client so that the product of the money and time for which the money is given is the same in both cases. It would, however, not be correct to use this method by way of a permanent alternative system to the interest-based system. However, in order to provide personal loans to people of small means banks may instead of the above stipulations, adopt it as a principle that they would provide loans for personal and non-productive purposes to those persons who already hold accounts with them. In laying down the repayment schedule and the amount of the loan, however, the banks may keep in view the amount of the deposit of the applicant for the loan and the period over which he has maintained his deposit with the bank".*

"The Council considered three different options with a view to suggesting an action plan for the elimination of interest from the economy. These were : (a) a model bank may be set up which may start operations on interest-free basis and, on the basis of experience gained from its working, the operations of the commercial banks and other financial institutions may be reorganized on interest-free basis subsequently; (b) a comprehensive scheme may be prepared for a complete switch-over to the interest-free economic system and then the timing of a switch-over may be decided; (c) interest may be eliminated from the economic system in a phased manner. The third option was considered to be the most practical and reasonable."

"The Council has recommended that during the period of about 1 year and 8 months that now remains within the 3 years time limit set by the President the rest of the measures for the elimination of interest from the domestic transactions should be taken in three clearly defined phases with specific time schedule."

"The operations of foreign branches of Pakistani banks, foreign currency deposits held with commercial banks in Pakistan and certain other transactions of banks with banks abroad would have to continue on the basis of interest."

"PICIC's foreign currency borrowings may continue to be on interest-basis until a viable alternative conforming to Shariah is available."

"In the case of Agricultural Development Bank of Pakistan (ADBP),deposits accepted by it should be subject to similar arrangements as those suggested for commercial banks. Loans received from the State Bank may either be on PLS basis or free of cost. Borrowings from international agencies may continue to be interest bearing until alternative arrangements compatible with Shariah become available."

"The interest-bearing foreign loans channeled by the Federal Government to the Provincial Governments may, however, continue on the basis of interest till a viable alternative compatible with Shariah is found in respect of borrowings from abroad."

"Government's borrowings from external sources will have to be continued for the time being, on the basis of interest."

"Loans from the Federal and Provincial Governments to local bodies, autonomous corporations etc. may be provided free of interest for financing non-profit-earning essential projects. For profit-earning projects finance could also be obtained from banks and other financial institutions on a basis conforming with Shariah. Interest-bearing foreign loans channeled by the government to these bodies would, however, need to be continued on the existing basis."

In a nutshell the Council of Islamic Ideology recommendations to the government were:-

(i) Eliminate interest from domestic transactions in phases in twenty months by way of PLS (which on account of prevalent standards of morality in the society had difficulties in practical application).

(ii) Continue with interest-based foreign transactions till a viable alternative conforming to *Shariah* is available.

As Islam is the panacea for all evils and for all times and Quraanic precepts are applicable and required to be implemented in all circumstances, the above recommendations were highly disappointing and shockingly painful for all those who were keen to see interest eliminated and the country rid of unpardonable sin and criminal offence amounting to rebellion against Allah and His Rasool *s.a.w.s.*

It is not clear why in spite of there being no defect and no practical difficulty in its immediate application TMCL was not accepted especially when there was no other better or equally effective alternative of interest under consideration. If TMCL was adopted as an alternative of interest in 1980, Pakistan would have long ago got rid of the evil of interest, exuded unemployment and crime, come out of foreign debt-trap, and gained economic prosperity.

Having stated that PLS or *Qard hasan* were ideally the real alternatives of interest and having found that there were difficulties in practical application of PLS, the only logical choice left was TMCL which is practical form of *Qard hasan* for debt-financing in banking system. Islamic principles are not only to be adorned and praised, but they are to be applied in practical life as widely as possible. Practical application of the Islamic principle of *Qard hasan* for eliminating interest is strongly recommended in the research thesis "*Preventive measures in Islam against interest*" on which Dr.Fazl-e-Illahi was awarded doctorate's degree. He has emphasized in his thesis the vital role which *Qard hasan* can play in abolishing interest. He concluded the chapter on *Qard hasan* with the assertion "*expanding the field of this way of lending will, by Allah's grace, aid in blocking the way of interest. Therefore in this context I urge upon all those who want to abolish interest to do whatever they can to expand the field of this way of lending.*" TMCL is actually institutionalization of *Qard hasan* and is the surest and simplest practical means of eliminating interest from the banking system, and the earlier it is realized better it would be for all.

The most unfortunate outcome of rejecting an practicable proposal for inception of TMCL as substitute of interest for getting rid of the malady and making unrealistic recommendations which were evident to be impractical due to moral hazard in the society, was that our rulers by design and default allowed interest to perpetuate and prosper and the country to drown ever deep into the debt morass so much so that we have to beg for fresh loans (which add to the debt burden on the country) to pay interest on outstanding debts and there is still no sign of any halt in the steep slide down of the economy and the continuous increase in unemployment, inflation and consequent rise in crime rate. *It is the unfortunate result of an inexplicable bias against TMCL!*

COMPLIANCE OF TMCL WITH *SHARIAH*

The Council of Islamic Ideology, Pakistan did not find any defect in TMCL from *Shariah* viewpoint as is clear from the paragraph on TMCL reproduced, in a previous chapter of this booklet, from CII report of June 1980. However, Dr.Mohmamed Ali Elgari and Mr.D.M.Qureshi raised the question of compatibility of TMCL with *Shariah*. As TMCL is entirely a new concept and a modern technique specifically designed to eliminate interest from the modern banking system, it is hardly possible that there would be any direct reference to it in traditional books of *Fiqh*. However, the writer requested Dr.Al-Ayachi Fedad *Shariah* expert in Islamic Research and Training Institute of Islamic Development Bank, to provide whatever material was available in Islamic literature which could relate to TMCL. He very kindly obliged by producing a computer statement of views expressed by some *Shaafi*, *Maleki* and *Hunbali* scholars but none from any *Hanafi* scholar. Upon specific enquiry regarding views of *Hanafi* scholars, Dr.Fedad said the computer record did not show any *Hanafi* scholar's view on the subject.

The logical conclusion from Dr.Fedad's advice and clearance by the CII is that TMCL is definitely acceptable in Pakistan where *Hanafi Fiqh* is followed.

To firmly establish acceptability of TMCL in other Islamic countries it is desirable to examine in detail the contents of the above mentioned computer statement Arabic text of which is reproduced at the end of this booklet. Hereunder are reproduced English versions of the texts in Arabic and the writer's comments on them.

The form of "you lend to me, and I will lend to you"

Muslim jurists have given the term ("You lend to me, and I will lend to you") to a loan agreement which includes a condition that the borrower, in exchange for the initial loan made to him, give a loan to his lender. For the Malikis, a loan with such a condition inclines toward being repugnant. The Hanbalis state that(such a condition) is not permitted, and if it occurs(in a loan agreement), the condition is invalid, while the loan itself (remains) valid.

Al-Mughni Volume 6, p. 437

Majallat-al Ahkam Ash-Shar'iyyah

al-Hanbaliyyah, p.272, Article 745

Al-Muntaqa Lil-Baji, Volume 5, p. 29

Kashaf Al-Qina'lil-Buhuti, Volume 3, p. 303-304

1. Al-Mughni (6/437)

"It is not permitted for a lender to make it a condition in loan (contract) that the borrower will give his house on rent to him or he will sell something to him or that the borrower will give to him a loan at another time, because Prophet s.a.w.s prohibited a sale and loan (being combined in a single transaction)and it is because he made a condition of another contract within a contract which is not permitted and it is as if someone sells his house on the condition that the other man will also sell his house to him. If the lender makes it a condition that the borrower will give his house to him on rent less than its value or that the borrower will take his house on rent at higher than its value, it is most severely prohibited."

According to this ruling it is not permissible for a lender to include a condition in loan contract that the borrower will give to him a loan at another time in future. As TMCL transaction is simultaneous exchange of two loans none of which includes any condition other than the repayment of the loan amount, the above ruling is not applicable to TMCL.

2. *Majallat Al-Ahkam Ash-Shar'iyyah 'ala Madhhab Ahmad (p 272)*

"It is not right to make a loan conditional upon including another contract in the loan contract. For example, if the lender included in the loan contract a condition for sale, rent, farming, irrigating or another loan, the condition is not right. The loan is not invalidated by wrong conditions but wrong conditions are invalidated."

According to this ruling it is not right to include a condition of another loan in a loan contract. Here another loan obviously refers to a loan in future, as it makes no sense that the lender having spare money to advance in loan will require a loan from the borrower at the same time when he himself is giving the loan. However, in TMCL transaction it makes sense because TMCL is a special device specifically designed for the noble purpose of eliminating interest from the banking system. In any of the two loans exchanged simultaneously in TMCL transaction there is no condition of another loan and as such this ruling is evidently not applicable to TMCL.

3. *Ighathat Al-Lahfan (1/363)*

"Combining of loan and sale (in one single transaction) is prohibited as in it there is means to get profit on loan by taking more than what is given in loan, and this profit is gained through sale or renting and it is as what happens in fact."

This ruling states combining of lending and selling together is prohibited. There is no selling involved in a TMCL transaction and as such this ruling cannot be applicable to TMCL.

4. *Tahdhib Ibn Al-Qayyim li Mukhtasar Sunan Abi Daud (5/149)*

"As regards (the combining of) a loan and a sale, if (a lender) lends to a borrower (a monetary amount of) one hundred for one year (and as part of the same transaction) sells to him the equivalent of fifty by one hundred, the sale becomes a means of increasing the amount of the loan which is to be returned in equal amount. If it were not for the sale the lender would not have given loan to the borrower and if it were not for the loan, the borrower would not have bought the house from him.

This ruling also relates to combining of lending with selling and as such this ruling also cannot be applicable to TMCL in which no selling is involved.

5. *Al-Muntaqa lil Baji (5/29)*

The reason from the aspect of concept is that loan is not included in (the category of) the contracts of recompense, rather it belongs to (the category of) the contracts of righteousness and nobility. Therefore, it is not right for a loan to draw recompense or return. If a loan is combined with a contract of recompense, it (the loan) receives a portion of the recompense, and thereby goes beyond its purpose and becomes void, together with the contract of recompense that was part of it. Another aspect (of the concept of a loan) is that if the loan has no time limit (specified for its repayment), then it is not (legally) binding on the lender, whereas(a contract of) sale and others like it (belonging to the category of legally) binding contracts, such as (contracts of) lease and marriage- (is legally binding and) is not allowed to be combined with a non-(legally) binding contract, because the rules relating to the two contracts (i.e., legally binding and non-legally binding) are mutually incompatible.

This ruling holds that the lender should not aim at earning any profit on loan. None of the two loans in TMCL transaction yields any profit as each of them is paid back without any increase. Whatever the bank earns, profit or loss, is accrued from investing the money borrowed in the form of counter loan. Similarly whatever the client earns, profit or loss, is accrued from investing the money borrowed from the bank. There is no bar on earning profit from investment of borrowed money and as such the above ruling is not applicable to TMCL.

6. *Al-Qawanin Al-Fiqhiyyah (p. 293)*

A loan is valid with two conditions.

The first condition is that no benefit should accrue (to the lender). If the lender receives a benefit, this is prohibited by mutual agreement (of the Muslim jurists), based (both) on the prohibition (against a loan drawing any benefit) and (due to the fact that) it goes beyond what is (considered) good and equitable. However, if the borrower receives some benefit, this is allowed. And if a benefit accrues to both (lender and borrower), this is not permitted unless it is deemed necessary. The second condition is that a loan should not be combined with another contract, such as (a contract) of sale, etc.

According to this ruling what is forbidden is accrual of benefit from loan to the lender and what is permissible under necessity is accrual of benefit to lender and borrower both. In the context of a loan, accrual of benefit in reality means excess amount earned over and above the amount of loan which is not at all the case with any of the two loans exchanged in a TMCL transaction. However, if it is insisted that benefit accrues from both the loans in TMCL transaction then the benefit accrues to the bank from the counter loan as borrower and also benefit accrues to the client from the principal loan as borrower. Moreover interest-free loan is a necessity for the client for running his business and interest-free counter loan is necessary for the bank to run interest-free banking system which actually is the necessity of the entire Muslim ummah. It is therefore quiet evident that this ruling does not disqualify TMCL from *Shariah* viewpoint.

7. *Kifayat at-Talib ar-Rabbaniyy wa Hashiyat al-Adawi (2/149-150)*

It is not permitted to (combine) a sale and a loan (in the same contract), similarly loan becoming associated with leasing or renting is not permitted. The reason for (the prohibition) is that both (a lease and a rental agreement) are among (the category of) contracts of sale. Therefore, it is not permitted to combine a loan with (the condition of) a lease or renting, because both lease and renting are like a sale (contract) and cannot be combined with a loan as a (contract of) sale. However, also know that it is not only lease and renting (which cannot be combined with a loan), rather (contracts of) marriage, partnership, qiraad, irrigation and barter are also not allowed to be combined with a loan (agreement). The essence of the foregoing is that it is prohibited to combine any contract (that results in) compensation with a loan (agreement). As regards combining a loan with alms or a gift, if the loan is from an almsgiver or donor, then it is permissible, but if the opposite is the case (i.e. the borrower is required to give alms or a gift), then it is not allowed."

This ruling refers to linking of a loan contract with several other contracts of which *qiraad* is the one which is a loan contract. (*Qiraad* is a type of loan in which a lender has some claim in the profit earned by the borrower from investing the borrowed amount in profit earning activity). In a TMCL transaction each party returns only the amount of loan to the other party and there is no claim of any share in the profit earned by any of the parties by investing the amount of loan. It is therefore evident that this ruling is not applicable to TMCL.

8. Al-Muhadhdhib (1/311)

The loan that results in a benefit (to the lender) is not permitted. An example of this is when a lender gives a loan of one thousand (in order that) the borrower sells him his house. The proof [of this prohibition] is that the Prophet s.a.w.s prohibited a sale and a loan (to be combined in a single transaction).

According to this ruling profit earned on a loan is prohibited. There is no profit earned on either of the two loans in a TMCL transaction as only actual amount of each loan is to be returned. Whatever profit or loss is earned by the bank or the client is accrued from investment of borrowed money. Therefore this ruling is not applicable to TMCL.

9. Kashshaf al Qina' (3/303, 304)

If (the loan agreement) stipulates that the borrower return (an amount) less than he borrowed, or one of the parties stipulates that the other sell, lease or loan him (an item), it is not permitted. The reason is that (the above stipulation amounts to) two sales (transactions) in a single sale (agreement), which is prohibited. If the lender imposes a condition on the borrower to sell him something at less than its market price, which is not permitted, because a benefit accrues (to the lender). (Similarly) if a lender stipulates that the borrower performs some work for him, or (the lender) benefits from a mortgage, that (the borrower) waters (the lender's) trees, or cultivate the lender's land, lease him real estate at more than the (market) rent, or sell him an item at more than its (market) value, or employ him in his industry and give him less than the (market) wage. All (of the preceding examples) involve the accrual of a benefit to the lender and are therefore prohibited because of what has been said previously. This ruling describes how the lender can make monetary gain by including in a loan contract condition of selling, renting, etc. which makes the transaction invalid. As regards the condition of another loan in a loan contract this can refer to a loan to be advanced in future. This matter has already been discussed under rulings *1* and *2* and as such this ruling is also not applicable to TMCL.

10. "You lend to me, and I will lend to you": Bidayat al Mujtahid

(Kitab al Sulh): For example, if two parties claim an amount of money from each other, with each side denying the other's claim, then they both agree to delay (payment) to the other of what was claimed, it is disliked (by the Muslim jurists).The reason for (their) dislike is the fear that both parties could be truthful, and by each allowing the other a mutual respite (for payment), [the agreement) enters (the category) of ("You lend to me, and I will lend to you").

This ruling refers to denial by one party of a financial claim of another party. This ruling does not in any way relate to TMCL.

11. The condition requiring an additional loan from the lender to the borrower: Rawdat-aTalibin (1/35)

If (the lender) stipulates (in the loan agreement) that he will lend an additional amount (to the borrower), it is valid, (for) the stipulation is not binding on the lender, rather it is (considered) a promise, as if (the lender) were to gift (the borrower) a thawb with the condition that he will gift him another one (at a later date).

This ruling has no consequence as far as TMCL is concerned.

12. Fath al Aziz (9/382)

If (the lender) gives a loan with the condition that he will lend an additional amount (to the borrower), (the loan) is valid, and the condition is not binding on the lender.

This ruling has also no consequence as far as TMCL is concerned.

From the above discussion on the rulings purported to be related to TMCL it is quiet evident that TMCL does not suffer from any defect preventing it from being acceptable by all Islamic schools of thought. However, for the satisfaction of those who are TMCL averse and insist on linking it with "*you lend to me and I will lend to you*", following further discussion is in order.

Even after more than twenty years of profitable operation of many Islamic banks and academic effort of Islamic economists and in spite of tremendous financial resources available to them, Islamic banks and governments are forced to take loans on interest from conventional banks only because of non-existence of a central organization which can function as a lender of last resort capable of providing interest-free loans to Islamic banks and governments. Establishment of such an organization is the most urgent need of the entire Muslim ummah which can be fulfilled by no known means other than TMCL. Hence Islamic banks should either adopt TMCL and manage to obtain interest-free loans in times of need or reject TMCL and depend on interest-bearing loans from Western banks. There is no third alternative. Common sense demands that TMCL must be adopted because interest is a glaring sin and definitely *haraam* whereas TMCL can be held by its critics at the most to be undesirable. What happens in a TMCL transaction is that a man needing a loan of say Rs. ten thousand for one year advances to the bank a loan of Rs. one thousand for ten years and at the same time the bank gives to him a loan of Rs. ten thousand for one year. The two loan contracts, one for the loan from the borrower to the bank and the other from the bank to the borrower, stipulate no condition other than returning the amount of loan, are executed simultaneously. The two loan contracts are distinct and separate and do not include any reference to each other. In this transaction there is no condition which allows what is prohibited or prohibits what is lawful in *Shariah.* Hence legitimacy of TMCL is fully established under the general principle laid down by our Prophet *s.a.w.s* in his famous *hadeeth* "*all the conditions agreed by the Muslims are upheld except a condition which allows what is prohibited or prohibits what is lawful.*" Hon.Justice Muhammad Taqi Usmani has quoted the above *hadeeth* at several places in his book "*An Introduction to Islamic Finance*" while discussing necessity of amending or adding new provisions in existing laws for meeting modern requirements like termination of *Musharakah* without closing business, termination of *Mudarabah* and running *Musharakah* accounts on the basis of daily products.

SOLUTIONS OF PROBLEMS RAISED IN GOVERNMENT'S PETITION OF 13-2-99 TO FEDERAL SHARIAT COURT

This booklet contains a fully satisfactory reply to the Government's petition of 13-2-99 to Federal Shariat Court on the question of interest about which the same court gave on 14-11-91 a fully documented, thoroughly argued, unanimous and authoritative decision after intensive hearings on petitions against interest, defended by the Government through legal talent of highest calibre available in the country.

It is not likely that the Federal Shariat Court will agree to hear arguments and open a debate all over again on an issue already thoroughly examined and comprehensively adjudicated upon and it is inconceivable that the court will make any amendment in its authoritative decision on which no objection has ever been raised by any Islamic scholar or modern economist and which remained unimplemented only because the Government never ordered the banking organizations to eliminate interest from the banking system.

Courts' normal function is to interpret laws and pass judgments on validity of laws and decide disputes and not to make laws or design systems and as such the request in the petition for proposing a model for economic system is an exercise in futility. However, this request reveals Government's concern about the harmful effects of interest on the society and economy and the urgent need for starting interest-free banking system in the country. Fortunately, this booklet is now available which demonstrates a practicable method for starting interest-free banking system immediately. Hence, there is no necessity to wait for a decision on the petition as there is a risk of long drawn proceedings to ensue which will unnecessarily delay our submitting to the Will of Allah and consequent result of fruitful gains therefrom.

For ready reference of the Prime Minister and those Government decision makers who are genuinely interested in starting the process of alleviating financial miseries of the people and taking the country out of debt-trap without any further delay, gist of each issue raised in the above petition is reproduced hereunder in italics with corresponding reply underneath.

2.1 Conflicting judgments, contrary view in earlier judgment of Sindh High Court (PLD 1989 Karachi 304)

For the first time in Pakistan history the question of interest came up for thorough examination and adjudication before the Federal Shariat Court in early 1990, and after the authoritative decision of 14-11-91 not a single differing opinion has so far come to light what to say of conflicting judgment. Sindh High Court's judgment of 1989 came up before Federal Shariat Court during the proceedings of 1990-1991. The court after detailed examination of the Sindh High Court's judgment dissented with it to the extent of allowing an additional amount on loan based on indexation on account of inflation.

3.1 The Government being cognizant of its responsibilities for ensuring a smooth and seamless transition to an economy based on Islamic principles is desirous of taking effective and immediate steps.

This nobly worded desire needs translation into action which is to order immediate elimination of interest which the banking organizations can execute without much ado by replacing interest with TMCL (Time Multiple Counter Loan) as explained in the chapter on "Operation Of Interest-Free Banking System" of this booklet. If the Government decision makers have any substantial objection or difficulty in implementing the proposal the writer shall travel at any time at short notice to meet the Prime Minister or any of his appointees anywhere for a discussion at his own expense. The writer also volunteers his services to the Government, without any status or remuneration, for any work required to be done for eliminating interest from the banking system.

4.1 It is the will of the people of Pakistan to establish an order wherein Muslims shall be enabled to order their lives in individual and collective spheres in accordance with the teachings and requirements of Islam as set out in the Holy Quraan and Sunnah.

The first and foremost requirement for fulfilling this objective is for the Government to finish the on-going war with Allah and His Rasool *s.a.w.s* by eliminating interest.

5.1 This Honourable court may be pleased to lay down an overarching schema with clearly delineated features providing for a comprehensive solution to the problem of creating an economy based on the elimination of Riba.

It is not the function of Federal Shariat Court to lay down schema which, as shown below, is un-necessary and even harmful.

It is well-known what is forbidden in Islam and whatever is not specifically forbidden can be practiced. Beyond certain "do's" and "don'ts" there are no constraints in Islam and it grants complete freedom of action and encourages competition which is necessary for progress and development and as such it will be harmful for the economy and unfair to individuals and enterprises to specify any particular scheme for all business houses and banks. Upon elimination of interest insatiable lust for worldly riches created by it will die down and economic system will begin to take Islamic shape automatically. Solution of the economic problems lies in elimination of interest for which this booklet provides sufficient guidance.

5.1.2 *No sustained research or systematic application of mind.*

It is the duty of the Government to take action in this connection.

5.1.3 *Impact of inflation on the rights of borrowers and lenders.*

According to the Holy Quraan and Sunnah any amount charged by the lender over and above the principal amount of loan on any account is *riba*. Interest is the main cause of inflation and in interest-free system there will be no significant impact of inflation. Islamic principles are simple to put into practice and are dispute-averse. Therefore, the simple and clear Islamic Law is that whatever amount is borrowed same amount has to be returned and there is no mention of the value of loan and also no provision for making any change on any account whatsoever. There is no exact unit of measure for calculating the value of money at different times. Therefore the simple way to avoid any dispute is to receive back only whatever is given in loan.

This issue was brought up in defense of interest by its advocates before the Federal Shariat Court during 1990-91. It was thoroughly examined argued and settled. It is not understood why this issue is again being raised. Apparently the authors of the petition have not cared to study the contents of the momentous judgment of the Federal Shariat Court given in November 1991.

5.1.4 *Right of banks to levy service charges.*

There will be no service charge on loans in TMCL-based interest-free banking system.

5.1.5 *Returns to banks in profit sharing, unsatisfactory experience of profit sharing agreements, false and inaccurate books of accounts by companies showing loss in profit-sharing transactions, injustice to small depositors.*

In TMCL-based banking system banks will issue loans on the basis of TMCL against collateral and they will not be under any compulsion to provide finance on profit-sharing basis. However, the banks will be free to enter into profit-sharing agreements with companies of their choice. In their own interest and in the interest of their depositors the banks themselves will take care to enter into profit-sharing agreements with only reputable organizations who maintain transparent accounts.

As regards profit-sharing ratio, it will be left to the market forces and competition. Market economy does not encourage unnecessary constraints and encourages open competition. In TMCL-based interest-free banking system there will be two types of deposits i.e. demand deposits and investment deposits. On demand deposits bank will not give any profit but return of full amount as and when demanded will be guaranteed. On investment deposits banks will give a portion of profit earned by them to the account holders. If the bank incurs loss on investment then the depositors will also share the loss. In the interest of their business and in view of competition from other banks the banks will give a fair share to the investment deposit account holders from the profits earned by the bank. Otherwise the bank will run the risk of deposits being shifted to other banks.

As regards maintenance of false accounts by companies, the Government can and must take stern administrative measures and punish the culprits irrespective of their political affiliation so as to stop leakage of taxes and loss of revenue. Federal Shariat Court can provide no help to the Government as it is a matter of good governance which the Government itself must provide.

5.1.6 (e) Laws to prevent money lenders charging usurious rates of interest from persons in weak bargaining position, were intended to prevent exploitation.

5.1.6 (f) Lenders are now middle class individuals who deposit their savings for their future needs, whereas bulk of borrowing from banks is done by corporate or business entities some of which are very large or very wealthy.

These fallacious contentions in favour of banking interest put forward by advocates of interest have been repelled time and again by eminent Muslim scholars and economists. Allama Iqbal made a specific reference to modern banks in one of his famous verses condemning interest. According to Quraan and Sunnah any amount (big or small) in excess of the original amount of loan (advanced for any purpose - consumption, trade, industry or agriculture) charged from any one (rich or poor) is *riba* and strictly prohibited.

Raising of such settled issues does not behove a government seeking ways and means to eliminate interest from the economy in abidance of precepts of Quraan and Sunnah.

5.1.6 (g) Traditional Islamic methods of financing such as Mudaraba or Musharaka arrangements may simply lead to deprivation of the savings of the depositors. Large and wealthy companies will receive interest-free loans which they may or may not repay.

In TMCL-based interest-free banking system banks will advance loans on TMCL basis against collateral and they will not be under any compulsion to enter into profit-sharing agreements as already explained under item *5.1.5*. As regards the problem of non-payment of loans, it is not specifically related to interest-free banking. In the present interest-based banking system also billions of Rupees have not been repaid. Solution of this problem is the duty of the Government and can be achieved only through good governance. Federal Shariat Court cannot help the Government in this politically originated problem solution of which requires stern administrative measures by the Government. However, upon elimination of interest insatiable lust for worldly riches created by interest will die down and instances of non-repayment of loans in TMCL interest-free banking system, hopefully, will be rare.

5.1.6 (h) Productive utilization of deposits, discovery of profitable avenues of investment, risky investments to be eschewed, lending of banks to be biased in favour of conservatism, lending entails risks, compensation for the risks incurred by banks.

Not only banking but all businesses involve risks and it is their exclusive concern to manage their businesses prudently. Where fraud or other misconduct comes into play it becomes the duty of the Government to take stern administrative measures and punish the culprits. It is by no means the function of Federal Shariat Court to devise ways and means to avoid risks and losses in banking business. Moreover these problems exist in the present system also and it is not understood why these are raised in respect of interest-free system specifically.

5.1.7 Borrowers should not be saddled with exorbitant charges imposed by banks.

In TMCL-based interest-free system there will be no service charges on loans imposed by the banks.

5.1.7 (a) Loan on profit-sharing may end up in paying more to the bank, many companies do not maintain correct books of accounts.

In TMCL-based interest-free system, as opposed to profit-sharing based system, banks will not be under any compulsion to enter into profit-sharing agreements.

5.1.7 (b) High cost of bank borrowings adversely effects growth of the economy, is likely to lead to Pakistani manufacturers being priced out of foreign markets, internally it leads to price increases and higher rate of inflation and externally it leads to fall in exports and a greater dependence on foreign loans at high rates of interest and consequential transfer of economic sovereignty in favour of foreign countries.

Nothing can be as unpatriotic and disgusting as to be guilty of laxity in discarding interest even after realizing its devastating grievous effects listed above, and continue jeopardizing the country's economic sovereignty. Any more delay in eliminating interest may make it well nigh impossible to save our economic sovereignty and independence from foreign clutches.

5.1.7 (c) Via media for recovery of sick industrial units.

Owners of sick industries got away with looting of public money due to their political influence. They are living in luxury and have used share-holders' money and loans from nationalized banks in building big bank balances and buying property and other valuable assets. The solution of the problem does not lie in pumping more public money into the sick units but it lies in recovering by force the looted wealth from the owners' personal assets which are no secret and which are often brazenly exhibited in public. Stern action must be taken against all of them irrespective of their political affiliations. Nobody should be permitted to enjoy looted wealth.

***5.2** What is required is a reform of the banking system and not its destruction in the name of interest-free banking system. What is required is a detailed careful and systematic application of mind to restructure it in the light of the injunctions of Islam in such a manner that it leads to an improvement in efficiency and not a devastation of the economy.*

The proposal of replacing interest by TMCL put forward in this booklet is so much in line with the above requirements that this booklet can be held to be tailor made for meeting the above requirements fully and effectively. The proposal calls for only giving up interest and injecting TMCL as debt financing instrument in the banking system. No other means is yet known whereby interest-based system can be so smoothly converted into interest-free system and this can take place in no time without much ado. Now there should be no excuse for any body to delay this transformation any longer.

5.3 No modern economy can function without secure and vibrant banking sector.

The above contention is true and it is also true that with the inception of TMCL as substitute of interest the banking sector will not only become vibrant and secure but will also produce spiritual, ideological, moral, social, economic and financial benefits as depicted in various chapters of this booklet.

5.4 Banking system is the conduit through which money flows for investment and export and imports. It is not possible in the modern world for any country to subsist as an island of isolation. If the country is to act as one of the flag bearers of an Islamic renascence it cannot afford to lag behind in economic progress and development.

The above contentions are very true but it is also true that the banking system does not have to be interest-based which has led us into debt-trap and brought our credit rating down to an insulting low level which is far worse than living in isolation with self-respect not injured by dictation of lenders. Flag bearer we are, but on the wrong side of the war front. We are not qualified even to enter any Islamic team for which we must discard interest and only then we can aspire to achieve economic independence and prosperity and consequently place of respect in the world.

Too much time has already been wasted and to avoid further damage it is necessary to implement Federal Shariat Court's order of 14-11-91 immediately instead of waiting for an outcome of the present petition and letting, in the mean time, the country's economy to worsen further and become more dependent on foreign loans which increase the debt burden and provide only short breathing space at high price of passing of our profitable strategic national assets like PTCL permanently into foreign hands, and no real assistance for economic recovery.

Due to non-implementation of Federal Shariat Court's order we have lacked far behind in economic progress during the past seven years. In order to avoid lagging further behind it is necessary to implement the above order immediately.

6.1 Subsisting contracts entered into with foreign or domestic entities.

It is not clear what the petition requires from the Federal Shariat Court by raising this point. If the intention is to enquire what should be done about outstanding interest-based loans, then complete satisfactory answer of this question is given in chapters on "domestic debt retirement after inception of interest-free banking system" and "foreign debt retirement after inception of interest-free banking system" of this booklet.

***7.1** Crucial and central role of the banking system not realized. This honourable court should embark on a detailed and exhaustive exercise to authoritatively lay down the salient features of an Islamic economy. A system which conforms to the spirit and letter of Islamic provisions should be spelled out in terms of which the banking system can function efficiently and productively for the benefit of the people of Pakistan. Features which are Islamic must be isolated and separated from those which are un-Islamic.*

Ordering to eliminate interest from the banking system does not at all mean non-realization of the crucial and central role of banking system which does not necessarily have to be based on interest. After the Federal Shariat Court had given exhaustive judgment of 14-11-91, it was the duty of the Government to embark on detailed and exhaustive exercise to find a method to eliminate interest from the banking system. Now after more than seven years it is not right to say "the honourable court should (?) embark on detailed and exhaustive exercise..." because the function of Federal Shariat Court is to examine and pass judgments on specific laws and disputes and not to design systems. If the quest is for a suitable method to eliminate interest from the banking system, then the requirement is fully met with by this booklet. If the concerned authority has any doubt about the viability of the proposal given in the booklet, the writer will be only too glad to have a meaningful discussion for which he will travel at his own expense.

Interest-free banking system is the foundation for Islamic economic system and laying of this foundation is the most urgent need of the hour and must be accomplished immediately. However, to work out details of a complete Islamic economic system for the country is a big task and the Government should set up a commission of Islamic scholars and economists of integrity to prepare recommendations on important issues like land reforms, equitable taxation, collection of revenues, proper *zakat* system (present system is an insult to the Islamic concept of *zakat*), prudent expenditure of revenues, stoppage of expenditure on luxurious amenities for Government executives and parliamentarians, provision of basic necessities of life for all including employment, housing, education, and health services etc. It may take quite some time in the preparation of these recommendations but elimination of interest from the banking system is not dependent on them and must on no account be delayed any further.

***8.1** Existing system may be destroyed without creating an alternative system. This can only be a recipe for economic and social disaster.*

Inception of TMCL as substitute of interest in the existing system will be smoothest possible transition of interest-based un-Islamic system into interest-free Islamic banking system. The existing interest-based banking system has already proved to be a recipe for social and economic disaster and there is no justification at all to let it continue any longer.

***9.1** Obligation in excess of US$ 60 billion (foreign debt in excess of US$ 34 billion, domestic debt in excess of RS 1200 billion) debt servicing running into billions of dollars annually. With a decision not to pay interest, the country may become a defaulter with potentially extremely serious implications.*

The miserable situation of the economy as depicted is the result of excessive import of luxuries far in excess of the value of exports, excessive budget deficits resulting from spending far in excess of the revenues, and indiscriminate borrowing on interest. The situation can be improved only by adopting the cult of inexpensive simple living within the available honest means of income at individual and national level, the example of which must be set by the ruling elite.

For taking the country out of the debt trap it is absolutely essential to convert the existing system into TMCL-based interest-free banking system. The two chapters of this booklet on domestic and foreign debt retirement demonstrate with mathematical calculations how we can meet the obligations of repaying our debts in full and proceed on the path of progress and development. Anybody in authority who rejects the writer's proposal must give a well-defined alternative and explain how the country can be pulled out of the debt-trap. If such an alternative is not available, which certainly is the case, the Government should have no hesitation to order immediate implementation of the writer's proposal.

10.1 *Importance of honouring contractual stipulation.*

As is clear from the answer to the issue *9.1* the contractual stipulations will be fully honoured under the procedures laid down in this booklet for domestic and foreign debt retirement.

11.1 (a) *A smooth and non-disruptive transition to an economy based on the principle of Ehsan and Adl which is free from the taint of Riba.*

Adoption of the writer's proposal to replace interest with TMCL will result in a smooth and non-disruptive transition of interest-based un-Islamic banking system to interest-free Islamic banking system which is a pre-requisite for structuring complete Islamic economic system based on the principles of *Ehsan* and *Adl*, on which the writer has already commented in answer to issue *7.1*. If and when interest-free banking system is established in the country the writer will offer his humble services to the Government, without any status or remuneration, for any work required to be done in preparation of full Islamic economic system.

11.1 (b) *A workable economic system which will enable Pakistan to flourish and prosper in the light of the principles of Quraan and Sunnah.*

The shown in the booklet TMCL-based interest-free banking is workable and will surely bring prosperity in the country.

Prayer (I) *Lay down declare the principles of Islam on the basis of which the existing laws, for and in relation to the question of Riba, are scrutinized and examined and an authoritative verdict given as to the lines along which the existing system can be remodeled so as to bring it in conformity with the requirements of Islam.*

Existing laws, for and in relation to interest which were defended on behalf of the Government by best available legal talent, were thoroughly examined and scrutinized on the basis of the principles of Islam adequately explained and documented in its exhaustive judgment and then the authoritative verdict was given by the Federal Shariat Court vide its order of 14-11-91. Any further laying down of principles in this connection will be superfluous.

As regards remodeling of the existing banking system so as to bring it in conformity with the requirements of Islam it was the duty of the Government to find out a method to accomplish this task. However, a ready answer for enabling the Government to proceed immediately to re-model the existing system is available in this booklet which illustrates workable method for starting interest-free banking system.

Prayer (ii) *Direct that in order to avoid creating a vacuum, the functioning of the existing system may not be disrupted until such time that a modified system has been put in place.*

This prayer seeks permission of the Federal Shariat Court for the Government to delay elimination of interest which is so severe a crime in Islam that Allah has given in Quraan warning of war from Allah and His Rasool *s.a.w.s* against those who do not give it up. The most extra-ordinary warning of war shows that interest cannot be permitted in any circumstances for any duration and that it can be given up without any difficulty because Allah says "*Allah intends every facility for you; He does not want to put you in difficulties*"(2:185). It is absolutely wrong and baseless contention that interest cannot be eliminated at once and that it should be done gradually and completely eliminated when an interest-free banking model has been put in place. Syed Abou-al-Aala Maudoodi wrote in his authentic book "*sood*" in Urdu "so long as interest is permitted by law and interest-based contracts are admitted and enforced by courts and money lenders are allowed to collect deposits by giving temptation of earning interest it is not at all possible for an interest-free financial system to come into existence and grow... . Whenever it (elimination of interest) is to be accomplished interest shall have to be banned by law in one single starting step. Then interest-free financial system will come into being automatically and necessity, which is the mother of invention, will pave the way for it to develop and expand in all fields".

As regards the fear of a vacuum or disruption, nothing like that can happen in converting the existing system into interest-free banking system in one single step by substituting interest with TMCL.

In Islam there is no papalism and no body howsoever high in status or learning has the authority to grant permission to any one, in any circumstances and on any account, to violate Allah's commands. Any one granting such an un-authorized permission will be crossing into Divine Realm. Even in secular systems no body is allowed to rebel or act against law.

The above discussion leads to the conclusion that the Government of Islamic Republic of Pakistan, as a first vital step towards fulfillment of its declared commitment to establish Islamic order in the country, must at least order immediate elimination of Interest and stop the on-going war against Allah and His Rasool *s.a.w.s*, without waiting for the outcome of the petition to the Federal Shariat Court.

PROHIBITION OF INTEREST AND GOVERNMENT'S DUTY

Interest is so severely prohibited that Quraan holds warding off interest as condition of *Iman* and declares war from Allah and His Rasool *saws* against perpetrators. If Allah's message has any meaning interest cannot exist in any Muslim society. However during the past several decades our economy managers promoted interest-based policies which ruined the country's economy.

In its exhaustive judgment of 23rd Dec. 1999, Supreme Court of Pakistan (*Shariat* Appellate Bench) finally set aside all the misleading contentions in support of interest and held that interest in all its forms, big or small, and regardless of the purpose of loan, is *Riba* prohibited by the Holy Quraan. The apex court also passed an order to transform the existing financial system to the one conforming to *shariah*.

Now the die-hard advocates of interest have started propagating that there is no viable alternative of interest and that the whole banking system will be disrupted if any attempt is made to eliminate interest. This booklet demonstrates that TMCL (Time Multiple Counter Loan) is as good a loaning instrument as interest and that it can effectively replace interest instantly without any difficulty and disruption in the banking system. The last chapter gives solutions of all the problems regarding elimination of interest, raised by the previous government in its petition of 13-2-1999 to the Federal Shariat Court.

Elimination of interest is the fundamental prerequisite for Islamizing the banking system and saving the country from drowning ever deep into the debt morass. It is a wrong notion that elimination of interest will be harmful if it is enforced without first bringing about other radical improvements in the socio-economic structure. Islamic way of evolutionary process for eradicating evils from the society is to struggle for finishing all evils and not to make elimination of one evil dependent on the elimination of other evils because such an approach sets up a vicious circle of evils and no evil is finished. Extinction of interest alone may not cure all economic evils, but it will certainly bring immense good as it will finish the on-going war with Allah and His Rasool *saws*. Task to reform the entire socio-economic structure must be undertaken but it will be a folly to postpone elimination of interest and continue warring against Allah and His Rasool *saws* which would only aggravate socio-economic miseries and render accomplishment of reform task impossible.

Our finance and economy managers will do well if they ignore baseless contentions and unfounded fears propagated by advocates of interest and instead pay heed to Allah's warning in Quraan: "*WHOSOEVER VIOLATES MY COMMANDS VERILY FOR HIM LIVELIHOOD WILL BECOME DISTRESSFUL*" (20:124).

They should proceed unhesitatingly to implement Divine Command to abolish interest laying trust in Allah's assurances in Quraan : "*WHOSOEVER FOLLOWS MY GUIDANCE WILL NOT LOSE HIS WAY NOR FALL INTO MISERY*" (20:123) and : "*TO HIM WHO BELIEVES*

IN ALLAH AND THE LAST DAY AND FOR THOSE WHO FEAR ALLAH HE (ever) PREPARES A WAY OUT. AND HE PROVIDES FOR HIM FROM (sources) HE NEVER COULD IMAGINE. AND IF ANYONE PUTS HIS TRUST IN ALLAH, SUFFICIENT IS ALLAH FOR HIM' (65:2,3).

The apex court order is final, unchallengeable and binding upon the government. It is comprehensive, unequivocal and exact and leaves no loop-hole or excuse whatsoever for allowing the curse of interest to continue to ravage our economy.

Rule of law demands enforcement of the apex court order and as such it is the bounden duty of the government to ensure elimination of interest and earn Allah's blessings which are necessary for taking the country out of the social and economic turmoil.

Nothing can be as repugnant to common sense as to suggest division of a Divine Command into parts and recommend elimination of interest in several phases. At any point of time one can be either a faithful or a rebel and either at peace or at war but in no case both faithful and rebel or partly at peace and partly at war. Fundamental principle of Islamic jurisprudence is that the shariah laws which had reached finality during the lifetime of our Prophet saws must be fully implemented at once and not in parts. Every Divine Command was acted upon immediately after revelation. Clearly gradualism in abolishing interest is an absurdity.

Upshot of the above discussion is that in order to save themselves and the nation from Allah's wrath arising from indulgence in the most heinous crime in Islamic jurisprudence, our rulers should at once stop interest-bearing savings schemes and put a complete ban on taking fresh loans on interest and on paying and charging of interest and declare it to be a cognizable offence with immediate effect. This can be done by issuing an ordinance as has been done in the past on many occasions. The time schedule given in the apex court order should be used only for legislation and framing of rules and procedures and not for continuing interest-based activities. Hon. Justice Wajihuddin Ahmad has aptly stressed in the judgment *"There should be no misgivings, in any quarters that this or the Federal Shariat Court would brook any unnecessary delay during the implementation phase of the judgment of this Court. Thus, time schedule or not, no one, be it the government itself would any longer be countenanced to conduct any further avoidable Ribawi dealings, here or with the outside world. Transgressions, if any, can be appropriately brought to the notice of the Court"*.

ISLAMIC ALTERNATIVE OF INTEREST

Modern banking system has played a key role in the economic and industrial development by providing finance widely and freely to industry and trade through interest-based credit and loans, although interest payments are exploitative as these are from those who have money less than what they need to those who have money in excess of their needs. Islamic approach to un-Islamic institutions has throughout been to use them beneficially after eliminating un-Islamic elements from them. After the conquest of Makkah, only the idols from *Kaabah* were removed and every thing else was left intact. Umer-bin-Khattab *rta* instructed governors appointed in newly conquered territories not to interfere in the local customs and traditions unless there was something un-Islamic in them. In our case sensible strategy is to make the established banking system Islamically acceptable by injecting only essential modifications most important of which is to replace interest by a non-exploitative Islamic lending device which can perform in Islamic way all the financial intermediation functions performed by interest in the present system.

Basic objective of Islamic Financial System is need fulfilment and needs may be for financing industry, trade, agriculture or consumption. For need fulfilment *Zakat* and *Qard Hasan* are Islamic financial instruments. *Zakat* caters for the needs of the poor and destitute whereas *Qard Hasan* caters for financial needs of others. *Qard Hasan* is loaning without additional charge over and above the principal amount. It can be used widely and freely in financial intermediation between those having money in excess of their needs and those having money less than their needs and that is what the banks do. It is absolutely wrong notion that *Qard Hasan* is meant only for the poor and destitute and not for development financing. Islam actually encourages widespread use of *Qard Hasan* for need fulfilment as according to a *Hadith* of our Prophet *saws* reward for lending is eighteen times whereas reward for charity is ten times. There is no bar in Islam on borrowing for business or production. Only those borrowers who do not repay loans are severely reprimanded.

Practical application of *Qard Hasan* for eliminating interest is strongly recommended in the research thesis '*PREVENTIVE MEASURES IN ISLAM AGAINST INTEREST*' on which Dr.Fazl-e-Ilahi was awarded Ph.D. He has emphasized in his thesis the vital role which *Qard Hasan* can play in abolishing interest. He concluded the chapter on *Qard Hasan* with the assertion *"expanding the field of this way of lending will by Allah's grace, aid in blocking the way of interest. Therefore in this context I urge upon all those who want to abolish interest to do whatever they can to expand the field of this way of lending"*.

Council of Islamic Ideology in its report of June 1980 held profit/loss sharing or *Qard Hasan* to be ideally the real alternatives of interest under an Islamic Economic System. Profit/loss sharing system cannot meet the financial needs of credit-worthy entrepreneurs unwilling to share profit. Credibility of most of the entrepreneurs willing to share profit is doubtful. Council of Islamic Ideology also acknowledged in its report *"difficulties faced in the practical application of the profit/loss sharing system in its pure form on account of the prevalent standards of morality in the society"*. Thus in our circumstances *Qard Hasan* remains the only ideal practicable alternative of interest.

Late Professor Shaikh Mahmud Ahmad (identified in the apex court judgment as our country's most outstanding economist and researcher) devised a financial instrument based on *Qard Hasan* and named it TMCL-Time Multiple Counter Loan. It can perform in Islamic way all the financial intermediation functions of interest-based banks. Perhaps because he was not a professional economist TMCL did not get any publicity. Also it did not receive any official attention because self-serving past rulers of our country had no will to abolish interest and pull the country out of the debt morass. Now, for implementing the apex court's order, our economy managers must genuinely be looking for a true Islamic alternative of interest which can effectively replace interest swiftly and easily without any disruption in the banking system. TMCL meets all these requirements and it is the surest, simplest and quickest means to convert the present banking system into interest-free system. This objective cannot be achieved by the banking products currently used by Islamic banks.

A TMCL transaction between two parties consists of two simultaneously executed separate interest-free loan (*Qard Hasan*) contracts such that the multiple of the amount and period of one loan equals the multiple of the amount and period of the other loan. It facilitates interest-free borrowing of large amounts against counter loans of much smaller amounts advanced for proportionately longer periods. For example, an entrepreneur needing Rs. 10 million for one year can get this loan (against collateral as at present) by advancing a loan of Rs. 1 million to the bank for 10 years. Thus TMCL fulfils the client's financial need and also enables the bank to earn profit from long-term investment of the counter-loan money. The bank does not earn any interest on the loans advanced by it and whatever gain or loss it earns comes from long-term investment of counter-loan amounts which are actually borrowed sums and in Islam there is no bar on investing borrowed sums in business.

In a TMCL transaction the bank and the client do good to each other and as such it conforms with the Quraanic precept "*HAL JAZA-UL-IHSAN ILLA-AL-IHSAN*" and the noble teaching of our Prophet *saws* that a favour done to any one should be reciprocated. TMCL also paves the way to interest-free banking which is the most urgent need of the Muslim *ummah* and particularly of Pakistan at the present juncture.

OPERATION OF TMCL-BASED INTEREST-FREE BANKING SYSTEM

General

Replacement of interest by TMCL is the surest, simplest and instant means to eliminate interest without any disruption in the banking system. In the interest-free regime banks will continue to function as at present with the following basic changes.:

(i) No interest will be charged or paid

(ii) Transactions involving credit will be based on TMCL

(iii) Instead of earning interest, banks will earn profit by investing in *shariah*-compliant modes of their choice

Excepting compliance with applicable foreign exchange regulations same procedures will apply to local and foreign currency accounts and transactions. Following salient features of TMCL-based Banking make it quite clear that switch-over to interest-free system can be carried out smoothly without any interruption or difficulty.

Advancement of Loans

All loans will be interest-free and will be advanced on TMCL basis (against collateral as at present). In the beginning time multiple ratio in TMCL is proposed to be ten which can be altered later on, if necessary.

For example a loan of Rs 10.0 M required for one year will be granted against counter-loan of Rs 1.0 M advanced to the bank for 10 years. If the borrower requires extension in the repayment period the bank may agree to it if the borrower advances another appropriate counter-loan to the bank. For example if an extension of 3 months is required in the above mentioned case the bank would require the borrower to advance another counter-loan of Rs. 0.25 M for 10 years. If the borrower is unable to advance another counter-loan, the bank may accept his request if he agrees to receive his original counter-loan money from the bank in 12 ½ years instead of 10 years. In the event of default the bank may make recovery from collateral or through legal action as at present. In case of delay in recovery the bank may retain the borrower's counter-loan money for an appropriate extended period.

In certain cases, if so needed by the borrower or the bank, they may agree on any time multiple ratio other than the normal ratio. Normally the Monetary Authority need not interfere in this matter, but if at any stage it is considered necessary, for controlling the credit availability or for any other reason, the Monetary Authority may fix the time multiple ratio or vary it periodically.

Settlement of Outstanding Interest-based Loans

Upon interest becoming illegal, outstanding interest based loans will have to be converted into TMCL-based transactions. The borrower will repay the principal amount of the loan on due date and instead of paying interest, the borrower will advance to the bank a counter-loan such that the multiple of the loan amount he took and the period of the loan availed equals the multiple of the counter-loan amount and the period of counter-loan. Interest already paid prior to initiation of interest-free regime will not be subject to recovery.

Example 1: Loan of Rs. 10.0 M was taken from bank for 1 year and is now due for repayment in the interest-free regime. The borrower will repay the principal amount Rs. 10.0 M to the bank and instead of paying interest will advance to the bank counter-loan of Rs. 10.0 M for 1 year or by mutual agreement Rs. 5.0 M for 2 years, or Rs. 2.0 M for 5 years, or Rs. 1.0 M for 10 years etc.

Example 2: Loan of Rs. 10.0 M was taken from bank for 2 years of which 1 year has passed and no interest has been paid. The borrower will return the principal amount Rs. 10.0 M on due date and instead of paying interest will advance a counter-loan of Rs. 10.0 M to the bank for 2 years or by mutual agreement Rs. 5.0 M for 4 years, or Rs. 4.0 M for 5 years or Rs. 2.0 M for 10 years etc.

Example 3: Loan of Rs. 10.0 M was taken from bank for 2 years of which 1 year has passed and interest for 1 year has been paid. On due date falling in interest-free regime the borrower will return the principal amount Rs. 10.0 M to the bank and instead of paying interest for the 2nd year will advance counter-loan of Rs. 10.0 M to the bank for 1 year or by mutual agreement Rs. 5.0 M for 2 years, or Rs. 2.0 M for 5 years, or Rs 1.0 M for 10 years etc.

Encashment of Bills, Bonds, Debentures Etc.

As no interest will be payable in interest-free regime bills, bonds and all such other interest-bearing documents will be encashed at face value and the interest content in them will be converted into appropriate TMCL such that the multiple of the amount and the period availed equals the multiple of the amount and the period of counter-loan. Interest payments already made prior to initiation of interest-free regime will not be subject to recovery.

Example 1: As per contract A provided to B goods/services for Rs. 1.0 M payable after 1 year. A draws a bill of Rs. 1.0 M on B payable after 1 year and sells the bill to C against cash payment of Rs. 0.90 M. On maturity date falling in interest-free regime C presents the bill to B for payment. B will pay Rs. 0.90 M to C and Rs. 0.10 M to A and A will advance an interest-free loan of Rs. 0.90 M to C for 1 year or by mutual agreement Rs. 0.45 M for 2 years or Rs. 0.10 M for 9 years or Rs. 0.09 M for 10 years etc.

Example 2: As per contract A provided to B goods/services for Rs.1.0 M payable after 1 year. A draws a bill of Rs. 1.0 M on B payable after 1 year. A sells the bill to C against cash payment of Rs. 0.95 M half year before maturity date. On the maturity date falling in interest-free regime C presents the bill to B for payment. B will pay Rs. 0.95 M to C and Rs. 0.05 M to A and A will advance to C an interest-free loan of Rs. 0.95 M for ½ year or by mutual agreement Rs. 0.475 M for 1 year or Rs. 0.095 M for 5 years, or Rs. 0.0475 M for 10 years etc.

Example 3: As per contract A provided to B goods/services for Rs. 1.0 M payable after 1 year. A draws a bill of Rs. 1.0 M on B payable after 1 year. A sells the bill to C against cash payment of Rs. 0.95 M ½ year before maturity date. C sells the bill to D against cash payment of Rs. 0.975 M ¼ year before maturity. On the maturity date falling in interest-free regime D presents the bill to B for payment. B will pay Rs. 0.975 M to D and Rs. 0.025 M to A and A will advance to D an interest-free loan of Rs. 0.975 M for ¼ year or by mutual agreement Rs. 0.4875 M for ½ year or Rs. 0.24375 M for 1 year or Rs. 0.024375 M for 10 years etc.

Example 4: 4 ½ years prior to initiation of interest-free regime A issued a bond of Rs. 1.0 M face value at discount of 2 percent with interest payable every year and maturity period 5 years. B bought the bond at the time of issue against cash payment of Rs. 0.98 M and received interest from A for 4 years. On the maturity date falling in interest-free regime A will pay to B Rs. 0.98 M and instead of paying interest for the last year A will advance to B interest-free loan of Rs. 0.98 M for 1 year or by mutual agreement Rs. 0.098 M for 10 years or Rs. 0.49 M for 2 years etc.

Example 5: 4 ½ years prior to initiation of interest-free regime A issued a bond of Rs. 1.0 M face value at 2 % discount, interest payable every year and maturity period 5 years. B bought the bond at the time of issue against cash payment of Rs. 0.98 M to A. After 4 years, having received interest for 4 years, B sold the bond to C against cash payment of Rs. 1.02 M. On the maturity date falling in interest-free regime A will pay Rs. 1.02 M to C and instead of paying interest for the last year A will advance to C an interest-free loan of Rs. 1.02 M for 1 year or by mutual agreement Rs. 0.51 M for 2 years or Rs. 0.102 M for 10 years etc.

Example 6: A is a holder of a bill of face value Rs. 1.0 M drawn on B. A wants to encash the bill 30 days before maturity. The bank will pay Rs. 1.0 M to A against a counter-loan of Rs. 0.10 M for 300 days or by mutual agreement Rs.0.20 M for 150 days or Rs. 0.05 M for 600 days etc. The bank will recover Rs. 1.0 M from B on the maturity date and will return the counter-loan money to A on the agreed date.

Customers' Bank Accounts

Banks will continue to receive deposits in customers' accounts and issue cheque books to account holders. There will be two types of accounts, demand deposit and investment accounts. Existing account holders will be given the choice to convert their accounts into demand deposit and/or investment accounts.

Demand Deposit Accounts: Refund on demand of part or full amount in these accounts will be guaranteed by the bank. The bank will have the right to invest the amounts in these accounts at its own risk and responsibility. The bank will not share any profit or loss incurred with the account holders. Banks will have the discretion to fix minimum balance to be maintained in these accounts.

Investment Accounts: Banks at their own discretion will invest the amounts in these accounts in business or industry and will share the profit or loss earned with the account holders on daily product basis. Addition of profit or deduction of loss will be adjusted in the accounts on yearly or half-yearly basis. Withdrawals from these accounts may be subject to certain limitations as are savings accounts at present.

Interest-Earning Saving Accounts will cease to earn interest in the interest-free regime. All savings account holders will presumably opt for investment accounts. It is misleading contention of the advocates of interest that non-payment of interest will induce account holders to withdraw their savings from banks. No doubt interest earnings will cease but there would be positive chances to earn more profit from investment accounts in banks. Moreover it would be very unwise for savings account holders to withdraw their money from banks because there is no alternative available to them to keep their money in safe custody with facility of making payments by cheques and receiving payments against crossed cheques marked "payee's account only". Even if some account holders angered by non-payment of interest to them withdraw their deposits from banks, their money will come back to the banking system through somebody else's account as and when they invest or spend the withdrawn money.

Issue Of Letters Of Credit, Bank Drafts, Bank Gurantees Etc.

Legal and financial papers not involving any credit will be issued by banks as at present against appropriate fees and charges. In the event of bank having to advance any credit or blocking its money for the client, the client will advance an appropriate interest-free loan to the bank such that the multiple of the loan amount and its period equals the multiple of the credit advanced by the bank or the money blocked by it and its period. For such eventuality the bank may require the client to make some deposit in advance, but in no case interest will be charged or paid. For example, if the bank has to part with or block Rs. 1.0 M for one week the client will advance to the bank Rs. 1.0 M for 1 week or by mutual agreement Rs. 0.1 M for 10 weeks or Rs. 0.05 M for 20 weeks etc.

Centeral Bank And Depository-cum-lender Of Last Resort

In the interest-free regime there will be no role of interest-based treasury bills and bonds etc. and all such documents will cease to be issued and no function involving interest will be undertaken by the Central Bank. Other functions not involving interest will be performed as at present. The Central Bank will set up under its auspices a framework of Central Depository-cum-lender of last resort for mobilizing surplus funds of banks and federal and provincial governments and autonomous bodies and advancing interest-free loans to them in times of need. The Central Depository will receive deposits and advance interest-free loans on TMCL basis. For example, if a bank has a surplus of Rs. 5.0 M for 1 month, it may deposit this sum for 1 month with the Central Depository and obtain an interest-free loan of Rs. 0.5 M for 10 months. If a bank is short of liquidity and requires Rs. 10.0 M for 1 week, it will obtain from the Central Depository an interest-free loan of Rs. 10.0 M for 1 week by depositing Rs. 1.0 M with the Central Depository for 10 weeks.

Open Market Operations

In the interest-free regime open market operations will be confined to exchange of interest-free loans and counter-loans with the Central Depository and commercial banks and purchase and sale of stocks and shares until such time as Islamic Economists and Bankers come up with some other marketable asset-based *shariah*-compliant instruments.

Government Borrowings

In the interest-free regime interest-bearing saving schemes, treasury bills and bonds etc. will not be available to the government for raising funds. For financing budgetary deficit and meeting other urgent financial requirements like procurement of war funds, the government will borrow from Central Depository and/or commercial banks on TMCL basis.

Liquidity Arrangement

Banks will deposit 20% of each counter-loan amount with the Central-Depository for 10 years against which Central Depository will allow banks to draw 200% of counter-loan amount for 1 year. This will provide 20% liquidity for the banks. Additional 2% liquidity will be obtained by keeping 20% of counter-loan amount as till money in the banks. Thus total liquidity achieved by the banking sector will be 22%. For example, let total deposit in a bank be Rs. 100.0 M all of which is loaned out against receipt of counter-loans totaling Rs. 10.0 M. 20% of Rs. 10.0 M (=2 M) will be deposited with the Central Depository for 10 years against which the bank will be able to draw 200% of Rs. 10 M (= 20 M) for 1 year. This will provide 20% liquidity for the bank. Additional 2% liquidity will be obtained by keeping 20% of total counter-loan amount (i.e. Rs. 2.0 M) as till money. This will raise the liquidity of the bank to 22% which is more than sufficient. However if the Monetary Authority so desires the liquidity percentage can be raised or lowered by varying the percentage of counter-loan money to be deposited with the Central Depository.

Profit Earning By Banks

As shown in the previous clause on liquidity arrangement, from the total counter-loan money received by the banks 20% will go to the Central Depository and 20% will be held as till money. The remaining 60% of the total counter-loan money will be available to the banks for long-term investment in *shariah*-compliant profitable modes of their choice. The banks will be free to enter into profit/loss sharing arrangement with entrepreneurs whom they consider to be trust-worthy. Banks themselves will decide how much and where they should invest.

Credit Control

At present interest rate mechanism is used to control credit availability. In the interest-free regime this function will be performed by raising or lowering the time multiple ratio in TMCL.

DOMESTIC DEBT RETIREMENT IN TMCL-BASED INTEREST-FREE REGIME

Following are the relevant extracts from the writer's book 'METHOD FOR STARTING INTEREST-FREE BANKING' printed in Feb'99

With the government's declaration to abolish interest, all interest earnings will cease to be paid with immediate effect. Lenders of money with no ideological allegiance and for whom money is above every thing will be shocked and displeased with the stoppage of their income from interest-bearing instruments (forbidden by Allah), and they may claim that the government has no right to go back on its commitment and arbitrarily stop payment of interest. In this connection it would suffice to say that our Prophet Muhammad *saws* said "*what about the people who stipulate conditions which are not present in Allah's Laws? Whoever imposes conditions which are not present in Allah's Laws, then those conditions will be invalid, even if he imposed these conditions a hundred times. Allah's conditions*

(Laws) *are truth and are more solid*'. The government, by freezing foreign currency accounts, has already demonstrated its power and capability to take drastic measures violating its own commitments and solemn guarantees. There is no valid reason whatsoever which should deter the government from complying with Allah's Law and the ruling of His Rasool *saws.*

Stoppage of interest payments will be far less shocking and much less grievous for the interest earners than freezing of foreign currency accounts and compelling the account holders to buy Dollars in the black market for meeting their foreign exchange needs and convert their Dollars into Rupees at a rate much lower than prevalent market rate or accept interest-bearing bonds sale and purchase of which flagrantly violate Quraanic injunction. It goes without saying that stoppage of interest will be for much nobler cause and good of the people and must be welcomed by all who have any allegiance to Islam and the government should consider it to be an honour to follow the example of our Prophet Muhammad *saws*, who upon revelation of the Quraanic injunction to give up interest, stopped payment of all interest earnings including even those which had accrued in the past and were outstanding for payment.

According to the Quraanic injunction to give up interest, the lenders are entitled to receive their original sums only. Therefore whilst the lenders will not be paid any interest, their original sums will have to be returned to them by the government. According to a statement of our Finance Minister, government's total domestic debt burden is worth $31 billion = Rs1,426 billion which is the total of the capital sums of the lenders and interest accrued on them. In the absence of any definite information on the build-up of the total debt it can be assumed that out of Rs1,426 billion an amount of Rs426 billion is interest and the remaining balance of Rs1000 billion is the total of original sums which the government must return to the lenders. Inception of interest-free TMCL-based banking system will enable the government to retire the entire domestic debt within a few years as explained below. The fast deteriorating state of our economy which may compel the government to declare moratorium on foreign debt servicing, unless a bail-out package is doled out to us, should move the rulers to look towards Allah and declare abolition of interest immediately.

Hopefully if 1998-99 is the first financial year of inception of interest-free banking system, the government will require Rs1000 billion to meet the demand of the lenders to return their capital sums. As is shown in the chapter 'economic and financial benefits of interest-free banking' of this booklet, interest-free banking will facilitate conversion of the Federal Budget deficit of Rs197.6 billion into surplus of Rs232.6 billion.

From the above mentioned surplus of Rs232.6 billion, Rs147 billion will be used to retire a portion of the domestic debt leaving balance debt of Rs853 billion. After settling debt of Rs147 billion the balance from surplus of Rs232.6 billion will be Rs85.6 billion.

For clearing the balance debt of Rs853 billion the government will obtain a loan of Rs853 billion for one year from the money market by advancing counter loan of Rs85.3 billion for 10 years. Thus in the first year of inception of interest-free banking the government will have cleared the entire domestic debt accumulated during the past several decades. However the fresh loan of Rs853 billion taken by the government will be required to be paid back in the next financial year. In the next financial year interest-free banking is expected to make surplus available in the budget more than that in the previous year, but assuming it to remain the same Rs232.6 billion will be available to the government for paying back the loan of Rs853 billion taken by it in the last year. Out of the available Rs232.6 billion the government will use Rs163 billion in repaying part of the loan of Rs853 billion carried over from last year leaving balance loan of Rs690 billion for settlement of which the government will take a loan of Rs690 billion from the money market for one year by advancing counter loan of Rs69 billion for ten years. Thus the debt burden to be carried over to third financial year will be Rs690 billion.

In the third financial year, again from the available surplus of Rs232.6 billion Rs181 billion will be used in repaying a part of the loan of Rs690 billion carried over from the last year leaving balance loan of Rs509 billion for settlement of which the government will take a loan of Rs509 billion from the money market for one year by advancing counter loan of Rs50.9 billion for ten years. Thus the debt burden to be carried over to fourth financial year will be Rs509 billion.

In the fourth financial year, again from the available surplus of Rs232.6 billion Rs200 billion will be used in repaying a part of the loan of Rs509 billion carried over from the last year leaving balance loan of Rs309 billion for settlement of which the government will take a loan of Rs309 billion from the money market for one year by advancing counter loan of Rs30.9 billion for ten years. Thus the debt burden to be carried over to fifth financial year will be Rs309 billion.

In the fifth financial year, again from the surplus of Rs232.6 billion Rs224 billion will be used in repaying a part of the loan of Rs309 billion carried over from the last year leaving balance loan of Rs85 billion for settlement of which the government will take a loan of Rs85 billion from the money market for one year by advancing counter loan of Rs8.5 billion for ten years. Thus the debt burden to be carried over to sixth financial year will be Rs85 billion.

In the sixth financial year, again from the surplus of Rs232.6 billion Rs85 billion will be paid in full settlement of the loan carried over from the last year. This will leave surplus of Rs147.6 billion with the government.

Thus within six years after inception of interest-free system the government will not only have retired the entire domestic debt, but will also have surplus of Rs147.6 billion in hand for development projects and Rs244.6 billion in five counter loans receivable after ten years of each advancement.

Conclusion : From the above calculations it is quite clear that with the inception of interest-free banking system we will be able to retire the entire domestic debt and will also have sufficient funds available for education, health, and provision of other basic necessities of life like clean drinking water, construction of roads and sewage services on which the government at present spends very little sums which do not fulfill even ten percent of the requirements.

N.B. As mentioned above, lenders should be paid only their original sums and no interest. However, if the concerned authorities are adamant to pay interest as well, the government will proceed as follows and come out of the debt trap in ten years instead of six years.

In the first year Rs100 billion from the available surplus of Rs232.6 billion will be paid in part payment of the total debt of Rs1,426 billion leaving balance debt of Rs1,326 billion and surplus balance of Rs132.6 billion. For paying balance debt of Rs1,326 billion, a loan of Rs1,326 billion will be taken from the money market for one year by advancing counter loan of Rs132.6 billion for ten years.

In the second year Rs111 billion will be paid in part payment of loan of Rs1,326 billion carried over from the first year leaving balance loan of Rs1,215 billion for settlement of which a loan of Rs1,215 billion will be taken for one year from the money market by advancing counter loan of Rs121.5 billion for ten years.

In the third year Rs123.4 billion will be paid in part payment of loan of Rs1,215 billion carried over from the second year leaving balance loan of Rs 1,091.6 billion for settlement of which a loan of Rs1,091.6 billion will be taken for one year from the money market by advancing counter loan of Rs109.16 billion for ten years.

In the fourth year Rs137.1billion will be paid in part payment of loan of Rs1,091.6 billion carried over from the third year leaving balance loan of Rs954.5 billion for settlement of which a loan of Rs954.5 billion will be taken for one year from the money market by advancing counter loan of Rs95.45 billion for ten years.

In the fifth year Rs152.3 billion will be paid in part payment of loan of Rs954.5 billion carried over from the fourth year leaving balance loan of Rs802.2 billion for settlement of which a loan of Rs802.2 billion will be taken for one year from the money market by advancing counter loan of Rs80.22 billion for ten years.

In the sixth year Rs169.3 billion will be paid in part payment of loan of Rs802.2 billion carried over from the fifth year leaving balance loan of Rs632.9 billion for settlement of which a loan of Rs632.9 billion will be taken for one year from the money market by advancing counter loan of Rs63.29 billion for ten years.

In the seventh year Rs188.1 billion will be paid in part payment of loan of Rs632.9 billion carried over from the sixth year leaving balance loan of Rs444.8 billion for settlement of which a loan of Rs444.8 billion will be taken for one year from the money market by advancing counter loan of Rs44.48 billion for ten years.

In the eighth year Rs209 billion will be paid in part payment of loan of Rs444.8 billion carried over from the seventh year leaving balance loan of Rs235.8 billion for settlement of which a loan of Rs235.8 billion will be taken for one year from the money market by advancing counter loan of Rs23.58 billion for ten years.

In the ninth year Rs232.1 billion will be paid in part payment of loan of Rs235.8 billion carried over from the eighth year leaving balance loan of Rs3.7 billion for settlement of which a loan of Rs3.7 billion will be taken for one year from the money market by advancing counter loan of Rs0.37 billion for ten years.

In the tenth year, after paying the loan of Rs3.7 billion carried over from the ninth year, from the available balance of Rs232.6 billion, amount of Rs228.8 billion will be left in hand with the government and Rs670.65 billion in nine counter loans receivable after ten years of advancement of each counter loan.

FOREIGN DEBT RETIREMENT IN TMCL-BASED INTEREST-FREE REGIME

Following are the relevant extracts from the writer's book 'METHOD FOR STARTING INTEREST-FREE BANKING' printed in Feb'99

Pakistan's predicament of foreign debt-trap is depicted in Research paper no.44 published by Islamic Research and Training Institute of Islamic Development Bank Jeddah as follows:-

"Despite the awareness about *riba* as cited above, at the present, Pakistan is posed to face a real debt crises: all new foreign borrowings of the country are exhausted in servicing existing *riba-based* debts. Total internal and external outstanding public debt of the country is equivalent to about 90% of its gross domestic product, servicing this debt yearly requires 3.2 billion US dollars, making it the first largest expenditure item of the nation's fiscal year 1996 budget. In March 1996, the governor State Bank of Pakistan warned that his country is likely to enter the 'debt-trap'; Pakistan may accumulate *riba* arrears, and continuously request for debt rescheduling. Pakistan - a nation committed to eliminate *riba*, during 1996, spent more on servicing *riba-based* debts than even on its national defense. This is a predicament of a country where a lucid definition of *riba* in the form of the above quotation has long been known, where the goal of replacing the *riba-based* financial transactions with some alternatives consistent with the Islamic Law has always remained in the national agenda and where political will in this regard has always been visible throughout the process of forming a national consensus on constitutional issues."

Our Finance Minister mentioned in May'98 that foreign debt liability was $30 billion which according to some analysts has gone up to $32 billion by the end of July'98.

Whilst the government can very well stop payment of interest on domestic debt it cannot do so for foreign debt and the total foreign debt of $32 billion which includes substantial amount of interest will have to be paid in full. However the government can and must avoid to receive any further foreign loans on interest. For retiring the foreign debt no concrete steps have so far been taken nor there is anything in sight except abolition of interest which can enable the government to take the country out of the foreign debt trap. According to a statement of our Finance Minister an amount of $3 billion is required for servicing the total debt every year. As is shown in the chapter 'economic and financial benefits of interest-free banking' of this booklet, interest-free banking will facilitate conversion of annual deficit of $1.5 billion into surplus of $4.6 billion in our balance of payments.

Foreign debt can be retired in one of the two following ways depending upon whether or not dollarization of our economy continues and sufficient foreign currency is available in the local money market :-

A. FOREIGN DEBT RETIREMENT WITH SUFFICIENT FOREIGN CURRENCY AVAILABLE IN THE LOCAL MONEY MARKET :

A1. $1.55 billion from the above mentioned available surplus of $4.6 billion will be used to retire a portion of the foreign debt of $32 billion leaving balance debt of $30.45 billion and surplus of $3.05 billion in hand. For retiring the balance debt of $30.45 billion the government will obtain a loan of $30.45 billion from the money market by advancing counter loan of $3.045 billion for ten years. Thus within the first year of inception of interest-free banking the government will have cleared the entire foreign debt accumulated during the past several decades. However the fresh loan of $30.45 billion taken by the government will be required to be paid back in the next financial year.

A2. In the second financial year, interest-free banking is expected to make foreign exchange surplus available higher than that in the first year, but assuming it to remain the same, $4.6 billion will be available to the government for paying back the loan of $30.45 billion taken by it in the first year. Out of the available surplus of $4.6 billion the government will use $1.72 billion in repaying part of the loan of $30.45 billion carried over from last year leaving balance loan of $28.73 billion for settlement of which the government will take a loan of $28.73 billion from the money market for one year by advancing counter loan of $2.873 billion for ten years.

A3. In the third financial year, again from the available surplus of $4.6 billion, $1.91 billion will be used in repaying a part of the loan of $28.73 billion carried over from the last year leaving balance loan of $26.82 billion for settlement of which the government will take a loan of $26.82 billion from the money market for one year by advancing a counter loan of $2.682 billion for ten years.

A4. In the fourth financial year, from the available surplus of $4.6 billion, $2.13 billion will be used in repaying a part of the loan of $26.82 billion carried over from the last year leaving balance loan of $24.69 billion for settlement of which the government will take a loan of $24.69 from the money market for one year by advancing counter loan of $2.469 billion for ten years.

A5. In the fifth financial year, from the available surplus of $4.6 billion, $2.25 billion will be used in repaying a part of the loan of $24.69 billion carried over from the last year leaving balance loan of $22.44 billion for settlement of which the government will take a loan of $22.44 billion from the money market for one year by advancing counter loan of $2.244 billion for ten years.

A6. In the sixth financial year, from the available surplus of $4.6 billion, $2.61 billion will be used in repaying a part of the loan of $22.44 billion carried over from the last year leaving balance loan of $19.83 billion for settlement of which the government will take a loan of $19.83 billion from the money market for one year by advancing counter loan of $1.983 billion for ten years.

A7. In the seventh financial year, from the available surplus of $4.6 billion, $2.90 will be used in repaying a part of the loan of $19.83 billion carried over from the last year leaving balance of $16.93 billion for settlement of which the government will take a loan of $16.93 billion from the money market for one year by advancing counter loan of $1.693 billion for ten years.

A8. In the eighth financial year, from the available surplus of $4.6 billion, $3.23 billion will be used in repaying a part of the loan of $16.93 billion carried over from last year leaving balance loan of $13.70 billion for settlement of which the government will take loan of $13.70 from the money market for one year by advancing counter loan of $1.370 billion for ten years.

A9. In the ninth financial year, from the available surplus of $4.6 billion, $3.58 billion will be used in repaying a part of the loan of $13.70 carried over from the last year leaving balance loan of $10.12 billion for settlement of which the government will take a loan of $10.12 billion from the money market for one year by advancing a counter loan of $1.012 billion for ten years.

A10. In the tenth financial year, from the available surplus of $4.6 billion, $3.98 billion will be used in repaying a part of the loan of $10.12 billion carried over from the last year leaving balance loan of $6.14 billion for settlement of which the government will take a loan of $6.14 billion from the money market by advancing counter loan of $0.614 billion for ten years.

A11. In the eleventh financial year, from the available surplus of $4.6 billion, $4.42 billion will be used in repaying a part of the loan of $6.14 billion carried over form the last year leaving balance loan of $1.72 billion for settlement of which the government will take loan of $1.72 billion form the money market for one year by advancing a counter loan of $0.172 billion for ten years.

A12. In the twelfth financial year, from the available surplus of $4.6 billion. $1.72 billion will be paid in full settlement of the loan carried over from the last year. This will leave balance surplus of $2.88 billion with the government.

Thus within twelve years after inception of interest-free banking system, the government will not only retire the entire foreign debt, but will also have minimum surplus of $2.88 billion in hand and also $20.157 billion in eleven counter-loans receivable after ten years of each advancement.

B. FOREIGN DEBT RETIREMENT WITH SUFFICIENT FOREIGN CURRENCY NOT AVAILABLE IN THE LOCAL MONEY MARKET :

B1. In the first financial year of inception of interest-free banking the government will pay the entire available surplus of $4.6 billion in debt retirement which will leave balance of $27.4 billion from the total debt of $32 billion.

B2. In the second financial year debt liability will be $27.4 billion plus interest payable on it. Assuming rate of interest to be 10% p.a., total debt liability will be $30.14 billion. Again the entire surplus of $4.6 billion will be paid in debt retirement leaving balance of $25.54 billion.

B3. In the third financial year debt liability including interest will be $28.094 billion. Again after paying the entire surplus of $4.6 billion in debt retirement balance of debt will be $23.494 billion.

B4. In the fourth financial year the debt liability including interest will be 25.8434 billion. Again after paying the entire surplus of $4.6 billion in debt retirement balance of debt will be $21.2434 billion.

B5. In the fifth financial year debt liability including interest will be $23.3677 billion. Again after paying the entire surplus of $4.6 billion in debt retirement balance of debt will be $18.7677 billion.

B6. In the sixth financial year debt liability including interest will be $20.6444 billion. Again after paying the entire surplus of $4.6 billion in debt retirement balance of debt will be $16.0444 billion.

B7. In the seventh financial year debt liability including interest will be $17.6488 billion. Again after paying the entire surplus of $4.6 billion in debt retirement balance of debt will be $13.0488 billion.

B8. In the eighth financial year debt liability including interest will be $14.3536 billion. Again after paying $4.6 billion in debt retirement balance of debt will be $9.7536 billion.

B9. In the ninth financial year debt liability including interest will be $10.7289 billion. Again after paying $4.6 billion in debt retirement balance of debt will be $6.1289 billion.

B10. In the tenth financial year debt liability including interest will be $6.7417 billion. Again after paying $4.6 billion in debt retirement balance debt will be $2.1417 billion.

B11. In the eleventh financial year debt liability including interest will be $2.3558 billion. Again after paying $2.3558 billion in debt retirement from the available surplus of 4.6 billion the government will have in hand $2.2442 billion.

Thus within eleven years of inception of interest-free banking system, the government will not only have retired the entire foreign debt but will also have available surplus foreign exchange.

UNJUSTIFIED BIAS AGAINST TMCL

Some times logic fails to prevail upon prejudice and innovative fruitful ideas are arbitrarily rejected to the detriment of mankind. This happened in Pakistan with TMCL (Time Multiple Counter Loan) conceived and presented by Late Professor Shaikh Mahmud Ahmad who was undoubtedly our country's most outstanding economist and researcher. Perhaps because he was not a professional economist TMCL did not get any publicity and it remained unknown outside Pakistan. Allah's laws are all enforceable and easy to implement in all times and climes because Quraan declares "*ALLAH INTENDS EVERY FACILITY FOR YOU; HE DOES NOT WANT TO PUT YOU IN DIFFICULTIES*" (2:185). Syed Abou-al-Aala Maudoodi in his famous book 'SOOD' in Urdu stressed "*interest shall have to be banned by law in one single starting step*".

Council Of Islamic Ideology (CII) accepted the principle of TMCL but unfortunately without giving any reason did not approve of its use for eliminating interest from the banking system. Relevant paragraph in CII report of June 1980 reads "*Time Multiple Counter Loans - Under this method a bank may give by way of interest-free loan a multiple of interest-free deposit by a client so that the product of the money and time for which the money is given is the same in both cases. It would, however, not be correct to use this method by way of a permanent alternative system to the interest-based system. However, in order to provide personal loans to people of small means banks may instead of the above stipulations, adopt it as a principle that they would provide loans for personal and non-productive purposes to those persons who already hold accounts with them. In laying down the repayment schedule and the amount of the loan, however, the banks may keep in view the amount of the deposit of the applicant for the loan and the period over which he has maintained his deposit with the bank*".

Queerly CII rejected TMCL which could eliminate interest instantly without any disruption in the banking system and made recommendations such as the following without defining any specific plan of action and which could only produce faint hope of elimination of interest in some distant time :-

(i) *during the period of about 1 year and 8 months that now remains within the 3 years time limit set by the President the rest of the measures for the elimination of interest from the domestic transactions should be taken in three clearly defined phases with specific time schedule,*

(ii) *The interest-bearing foreign loans channeled by the Federal Government to the Provincial Governments may, however, continue on the basis of interest till a viable alternative compatible with Shariah is found in respect of borrowings from abroad,*

(iii) *Government's borrowings from external sources will have to be continued for the time being, on the basis of interest,*

(iv) *The operations of foreign branches of Pakistani banks, foreign currency deposits held with commercial banks in Pakistan and certain other transactions of banks with banks abroad would have to continue on the basis of interest,*

(v) *PICIC's foreign currency borrowings may continue to be on interest-basis until a viable alternative conforming to Shariah is available*".

Only God knows what prompted CII to reject one readily available *shariah*-compliant means to finish interest and to recommend continuation of an act of war against Allah and His Rasool *saws* for an indefinite period. About twenty years have already passed and still the awaited alternative arrangements have not become available.

Following writings show that Islamic economists neither offer a *shariah* compliant alternative of interest workable in the prevailing low standard of morality in the society nor do they accept TMCL, which is neutral to moral hazard, as a means to eliminate interest from the banking system.

In his book 'TOWARDS A JUST MONETARY SYSTEM' Dr. M. Umer Chapra writes :-

(i) If the Islamic commercial bank faces a liquidity crisis and is unable to make an alternate arrangement for liquidity, the central bank cannot afford to remain indifferent. It should act as lender of last resort within the framework suggested later, but, of course, with appropriate penalties and warnings accompanied by a specially-tailored corrective program,

(ii) The method of Time Multiple Counter Loans could be adapted for small-scale financing particularly within the framework of co-operative institutions. For commercial banks, it would be of limited applicability,

(iii) It would, nevertheless, be a mistake to try to achieve the transition from the conventional capitalist money and banking system now prevalent in the Muslim world to the just Islamic model in one stroke or over a very short period of time,

(iv) Interest should be declared illegal, allowing a certain grace period over which it may be tolerated as a necessary evil, but after the expiry of which it should be abolished from all domestic transactions,

(v) All interest-oriented financial institutions should be converted gradually, irrespective of whether they are domestic or foreign origin, into profit-sharing institutions,

(vi) The best way to accomplish the conversion would be to enable all financial institutions to bring about a certain percentage decrease in their interest-based assets and liabilities with a corresponding percentage increase in their profit-and-loss-sharing assets and liabilities until the total transformation has taken place over an agreed number of years,

(vii) All normal international transactions would, however, have to remain on the basis of interest until the Muslim countries can free themselves from the interest element through an expansion in their mutual relations and some reciprocal arrangement with non-Muslim countries. This cannot be done until the economies of Muslim countries become stronger and capable of satisfying their mutual needs.

Whilst TMCL can easily fulfil banks' short-term needs of liquidity Dr. Chapra prefers unspecified procedures which may or may not be workable! Dr. Chapra does not give any reason as to why TMCL will be of limited applicability for commercial banks and as to what is the logic behind continuing an act of war against Allah and His Rasool *saws* for indefinite period or for agreed number of years especially when it can be finished in one stroke by replacing interest with TMCL in the banking system.

The contention that TMCL can be used only for small scale financing is unfounded and misleading. Use of TMCL for large scale financing is demonstrated in tabular form in ANNEX-1 which shows how a large industrial project currently under execution in Saudi Arabia could have been financed on TMCL basis. Particulars of the project and financing agreement between the Industrialist and Bank are as follows:-

Total capital requirement = SR 133.0M

Owner's equity = SR 33.0M

Bank loan requirement = SR 100.0M

Loan advanced by bank in year 1 = SR 50.0M

Loan advanced by bank in year 2 = SR 50.0M

Rate of interest on bank loan = 8 % p.a.

Project construction period = 2 years

Commencement of production and earning from project = 3years after completion

Repayment of bank loan and interest from project earnings to commence in year 6 and completed in 10 yearly installments of SR 25.2, 24.1, 22.96, 21.84,20.72, 19.60, 18.48, 17.36, 16.24, 15.12M.

Total amount to be paid to the bank = Principal 100.0M + interest 101.62M = 201.62M

The executives of the project and the bank who negotiated the financing agreement, during a discussion on TMCL in Jeddah, asked the writer as to how the above project could be financed under TMCL.

Thereupon the writer prepared ANNEX-1 which shows how the project worth SR 133.0M could be completed under TMCL system with the available equity of SR 33M and without having to pay any interest and without any profit-sharing with the finance provider. Following are narrated the steps to be taken for financing the project under TMCL System :-

Year 1 – a loan of 66.8M for 5 years (repayable in year 6) is taken against counter-loan of 16.7M for 20 years (66.8 X 5 = 16.7 X 20)

Year 2 – a loan of 66.3M for 4 years (repayable in year 6) is taken against counter-loan of 15.6M for 17 years (66.3 X 4 = 15.6 X 17)

Year 6 – amount of loan to be repaid to bank = 66.8 + 66.3 = 131.1M

Cash available = (Balance from capital) + (Loans received – Expenditure on project) + Amount from project earning

= (33.0 – 16.7 – 15.6) + (133.1 – 133) + 25.2 = 0.7 + 0.1 + 25.2 = 26M.

13.1M paid to the bank from 26M leaves balance of 12.9M and bank loan of 131.1 – 13.1 = 120M for settlement of which loan of 120M is taken for 1 year against counter-loan of 12M for 10 years. Thus cash balance of 0.9M is carried forward and loan of 120M for settlement in year 7.

Year 7 – Loan to be repaid to the bank = 120M

Cash available = Balance from year 6 + amount from project earning = 0.9 + 24.1 = 25M

12M paid to bank from 25M leaves balance of 13M and bank loan of 120 – 12 = 108M for settlement of which loan of 108M is taken for 1

year against counter-loan of 12M for 9 years. Thus cash balance of 1M is carried forward and loan of 108M for settlement in year 8

Year 8 – Loan to be repaid to the bank = 108M

Cash available = Balance from year 7 + amount from project earning = 1 + 22.96 = 23.96M

12M paid to bank from 23.96M leaves balance of 11.96M and bank loan of 108 – 12 = 96M for settlement of which loan of 96M is taken for 1 year against counter-loan of 9.6M for 10 years. Thus cash balance of 2.36M is carried forward & loan of 96M for settlement in year 9

Year 9 – Loan to be repaid to the bank = 96M

Cash available = Balance from year 8 + amount from project earning = 2.36 + 21.84=24.2M

12M paid to bank from 24.2M leaves balance of 12.2M and bank loan of 96 – 12 = 84M for settlement of which loan of 84M is taken for 1 year against counter-loan of 12M for 7 years. Thus cash balance of 0.2M is carried forward & loan of 84M for settlement in year 10

Year 10 – Loan to be repaid to the bank = 84M

Cash available = Balance from year 9 + amount from project earning = 0.2 + 20.72=20.92M

12M paid to bank from 20.92M leaves balance of 8.92M and bank loan of 84 – 12 = 72M for settlement of which loan of 72M is taken for 1 year against counter-loan of 8M for 9 years. Thus cash balance of .92M is carried forward & loan of 72M for settlement in year 11

Year 11 – Loan to be repaid to the bank = 72M

Cash available = Balance from year 10 + amount from project earning=0.92 + 19.6=20.52M

12M paid to bank from 20.52M leaves balance of 8.52M and bank loan of 72 – 12 = 60M for settlement of which loan of 60M is taken for 1 year against counter-loan of 6M for 10 years. Thus cash balance of 2.52M is carried forward & loan of 60M for settlement in year 12

Year 12 – Loan to be repaid to the bank = 60M

Cash available = Balance from year 11 + amount from project earning = 2.52 + 18.48 =21M

10M paid to bank from 21M leaves balance of 11M and bank loan of 60 – 10 = 50M for settlement of which loan of 50M is taken for 1 year against counter-loan of 10M for 5 years. Thus cash balance of 1M is carried forward & loan of 50M for settlement in year 13

Year 13 - Loan to be repaid to the bank = 50M

Cash available = Balance from year 12 + amount from project earning = 1 + 17.36 = 18.36M

10M paid to bank from 18.36M leaves balance of 8.36M and bank loan of 50 – 10 = 40M for settlement of which loan of 40M is taken for 1 year against counter-loan of 8M for 5 years. Thus cash balance of .36M is carried forward & loan of 40M for settlement in year 14

Year 14 - Loan to be repaid to the bank = 40M

Cash available = Balance from year 13 + amount from project earning =0.36 + 16.24=16.6M

8M paid to bank from 16.6M leaves balance of 8.6M and bank loan of 40 – 8 = 32M for settlement of which loan of 32M is taken for 1 year against counter-loan of 8M for 4 years. Thus cash balance of .6M is carried forward & loan of 32M for settlement in year 15

Year 15 – Loan to be repaid to the bank = 32M

Cash available = Balance from year 14 + amount from project earning = 0.6 + 15.12=15.72M

8M paid to bank from 15.72M leaves balance of 7.72M and bank loan of 32 – 8 = 24M for settlement of which loan of 24M is taken for 1 year against counter-loan of 6M for 4 years. Thus cash balance of 1.72M is carried forward & loan of 24M for settlement in year16

Year 16 - Loan to be repaid to the bank = 24M

Cash available = Balance from year 15 + amounts of counter loans given in years 6, 7 and 9 receivable from bank = 1.72 + 12 + 12 +12 = 37.72M After repaying the bank loan of 24M cash balance left will be = 37.72 – 24 = 13.72M

Year 17 - Loan to be repaid to the bank = Nil

Cash available = balance from year 16 + amount of counter-loan given in year 12 receivable from bank = 13.72 + 10 = 23.72M

Year 18 - Cash available = Balance from year 17 + amounts of counter-loans given in years 8, 13 and 14 receivable from bank = 23.72 + 9.6 + 8 + 8 = 49.32M

Year 19 - Cash available = Balance from year 18 + amounts of counter-loans given in years 2, 10 and 15 receivable from bank = 49.32 + 15.6 + 8 + 6 = 78.92M

Year 21 - Cash available = Balance from year 19 + amounts of counter-loans given in years 1 and 11 receivable from bank = 78.92 + 16.7 + 6 = 101.62M. This is the amount of interest which the industrial unit has to pay to the bank in the interest-based system.

The above narration shows that the industrial unit if financed under TMCL system would have cost 101.62M less. Large saving of interest expense and no profit-sharing with finance provider will definitely reflect in prices of project products which would be available at much lower prices to the advantage of common man and society as a whole. Thus TMCL-based financing of even large projects is far superior to financing through interest-based loan and through profit-sharing.

Dr. M. Umer Chapra in his another book 'ISLAM AND ECONOMIC DEVELOPMENT' proclaimed immense benefit of ban on interest in the following words: -

> *"since borrowing does not obviate, but rather only postpones, the ultimate need for sacrifice, the ban on interest should prove to be a blessing by removing the long-run heavy debt-servicing burden it normally entails. The constraint it will impose on government spending in the short-run may tend to be more than offset by the healthy discipline it will impose on the governments, the sustained, steadier growth it will generate in the economy, the greater cooperation it will bring about between the governments and the private sector, and the much smaller debt-servicing burden it will create in both the domestic and external sectors of the economy".*

However ignoring or neglecting the potentiality of TMCL as an effective replacement of interest in one stroke, Dr. Chapra immediately after the above proclamation in his book negated the proclamation by stating:-

"To avoid an excessive squeeze in the initial stage, the governments may apply the prohibition gradually and not in one stroke".

It is not understood why Dr. Chapra prefers to continue an act of war against Allah and His Rasool *saws* over a mere excessive squeeze. He did not define the mechanics of the process of gradual prohibition of interest and also where to start.

The Blue Print Of Islamic Financial System Including Strategy For Elimination Of *Riba* published by International Institute Of Islamic Economics, International Islamic University, Islamabad includes short comment on TMCL: *"One may argue that TMCL instrument offers an ingenious solution to the problems of Riba, gharar and having two mutually exclusive conditions in one contract. But its viability is questionable for several reasons. Some of these are as follows. Counter loans would be liability of the banks. Therefore, while the sum generated might be used to meet their operating expenses it would not be distributable as profits among their share holders or depositors who provide funds on partnership basis. This will compel the banks to turn to trading, leasing and other profitable options. It is also possible that clients may use loans from banks, whether directly or indirectly, to give, the counter-loans. This, in turn, casts further doubts on the usefulness of the TMCL option. Last but not the least, a recourse to TMCL is not advisable because the ensuing credit expansion is likely to fuel inflation."*

Obviously the above cursory remarks on TMCL have been made without taking into account the following important points. The sum generated by counter-loans will be invested in long-term profitable business. The profits earned by the banks will be shared with the depositors in investment accounts. There is no harm in the banks turning to *Shariah*-compliant trading modes as is done by all Islamic banks. Every loan will be advanced against collateral and will have to be returned on due date. There is no reason why any sensible person will use the loan from bank to give counter-loans for further loans instead of utilizing it in meeting his business requirements. Credit expansion will be controlled by raising or lowering the time-multiple ratio in TMCL just as it is controlled in the present system by raising or lowering interest rate.

In the chapter on strategy for elimination of *Riba* the Blue Print states "*The move towards Riba-free banking system may start in earnest with the establishment of one model Islamic branch each by all existing banks. This experience may be replicated by them and applied to their other branches such that all branches of a bank and, thereby, the entire banking system gets converted into the Islamic mode in approximately one and a half years.*", "*The terms of reference of the above Coordination Committee should be: i. to chalk out the blue print and documents for the model branches. ii. To recommend necessary action to the concerned quarters, such as the State Bank and the Ministry of Finance.*"

Strangely enough the authors of the blue print reject a definite one step action plan of replacing interest instantly by TMCL and recommend a plan blue print of which still remains to be chalked out and implementation of which would tentatively take one and a half years and no body knows how many more years it may take to eliminate interest completely from the banking system.

It would be appropriate to prove, by definite example, conspicuous superiority of TMCL-based financing over the proposition made in IIIE's blueprint which states:-

"**13.4.1** Asset *Ijarah* Securities involving a financial intermediary **(AIS-IFI).**

Suppose the Ministry of Defence needs a training field spread over a 10-acre piece of land in central location… .

13.4.2 The Ministry may contact an Islamic bank to prepare an issue of asset *Ijarah* securities that allows the Ministry to acquire the needed land.

13.4.3 The line of action on the bank's side can be as follows:

i. It may initially buy the lot for, say, Rs. 10 M in its own name.

ii. It may rent the lot to the Ministry for, say, Rs. 900,000 per year.

iii. The *Ijarah* contract with the Ministry may have a period of, say, 10 years after which it may be renewed for 10 years at a time.

iv. The bank may issue, for example, 1,000 asset *Ijarah* securities with each security representing 1,000th of the lot and a claim to Rs. 900 a year (=1,000th of Rs. 900,000) as rent.

v. The bank may claim an issuance commission of, say, 5%as a premium above the purchase price of land and, hence, sell the securities at Rs. 10,500 each".

In the above mode of financing the government will never own the defense facility and will have to continue to incur recurring expense of Rs. 0.9M as annual rent. In the first 12 years the government will have paid Rs. 10.8M which exceeds the actual cost of the facility by 0.8M. Under TMCL system of financing government will obtain a loan of Rs. 10.8M for 1 year against counter loan of Rs. 0.9M advanced to the bank for 12 years. From this loan the government will spend Rs. 10.0M to acquire the facility as state property. Calculations in ANNEX 2 show that under TMCL system government will clear the bank loan within 20 years and apart from having a surplus balance of Rs. 2.0M will have receivable counter-loan amounts from the bank Rs. 0.7 + 0.5 + 0.7 + 0.5 + 0.4 + 0.5 + 0.5 + 0.5 + 0.5 + 0.4 + 0.4 + 0.4 = 6.0M. As the government will own the facility it will permanently save Rs. 0.9M annually. If the project is financed under Asset *Ijarah* securities system as recommended in IIIE's blueprint the government will remain a tenant permanently incurring annual expense of Rs. 0.9M as rent of the facility. Is it not sadly astonishing that the blueprint rejects TMCL and prefers Asset *Ijarah* securities system?

Tragic result of the persistent bias against TMCL is that about 200 Islamic banks have mobilized Muslim *Ummah's* financial resources of billions of Dollars and are running profitably but they are unable to ward off interest which is the foremost fundamental requirement of Islamic financial system. Nothing can be so tragic and ridiculous as Islamic banks indulging in interest-based transactions. Against Pakistan's urgent requirement of funds in 1998 Islamic Development Bank Jeddah together with the large Islamic banking community could do no better than offering a loan on interest and that too at 5% above LIBOR!

Hon. Justice Muhammad Taqi Usmani is chairman/member *Shariah* Supervisory Boards of a dozen Islamic banks. In his recent book 'INTRODUCTION TO ISLAMIC FINANCE' he writes "*The case of Islamic banking cannot be advanced unless a strong system of inter-bank transactions based on Islamic principles is developed. The lack of such a system forces the Islamic banks to turn to the conventional banks for their short-term needs of liquidity which the conventional banks do not provide without either an open or camouflaged interest*".

In the seminar proceedings no.39 on 'Islamic Financial Instruments' published by IDB Islamic Research and Training Institute is stated "*But what if the government needs cash (to pay salaries or buy services) and needs it now. The options available, so far, is borrowing from the public or the banking sector at interest. It is no accident that while great advances had been taking place in the Islamization of the private financial transactions in many Muslim countries, very little has been done in the public sector. Almost all Islamic governments borrow on interest*". In another IDB IRTI publication 'CHALLENGES FACING ISLAMIC BANKING' is stated "*While Islamic banks and investment funds have so far mobilized huge financial resources, a large part of these resources have found its way into western financial markets*".

Adoption of TMCL as loaning instrument by Islamic banks will bring the following benefits to Islamic banks and the Muslim *ummah*;

1. It will facilitate inter-bank interest-free loan transactions.
2. It will facilitate setting up of a Central Depository for mobilizing surplus funds of Islamic banks and governments on TMCL basis and advancing to them in times of need TMCL-based interest-free loans.
3. It will facilitate utilization of the financial resources of the Muslim *ummah* in developing Muslim countries through the Central Depository, instead of being diverted to western financial markets.

Upshot of the above discussion is that Islamic economists and bankers with profound sense of urgency and dedication should strive for inception of TMCL as loaning instrument to replace interest in the banking system. It is indeed the entire Muslim *Ummah's* crucial need of the hour.

BASIC DEFICIENCY AND DEFECTS IN ISLAMIC BANKS AND THE REMEDY

Note : It is a commentary on IDB-IRTI occasional paper no. 4 'Islamic Banking: Answers to some frequently asked questions' authored by Dr.Munawar Iqbal, Dr.Mabid Ali Al-Jarhi and Dr.M.Umer Chapra. The comments relate mainly to the opinions and proposals which, though well-intentioned, are faulty and detrimental to the cause of elimination of interest. The comments are forthright made in right earnest and should be taken in that spirit. However, I offer my apologies if any comment hurts the feelings of any of the respected authors. Helpful response, queries and reasoned criticism will be gratefully received.

UNANSWERED QUESTIONS: Following challenging questions in a published article written by a highly placed bureaucrat in Pakistan trying to prove that Supreme Court order to eliminate interest cannot be implemented, remain unanswered.

(i) Is there any single bank in the Islamic or Non-Islamic world which is truly run on an interest-free basis?

(ii) Can a Central Bank conduct its monetary policy without a norm of interest?

(iii) Are not the practices of Islamic banks a queer blend of interest-based modes of finance carrying a façade of Islamic names?

(iv) What are exactly the Islamic compliant instruments of finance? Can these instruments meet the myriad and diverse needs of modern trade, finance and banking?

(v) When and where have these instruments been applied and with what degree of success?

(vi) Does the Islamic Development Bank as the model Islamic bank operate on interest-free basis? If that is the case why did it offer to extend a loan to the government of Pakistan after nuclear detonation at an interest rate of 5% above LIBOR?

(vii) By what mechanism can Islamic banks undertake financial intermediation

which is the primary function of all commercial banks throughout the world?

I have brought these questions to the attention of many Islamic economists pleading that these can be satisfactorily answered by inception of an interest-free lending instrument (TMCL) in Islamic banks. My several repeated appeals have remained un-replied. Whilst Islamic economists are keeping silent the advocates of interest have succeeded in getting one year extension in the period fixed in the Supreme Court order for eliminating interest and now they are trying to have the Supreme Court order set aside or shelved.

THE DEFICIENCY: The paper limits Islamic modes of finance to "carrying out of investment and / or the purchase of goods, services and assets". These modes cannot meet the financial needs of very large number of cost-conscious privately owned firms keen on protecting their independence and ownership structure. Such firms form large source of productive manpower employment and they cannot be ignored. Their financial needs in Islamic financial system can be fulfilled only through interest-free lending. Hence to satisfy the financial needs of all sectors of the economy interest-free lending must be included in the Islamic modes of finance.

THE DEFECTS: For meeting their own short-term needs of liquidity Islamic banks take loans on interest from conventional banks and almost all Muslim governments also do the same. Muhammad Taqi Usmani who is chairman / member on *Shariah* Supervisory Boards of a dozen Islamic banks and financial Institutions, in his book 'INTRODUCTION TO ISLAMIC FINANCE' writes "The case of Islamic banking cannot be advanced unless a strong system of inter-bank transactions based on Islamic principles is developed. The lack of such a system forces the Islamic banks to turn to the conventional banks for their short-term needs of liquidity which the conventional banks do not provide without either an open or camouflaged Interest".

The paper places modes of financing used by Islamic banks in two categories "advancing funds on a profit-and-loss sharing basis" and "financing the purchase / hire of goods (including assets) and services on a fixed-return basis". The paper mentions "the share of profit-sharing modes in the total financing by Islamic banks is very small. Most of the financing is provided on a *Murabahah* basis". *Murabahah* which is permissible in *Shariah* is a sales contract at a price markup between buyer and seller. In fake *Murabahah* transactions Islamic banks do not actually buy or sell and they simply provide finance to buyers in a round about manner through proxy buying and selling and use this mode only to legitimize fixed-return on capital which virtually is the same as interest earned by conventional banks. Following excerpts from an article written by Arshad Zaman and Asad Zaman published in April 2001 issue of 'Islamic Economic Studies' support this contention. "Thus in principle interest-based transactions have been replaced by those based on *Murabahah*, leasing and some *Musharakah* all of which are permissible under *Shariah*. Appearances are deceiving, however, and only the form of the transactions have changed with no change in the underlying transactions". "Another issue of importance to consumers is the financing of loans.... These can easily be handled via the instrument of *Murabahah*.... There are virtually no differences between it and the conventional interest-based financing".

The paper acclaims (i) "Islamic scholars and practical bankers took up the challenge and have made commendable progress in the last 25 years in providing a number of such instruments". (ii) "Another manifestation of the success of Islamic banking is the fact that many conventional banks have also started using Islamic banking techniques in the conduct of their business, particularly in dealing either with Muslim clients or in predominantly Muslim regions". However, borrowing on interest and earning profits akin to interest by Islamic banks show that the financing modes in their use bring prosperity to them and attract conventional bankers, having no ideological preference for Islamic ways, to open Islamic windows only to exploit religious sentiments of Muslims, but these modes cannot pave the way to Islamise the financial system. It is a matter of serious concern for committed practical bankers and hierarchy in IRTI who should either devise a new financial intermediation mechanism for getting the Islamic and conventional banks rid of interest or give serious consideration to accept the way shown by late Professor Sheikh Mahmud Ahmad. Upon my taking up the problem of shortcomings in Islamic banks personally with IDB President during Fourth International Conference on Islamic Economics and Banking held in UK in mid-August 2000 I received the following encouraging response from IDB: "REFERRING TO THE DOCUMENTS SUBMITTED TO H.E. THE PRESIDENT OF ISLAMIC DEVELOPMENT BANK (IDB) ABOUT YOUR OBSERVATION ON THE ISLAMIC BANKING MOVEMENT, WE APPRECIATE VERY MUCH YOUR GOOD EFFORTS AND INSIGHTS. THE ISLAMIC BANKS' OFFICE OF IDB WILL TRY TO DO ITS BEST TO COMMUNICATE TO THE ISLAMIC BANKS THE SHORTCOMINGS THAT YOU HAD MENTIONED IN YOUR DOCUMENT".

Unfortunately further to the above advice, nothing appears to have been done by Islamic Economists and Bankers towards eliminating interest from the banking system.

DESCRIPTION OF ISLAMIC BANK given in the paper needs to be modified to include interest-free lending and borrowing in the scope of activities and to exclude fixed-return on capital akin to interest. Without these modifications Islamic banks cannot qualify to be Islamic nor can they meet the financial needs of all sectors of the economy.

THE REMEDY: Interest-free lending and borrowing can remedy the deficiency and defects in Islamic banks and eliminate interest from the banking system. Hence the need for an interest-free lending instrument. Wide spread practical use of Islamic concept of *Qard Hasan* i.e. interest-free lending for productive purposes is highly commendable and deserves to be encouraged as according to a *Hadith* reward for lending is eighteen times. There are several authentic examples in Islamic history of staunch Muslims investing loaned sums in trade. It is a gross misconception that *Qard Hasan* is meant only for the poor and disabled whose needs are fulfilled through *zakah* and *sadaqaat* in Islamic economic system. It is a pity that nowhere in the paper under discussion interest-free lending is mentioned although it is the most useful and commendable means for economic development. The paper mentions "Monetary economists insist that a zero nominal interest rate is a necessary condition for optimal allocation of resources", "when this matter was investigated within general equilibrium modes it was found that a zero interest rate is both necessary and sufficient for allocative efficiency", "those studies have shown that a system which is based on profit-sharing is not only viable, but also carries with it many advantages which make it superior to interest-based ones". No doubt profit- sharing mode of financing is far superior to interest-based lending, but due to moral hazard profit-sharing on large scale has proved to be impracticable. In these circumstances it is necessary to put in use another zero interest rate mechanism i.e. interest-free lending as a mode of finance. Interest-based lending, though exploitative, has played a major role in the enormous economic development by providing finance freely and widely to industry, commerce and agriculture. Interest-free lending being commendable as a rewarding mode in *Shariah* will definitely bring economic development to an extent far greater than that brought by interest-based lending and what can be expected from wide spread use of profit-sharing which is permissible in Islam but not as rewarding as interest-free lending.

PLANNED GRADUALISM: The paper claims "gradualism in implementing the *Shariah* injunctions is well-recognised". It is a misconception because each and every Divine command was fully implemented immediately upon revelation. There is not a single instance of any sinful act being permitted to persist for any duration. The juristic rule quoted in the paper "what cannot be attained in its entirety should not be left entirely" applies to attainment of good and not to shedding of evil. Allah's laws are all for the good of mankind at all times and in all circumstances. It is inconceivable that elimination of interest even if it is done abruptly could bring any harm because Allah assures in Quraan "*those who act upon My instructions will have nothing to fear nor will they be sorry*". It is therefore wrong to contend as is done in the paper that "it is not advisable to carry out transformation from a conventional to an interest-free banking system abruptly, as this may subject the banking system as well as the rest of the economy to needless shocks". The paper does not specify what are those needless shocks to the economy and banking system which need to be avoided at the cost of earning Allah's wrath by maintaining interest in the banking system.

Gradualism is understandable and can be acceptable for transforming the whole economic system to Islamic System. However, gradualism in eliminating interest cannot be acceptable in any circumstances because giving up of interest is condition of *Iman* and Quraan declares war from Allah and His Rasool *saws* against perpetrators. Interest must, therefore, be eliminated forthwith and not gradually. No doubt "every system has its own institutional requirements" but these come into being through constant evolving process which goes on side by side with the expansion and development of the system. However, elimination of interest must not be delayed on any account.

HYPOTHETICAL PLAN TO APPLY THE ISLAMIC MONETARY SYSTEM AS PER TABLE 5 IN THE PAPER indicates universal + Islamic banking in the first two-year phase, no commercial banking during the second two-year phase and only Islamic banking in the third two-year phase. The plan states "Obviously, switching to universal banking and adapting to Islamic banking must be done within a specified time limit. A period of four years, extending to the end of the second phase would be reasonable".

The plan suggests a period of four years for adapting to Islamic banking without defining actual practical steps for achieving these objectives. The plan implies that interest will persist for at least four years from the day any establishment decides to implement Allah's Will or in other words it will take four years to bow to Allah! Allah's laws are enforceable at all times and in all circumstances. The paper does not indicate what are the obstacles in the way of eliminating interest removal of which will require as long a period as four years. The obstacles if any in eliminating interest will be either imaginary or man-made as there can be no real obstacle in the way of eliminating interest forthwith as Allah declares in Quraan "*He has not produced any obstacle for you in (the way to follow the edicts of) the religion*" and also "*whosoever fears Allah, He makes for him way out (of difficulties) and provides to him from (sources) which he cannot imagine and whosoever depends on Allah sufficient is He for him*".

DOCTRINE OF NECESSITY AND INTEREST-BASED FOREIGN BORROWING: The paper suggests "interest-based foreign borrowing can only be resorted to in case of compelling need for development purposes which amounts to 'necessity' as determined by the *Ulama*". Doctrine of necessity can be invoked only in cases where Allah Himself has allowed some concession like eating pork for saving life. It cannot be invoked for continuing interest for which Allah has not allowed any concession whatsoever. *Ulama* cannot permit what Allah has prohibited.

For Muslims nothing can be more compelling a need than desisting from committing a planned sinful act amounting to rebellion against Allah and His Rasool *saws*. Islamic countries can get rid of interest-based foreign borrowing by setting up a Central Depository-cum-lender of last resort for receiving deposits from Islamic banks and countries having surplus funds and advancing loans to other Islamic countries and banks needing funds for development. Central Depository will use same interest-free lending and borrowing mechanism as suggested for Islamic banks. The Central Depository will invest surplus available funds in profitable Islamic modes of business.

PUBLIC DEBT: The paper suggests "in the first phase the country must seek debt-relief (debt forgiveness as well as rescheduling) through active and energetic contacts with donors' forums. The fact that it is embarking on serious and rigorous financial and structural adjustment program would go a long way in persuading donors to provide debt-relief". So-called donors are in fact lenders of money on interest and they are no friends of the borrowers. Their recent behavior clearly shows that they want to dictate the borrowing countries. It is a mistake to expect them to do anything to help the borrowers to come out of the debt morass and become independent of them. Instead of begging for debt forgiveness or debt rescheduling Islamic countries must build self-sufficient interest-free financial system capable of clearing current debts and providing interest-free loans in times of need. These objectives can be very well achieved by utilizing interest-free lending and borrowing mechanism as suggested for Islamic banks.

NOVEL IDEA OF PRACTICAL APPLICATION OF *QARD HASAN* IN BANKING was presented by late Professor Sheikh Mahmud Ahmad applauded in Supreme Court of Pakistan judgment in *Riba* case as "*our country's most outstanding economist and researcher and a leading thinker—had devoted considerable part of his life in the study of the theory of interest*".

He devised interest-free lending instrument which he named as Time Multiple Counter Loan - TMCL consisting of two simultaneously exchanged interest-free loans between two parties such that the multiple of the amount and period of one loan equals the multiple of the amount and period of the other loan. It facilitates interest-free loaning of large sums against counter-loans of smaller sums advanced for proportionately longer periods. For example an entrepreneur requiring a loan of $10.0 Million for one year can get interest-free loan of $10.0 Million (against collateral as usual) for one year by advancing an interest-free counter loan of $1.0 Million to the bank for 10 years.

Thus TMCL fulfills the client's need of funds for the required period and also enables the bank to earn profit from long-term investment of counter-loan money. Whatever gain or loss the bank earns comes from investment of counter-loan amounts which are actually borrowed sums and in Islam there is no bar on earning profit by investing borrowed sums. In interest-based loaning the lender always gains because he earns interest whereas the borrower may gain or lose from investment of the borrowed sum.

Therefore interest-based loaning is inequitable and unjust. In TMCL transaction none of the two parties is a definite gainer and each one of them may gain or lose by investing the loan taken from the other party. Hence TMCL transaction is equitable and just. In TMCL transaction each party does good to the other party and as such TMCL-based loaning conforms with the Quraanic precept *Hal jaza-ul-ihsaan illa al-ihsaan* and the noble teaching of our Prophet *saws* that a favour done to any one should be reciprocated.

As TMCL can perform Islamically all legitimate financial intermediation functions which are performed by interest, it can instantly and effectively replace interest without any disruption in the banking system. After switching over to TMCL-based loaning system the banks will continue to function as usual with the basic change that no interest will be paid or charged. All loans will be advanced against counter-loans and all transactions involving credit will be executed on TMCL-basis. Banks will continue to receive deposits and issue cheque books as usual. Account holders will have the option to keep their money in investment or demand deposit accounts. Investment account holders will share profit/loss with the bank on daily product basis. Banks will earn profits by investing counter-loan amounts and surplus deposits in *Shariah*-compliant modes like stock exchange, real property, *musharakah*, *mudarabah*, etc. Outstanding interest-based loans will be converted into TMCL-based transactions. Each borrower will repay only the principal amount of loan on due date or earlier and instead of paying interest the borrower will advance to the bank a counter-loan of the same amount as he took in loan and for the same period for which he availed the loan. Alternatively the bank and the borrower may mutually agree to a different amount of counter-loan for proportionately longer or shorter period on TMCL-basis. Interest-bearing bills and bonds will be encashed at their face value and the holders will receive appropriate counter-loan on TMCL-basis from the issuer.

In the interest-free regime there will be no role of interest-based treasury bills and bonds etc. and all such documents will cease to be issued and no function involving interest will be undertaken by the Central Bank. Other functions not involving interest will be performed as usual. The Central Bank will set up a framework of Central Depository-cum-lender of last resort for mobilizing surplus funds of banks and federal and provincial governments and autonomous bodies and advancing interest-free loans to them in times of need. The Central Depository will receive deposits and advance interest-free loans on TMCL basis. For example, if a bank has a surplus of Rs. 5.0M for 1 month, it may deposit this sum for 1 month with the Central Depository and obtain an interest-free loan of Rs. 0.5M for 10 months. If a bank is short of liquidity and requires Rs. 10.0M for 1 week, it will obtain from the Central Depository an interest-free loan of Rs. 10.0M for 1 week by depositing Rs. 1.0M with the Central Depository for 10 weeks. Central Depository will also earn profits by investing surplus funds in *Shariah*-compliant businesses.

Adoption of TMCL as loaning instrument by Islamic banks will bring the following benefits to Islamic banks and the Muslim *ummah* as a whole.

1. It will open for Islamic banks the vast field of loaning to reliable and capable cost conscious entrepreneurs who want to remain independent and in full control of their enterprises and do not accept any sharing of profit or outside interference. Without providing loans to this big class of loan seekers, Islamic banks will not be able to compete with western banks who have started capturing business in Islamic investment field.
2. It will facilitate inter-bank interest-free loan transactions and Islamic banks will not have to turn to western banks for meeting their short-term needs of liquidity.
3. It will facilitate setting up of a central depository for mobilizing surplus funds of Islamic banks and governments on TMCL-basis and advancing to them in times of need TMCL-based interest-free loans.

It will facilitate utilization of the financial resources of the Muslim *ummah* in developing Muslim countries through the Central Depository, instead of being diverted to western financial markets.

UNJUSTIFIED BIAS AGAINST TMCL: Unfortunately mainstream thinking among Islamic economists and bankers mistakenly favours gradual elimination of interest whereas use of TMCL can eliminate interest forthwith and perhaps that is why they do not treat inception of TMCL in banking with the vigour and rigour it deserves. Following are three specific examples of unjustified bias against TMCL.

In his book 'Towards a Just Monetary System' Dr.M.Umar Chapra writes "*The method of Time Multiple Counter Loans could be adapted for small-scale financing particularly within the framework of co-operative institutions. For commercial banks, it would be of limited applicability*". He does not give any reason for putting limitations on the use of TMCL which can perform all functions as are performed by interest in the modern banking system.

'The Blue-print Of Islamic Financial System Including Strategy For Elimination Of *Riba*' published by International Institute Of Islamic Economics, International Islamic University, Islamabad includes short comment on TMCL: "*One may argue that TMCL instrument offers an ingenious solution to the problems of Riba, gharar and having two mutually exclusive conditions in one contract. But its viability is questionable for several reasons. Some of these are as follows. Counter loans would be liability of the banks. Therefore, while the sum generated might be used to meet their operating expenses it would not be distributable as profits among their share holders or depositors who provide funds on partnership basis. This will compel the banks to turn to trading, leasing and other profitable options. It is also possible that clients may use loans from banks, whether directly or indirectly, to give, the counter-loans. This, in turn, casts further doubts on the usefulness of the TMCL option. Last but not the least, a recourse to TMCL is not advisable because the ensuing credit expansion is likely to fuel inflation.*"

Obviously the above cursory remarks on TMCL have been made without taking into account the following important points. The sum generated by counter-loans will be invested in long-term profitable business. The profits earned by the banks will be shared with the depositors in investment accounts.

There is no harm in the banks turning to *shariah*-compliant trading modes as is done by all Islamic banks. Every loan will be advanced against collateral and will have to be returned on due date. There is no reason why any sensible person will use the loan from bank to give counter -loans for further loans instead of utilizing it in meeting his business requirements. Credit expansion will be controlled by raising or lowering the time multiple ratio in TMCL just as it is controlled in the present system by raising or lowering interest rate.

During question and answer hour at the end of a session at Fourth International Conference on Islamic Economics and Banking I raised the question as to why TMCL was not used for getting Islamic banks rid of interest and enhancing economic co-operation among Islamic countries. Dr.Najatullah Siddiqui answered every other question raised by the audience but he completely ignored my question and did not say a word about it.

SUCCESS, FAILURE AND THE RISK: Islamic scholars and economists won the battle against interest and Supreme Court of Pakistan settled once for all in Dec 1999 that interest is *Riba* and ordered its elimination by 30th June 2001. Soon after the Supreme Court Order was passed advocates of interest began striving to render the order ineffective. UBL filed a review petition in the Supreme Court which came up for hearing in June 2001 at which time UBL succeeded in getting one year extension in the date for elimination of interest on the plea that there was no viable interest-free banking plan available to replace the existing system. Eight months have passed since the extension was granted and still the above plea remains un-repelled. If on the next hearing of UBL review petition, any day before 30th June 2002, a viable interest-free banking plan to replace the existing system is not presented, then there is grave risk of Supreme Court Order being set aside or shelved. If, God forbid, it so happens it will be highly tragic as it would bring to naught more than half a century's strenuous efforts of dedicated Muslims to get the curse of interest banished from the country.

3

Interest-free Loaning

THE NEED, METHOD, AND BENEFITS

Capitalist system, though exploitative, has played a major role in the enormous industrial and agricultural development by providing finance for production and trade freely and widely on the basis of interest which is strictly prohibited in Islam. Quraanic command to believers to give up interest and warning of war from Allah and His Rasool *saws* against those who do not abide make it absolutely clear that what is required of Muslims is to eliminate interest instantly in one stroke and not in stages. It is a gross misconception that *Shariah* laws were implemented gradually. Our Prophet Muhammad *saws* enforced each and every Divine Command immediately upon revelation. Divine laws are all for the good of humanity and are enforceable at all times and in all circumstances. Hence an instrument for advancing interest-free loans freely and widely for production and trade must be available in Islamic financial system which aims at fulfilling the needs of all sectors of society. *Zakaat* caters for the poor and disabled. *Qard hasan* (Interest-free loaning) caters for the affluent needing funds on loan for production, trade and consumption. It is utterly wrong notion that *Qard hasan* is not meant for development financing. Islam encourages widespread use of *Qard hasan* for need fulfillment as according to a saying of our Prophet Muhammad *saws* the reward for lending is eighteen times and for charity it is ten times. Only those who do not repay loans are severely reprimanded. Late Shaikh Mahmud Ahmad, the most outstanding Islamic economist and research scholar of Pakistan, devised an Islamic financial instrument for interest-free lending based on *Qard hasan* and named it Time Multiple Counter Loan – TMCL.

A TMCL transaction between two parties comprises two simultaneously exchanged interest-free loans such that the multiple of the amount and period of one loan equals the multiple of the amount and period of the other loan. It facilitates interest-free loaning of large sums against counter-loans of smaller sums advanced for proportionately longer periods. For example an entrepreneur requiring a loan of $10.0 Million for one year can get interest-free loan of $10.0 Million (against collateral as usual) for one year by advancing an interest-free counter loan of $1.0 Million to the bank for 10 years. Thus TMCL fulfills the client's need of funds for the required period and also enables the bank to earn profit from long term investment of counter-loan money. Whatever gain or loss the bank earns comes from investment of counter-loan amounts which are actually borrowed sums and in Islam there is no bar on earning profit by investing borrowed sums. In interest-based loaning the lender always gains because he earns interest whereas the borrower may gain or lose from investment of the borrowed sum. Therefore interest-based loaning is inequitable and unjust. In TMCL transaction none of the two parties is a definite gainer and each one of them may gain or lose by investing the loan taken from the other party. Hence TMCL transaction is equitable and just. In TMCL transaction each party does good to the other party and as such TMCL-based loaning conforms with the Quraanic precept *Hal jaza-ul-ihsaan illa al-ihsaan* and the noble teaching of our Prophet *saws* that a favour done to any one should be reciprocated.

As TMCL can perform Islamically all legitimate financial intermediation functions which are performed by interest, it can instantly and effectively replace interest without any disruption in the banking system. After switching over to TMCL-based loaning system the banks will continue to function as usual with the basic change that no interest will be paid or charged. All loans will be advanced against counter-loans and all transactions involving credit will be executed on TMCL-basis. Banks will continue to receive deposits and issue cheque books as usual. Account holders will have the option to keep their money in investment or demand deposit accounts. Investment account holders will share profit/loss with the bank on daily product basis. Banks will earn profits by investing counter-loan amounts and surplus deposits in *Shariah*-compliant modes like stock exchange, real property, *musharakah*, *mudarabah*, etc. Outstanding interest-based loans will be converted into TMCL-based transactions. Each borrower will repay only the principal amount of loan on due date or earlier and instead of paying interest the borrower will advance to the bank a counter-loan of the same amount as he took in loan and for the same period for which he availed the loan. Alternatively the bank and the borrower may mutually agree to a different amount of counter-loan for proportionately longer or shorter period on TMCL-basis. Interest-bearing bills and bonds will be encashed at their face value and the holders will receive appropriate counter-loan on TMCL-basis from the issuer.

In the interest-free regime there will be no role of interest-based treasury bills and bonds etc. and all such documents will cease to be issued and no function involving interest will be undertaken by the Central Bank. Other functions not involving interest will be performed as usual. The Central Bank will set up a framework of Central Depository-cum-lender of last resort for mobilizing surplus funds of banks and federal and provincial governments and autonomous bodies and advancing interest-free loans to them in times of need. The Central Depository will receive deposits and advance interest-free loans on TMCL basis. For example, if a bank has a surplus of Rs. 5.0M for 1 month, it may deposit this sum for 1 month with the Central Depository and obtain an interest-free loan of Rs. 0.5M for 10 months. If a bank is short of liquidity and requires Rs. 10.0M for 1 week, it will obtain from the Central Depository an interest-free loan of Rs. 10.0M for 1 week by depositing Rs. 1.0M with the Central Depository for 10 weeks. Central Depository will also earn profits by investing surplus funds in *Shariah*-compliant businesses.

Banks will deposit 20% of each counter-loan amount with the Central-Depository for 10 years against which Central Depository will allow banks to draw 200% of counter-loan amount for 1 year. This will provide 20% liquidity for the banks. Additional 2% liquidity will be obtained by keeping 20% of counter-loan amount as till money in the bank. Thus total liquidity achieved by the banking sector will be 22%. At present interest rate mechanism is used to control credit availability. In the interest-free regime this function will be performed by raising or lowering the time-multiple ratio in TMCL.

Substitution of interest-based loaning by TMCL-based loaning will disprove the mischievous propaganda that interest cannot be abolished. It will finish the on-going war against Allah and His Rasool *saws* and will save the Muslim *ummah* from disastrous consequences thereof, both spiritual and temporal. Many tangible benefits for the Muslim *ummah* will also emanate from TMCL-based loaning system. The cost of capital in the form of interest charged on loans for production and trade adds to the cost of goods and commodities which results in increase of consumer prices. In TMCL-based loaning system no such cost is incurred and as such it will result in substantial decrease in consumer prices. According to a saying of our Prophet Muhammad *saws* Allah imposes dearness of necessities upon the society in which interest gets prevalence. Keynes, the most eminent economist of the past century, held that direct relationship between interest rate and prices is one of the most completely established empirical facts within the whole field of quantitative economics. Keynes also argued that lower the rate of interest, higher the level of investment, therefore higher the level of employment therefore higher the level of incomes therefore higher the level of savings. His contention was that highest level of savings can be obtained at the lowest level of interest. Empirical proof supports Keynes' contentions. According to the World Bank statistics gross domestic savings in Pakistan were 13% in 1965 when interest rate was 9% and savings fell to 5% in 1985 when interest rate had risen to 18%. Clearly highest possible savings must occur at zero rate of interest and in TMCL-based loaning system savings and consequently bank deposits will rise considerably. Higher level of deposits will raise lending capacity of banks and more funds will be available for industry and trade which will provide employment to many of the unemployed millions and hopefully no body willing to work will remain unemployed.

Adoption of TMCL as loaning instrument by Islamic banks will bring the following benefits to Islamic banks and the Muslim *ummah* as a whole.

1. It will open for Islamic banks the vast field of loaning to reliable and capable cost conscious entrepreneurs who want to remain independent and in full control of their enterprises and do not accept any sharing of profit or outside interference. Without providing loans to this big class of loan seekers, Islamic banks will not be able to compete with western banks who have started capturing business in Islamic investment field.
2. It will facilitate inter-bank interest-free loan transactions and Islamic banks will not have to turn to western banks for meeting their short-term needs of liquidity.
3. It will facilitate setting up of a central depository for mobilizing surplus funds of Islamic banks and governments on TMCL-basis and advancing to them in times of need TMCL-based interest-free loans.
4. It will facilitate utilization of the financial resources of the Muslim *ummah* in developing Muslim countries through the Central Depository, instead of being diverted to western financial markets.

ISLAMIC LENDING INSTRUMENT FOR MEETING SHORT-TERM NEEDS OF LIQUIDITY - TMCL

Following assertions in authentic publications on Islamic Finance highlight the need for a lending instrument to meet the short-term needs of liquidity of Government, banks and very large number of sole proprietorship enterprises forming vast source of productive manpower employment.

These short-term needs of liquidity cannot be fulfilled by the traditional Islamic financing modes currently in use by Islamic banks. Hence the necessity of an Islamic lending Instrument in Interest-free regime. TMCL (Time Multiple Counter Loan) is such an instrument as it facilitates Interest-free loans of large amounts for short periods against counter-loans of smaller sums for proportionately longer periods. It is institutionalization of the Islamic concept of Qard-Hasan and conforms with the Quraanic precept Hal Jaza-ul-Ihsan illa Al-ihsan and the noble teaching of our Prophet *saws* that a favour done to any one should be reciprocated. For fulfilling the financial needs of all types for all sectors of the economy it is absolutely necessary that TMCL is included in the list of Financial Instruments for use by Islamic banks in Interest-free regime. A document on the shortcomings of Islamic banks resulting from the lack of a lending instrument brought the following response from Islamic Development Bank Jeddah:

"REFERRING TO THE DOCUMENTS SUBMITTED TO H.E. THE PRESIDENT OF ISLAMIC DEVELOPMENT BANK (IDB) ABOUT YOUR OBSERVATION ON THE ISLAMIC BANKING MOVEMENT, WE APPRECIATE VERY MUCH YOUR GOOD EFFORTS AND INSIGHTS. THE ISLAMIC BANKS' OFFICE OF IDB WILL TRY TO DO ITS BEST TO COMMUNICATE TO THE ISLAMIC BANKS THE SHORTCOMINGS THAT YOU HAD MENTIONED IN YOUR DOCUMENT".

Research Paper No. 29 published by Islamic Research and Training Institute – Islamic Development Bank Jeddah:-

"...in order to effectively replace Interest, the Islamic Economy needs a comprehensive financing mechanism. In the absence of such a mechanism, even if the capital structure of an enterprise is cleansed from Interest, overtime, the maintenance of such an Interest-free capital structure may not be possible. On the other hand, if a comprehensive Islamic financing mechanism can be devised, not only Interest can be prevented from entering in the capital of enterprises but also existing enterprises may be able to replace their Interest-based debts at a larger scale. ....a comprehensive financing mechanism may be defined as a mechanism which provides monetary financial accommodation to enterprises but remains neutral with respect to their longer-run ownership structure. Although, hiring, installment purchase and spot sale of owned assets and Mudharabah etc, serve the purpose of financing but, neither of these can function as a comprehensive financing mechanism. ....For some reasons, if the company needs cash, installment purchase or hiring does not directly meet such requirements. Mudharabah and Musharakah arrangements directly meet the company's cash requirements. But both of these essentially lead to a change in the ownership structure of the enterprise. Thus enterprises which need cash, but, for the time being, not wanting or being able to change their ownership structure would find hard to compromise. An interest-free comprehensive financing mechanism is thus needed by an Islamic Economy.....if funds are needed for expansion and business sections cannot be identified for new Mudharabas and Musharakahs the enterprise has to admit new Mudharibs/Mushariks (Partners) by issuing profit sharing financial instruments. Besides the cost of such arrangements, this option is suitable only for those enterprises which are willing to change their ownership structure. Capital structure of sole Proprietorships: - these enterprises are effective source of productive engagement of manpower, particularly, in the capital-scarce developing countries. As sole proprietorships do not like to associate others with their enterprises, they cannot utilize Musharakah or Mudharabah finance. The capital structure of these enterprises may contain debt as a natural result of shortage of internal resources to finance either the establishment of the enterprise or its expansion. But, since these are solely owned by a single person, by definition, the capital structure of such firms shall never contain external funds such as Mudharabah, Musharakah, or common stock. In other words, due to their typical ownership structure, these enterprises could not benefit from the traditional Islamic participatory modes of financing or from the equity finance. It may not be just to ask the enterprises to sacrifice their ownership characteristics if they need financial accommodation. Nor, such an administrative arrangement sounds efficient or even logical economy-wise. The right approach, in our opinion, is therefore, to evolve a scheme of permissible financial accommodation which could also be consistent with the universal preference of these enterprises for the form of capital structure. The problem is one of meeting the cash needs of a sole proprietorship for establishment or growth, but at the same time, without changing the structure of the enterprise. Thus conceptual efforts as well as institutional arrangements are required to provide such a financing mechanism in conformity with the ban on interest.....the actual problem of the elimination of Interest also requires an alternative mechanism which can be used by common people and millions of sole proprietorships. ...there must be

hundreds of thousands of enterprises in the Muslim World which may not have interest-based funds in their capital structure. Many of these enterprises must be looking for funds in conformity with the shariah *requirements but due to their preference for strong internal ownership these enterprises may be in difficulty to compromise with the ownership structure underlying Mudharabah and Musharakah arrangements.......the problem of capital participation in enterprises is in fact a problem of devising a comprehensive Islamic Financing Mechanism – a mechanism which can provide financial accommodation in the form of money, but simultaneously remain neutral to the longer-run ownership structure of the enterprise. ....once a comprehensive Islamic Financing Mechanism is provided, the infant enterprises are expected to have a proper environment to avoid interest while financing their growth."*

Research Paper No. 41 published by Islamic Research and Training Institute-Islamic Development Bank Jeddah:-

'The issue of a short-term excess liquidity is one of the problems facing IBs (Islamic banks). However, this problem is exacerbated by the fact that there is neither a money market in the countries where most IBs operate, nor adequate and efficient financial instruments that can be used to manage these surplus funds in order to recycle them among IBs themselves or among other financial institutions. The seriousness of this problem is increased since some IBs hold temporarily idle balances whereas other IBs need these balances, and both groups are unable to benefit from these funds due to the lack of short-term financial instruments which are not in contradiction of shariah *laws.*

Seminar Proceedings No. 39 published by Islamic Research and Training Institute – Islamic Development Bank Jeddah:-

"When an Islamic Government (or any economic agent) needs money to acquire goods, they can buy them through Murabaha. If they need funds to build a road, they can use Istisna or Musharakah. But what if the government needs cash (to pay salaries or buy services) and needs it now. The options available, so far, is borrowing from the public or the banking sector at interest. It is no accident that while great advances had been taking place in the Islamization of the private financial transactions in many Muslim countries, very little has been done in the public sector. Almost all Islamic governments borrow on interest."

Occasional Paper No. 2 published by Islamic Research and Training Institute – Islamic Development Bank Jeddah:-

"While Islamic banks use Mudarabah on the resource mobilization side, they use a number of Shariah-compliant financial instruments on the asset side. It is generally observed that the modes of finance used by Islamic banks are dominated by fixed-return modes especially Murabahah ... .The profit-sharing modes account for less than 14 percent financing. In case of financing by sectors trading gets the biggest proportion i.e. 42 percent. The second largest sector is real estate which accounts for 13%. Agriculture claims only 2 percent and industry 12 percent of the financing. This calls for rethinking the role of Islamic banks in economic development against the hopes which had been raised in the past regarding their ability to finance agriculture and industry. While Islamic banks and investment funds have so

far mobilized huge financial resources, a large part of these resources have found its way into Western financial markets. Likewise, the same thing happened with resources mobilized by conventional banks. There is no Islamic (or for that matter, conventional indigenous) financial institution which has been able to channel savings from Western countries into Muslim countries in spite of the great demand for such resources in the latter countries. This is another challenge for Islamic banks with very important implications for Muslim countries. Islamic banks have succeeded in mobilizing large amounts of funds. However, it will require much more strenuous efforts to maintain a reasonable rate of growth in future. There are several reasons for that. Firstly, it must be realized that much of the deposits now with the Islamic banks came not due to the attraction of higher returns or better services but because of religious commitment of the clients. Most of this money has already found its way into the coffers of Islamic banks. Therefore this source has been almost dried up. Secondly, so far Islamic banks had a fairly large degree of 'monopoly' over the financial resources of Islamically motivated public. This situation is changing fast. Islamic banks are now facing ever-increasing competition."

Introduction to Islamic Finance by Hon. Justice Muhammad Taqi Usmani:-

"The case of Islamic banking cannot be advanced unless a strong system of inter-bank transactions based on Islamic principles is developed. The lack of such a system forces the Islamic banks to turn to the conventional banks for their short-term needs of liquidity which the conventional banks do not provide without either an open or camouflaged Interest".

Adoption of TMCL as loaning instrument by Islamic banks will bring the following benefits to Islamic banks and the Muslim ummah as a whole.

1. It will open for Islamic banks the vast field of loaning to reliable and capable cost conscious entrepreneurs who want to remain independent and in full control of their enterprises and do not accept any sharing of profit or outside interference. Without providing loans to this big class of loan seekers, Islamic banks will not be able to compete with western banks who have started capturing business in Islamic investment field.
2. It will facilitate inter-bank interest-free loan transactions and Islamic banks will not have to turn to western banks for meeting their short-term needs of liquidity.
3. It will facilitate setting up of a central depository for mobilizing surplus funds of Islamic banks and governments on TMCL-basis and advancing to them in times of need TMCL-based interest-free loans.
4. It will facilitate utilization of the financial resources of the Muslim ummah in developing Muslim countries through the Central Depository, instead of being diverted to western financial markets.

Usury & Interest

5. *[2:275] Those who charge usury are in the same position as those controlled by the devil's influence. This is because they claim that usury is the same as commerce. However, GOD permits commerce, and*

prohibits usury. Thus, whoever heeds this commandment from his Lord, and refrains from usury, he may keep his past earnings, and his judgment rests with GOD. As for those who persist in usury, they incur Hell, wherein they abide forever

6. The Quran forbids usury, not interest. Quite a few states in USA have laws against usury. Usury is defined as excessive interest. A Dictionary defines usury as "an excessive or inordinate premium for the use of money borrowed", "extortionate interest", or "the practice of taking exorbitant or excessive interest." The Arabic language also makes distinction between interest (Fa'eda) and usury (Reba). The Quran forbids Reba or usury.
7. Earning interest and paying interest is perfectly acceptable, as the Quran has not prohibited interest. Interest is an essential component of the financial aspect of an individual or an organization. Individuals may need to save money in a bank, may carry a credit card for convenience, or may borrow and pay interest for an automobile or to own a house. Borrowing money and thus paying interest for business loans is an essential component for business and organizations. Thus paying interest, as long as it is not considered excessive by the standard of the day and community, to a credit card company, to a financial institution for a loan of any kind (business, car, house mortgage) is allowed and perfectly legal from a Quranic point of view. Also earning interest from a financial institution like a bank or bonds or mutual fund is also fine.
8. As defined above usury is excessive interest. Unlicensed or illegal moneylenders (mafia as a well known example) charge usury, excessive interest. Such unlicensed or illegal moneylenders are all over the world and can easily be accessed by a few inquiries. For those who live in USA, any individual can find out about these moneylenders by asking about them within their ethnic business community. These illegal moneylenders have entirely separate standards for making loans - they charge excessive interest (usury) and usually rely on someone's life (guarantor) as collateral. The Quran forbids in dealing with usury - borrowing money and paying usury or earning money by charging usury. The Quran specifically states that usury cannot be equated to commerce or taken as a normal business practice. The practice of usury, unfortunately, is prevalent all over the world with individuals and business engaged in this practice.
9. In practical terms as long as we are dealing with any state-licensed institution like a bank, Mortgage Company, Credit Card Company, etc., we are not violating any Quranic commandment as these institutions usually follow the law of the land and do not charge excessive interest. They calculate their interest rate on daily basis considering the status of the economy and the need of the society. However, if we deal with the illegal moneylenders who practice usury, we are in violation of clear Quranic commandments. This is not to say that one may not borrow or lend money to a friend or relative and even charge interest. Such transaction must be in writing as the Quran cleary commands in verse 2:282 and may involve interest, to at least pay for the cost of the loan to the

lender if any, and compensate for any change in the value of the currency over the time of the loan, but should not involve usury.

10. [2:282] *O you who believe, when you transact a loan for any period, you shall write it down. An impartial scribe shall do the writing. No scribe shall refuse to perform this service, according to GOD's teachings. He shall write, while the debtor dictates the terms. He shall observe GOD his Lord and never cheat. If the debtor is mentally incapable, or helpless, or cannot dictate, his guardian shall dictate equitably. Two men shall serve as witnesses; if not two men, then a man and two women whose testimony is acceptable to all. Thus, if one woman becomes biased, the other will remind her. It is the obligation of the witnesses to testify when called upon to do so. Do not tire of writing the details, no matter how long, including the time of repayment. This is equitable in the sight of GOD, assures better witnessing, and eliminates any doubts you may have. Business transactions that you execute on the spot need not be recorded, but have them witnessed. No scribe or witness shall be harmed on account of his services. If you harm them, it would be wickedness on your part. You shall observe GOD, and GOD will teach you. GOD is Omniscient.*

11. A note should be made that the Quran, which spells out religious laws for our great religion, removes the shackles and burdens imposed on us by the ignorant scholars and religious leaders. Most of the "Muslim" countries have various laws against interest and have sham "interest-free banking" reflecting their ignorance of this simple Quranic truth. Unfortunately, quite a few of those who call themselves Muslims fall victims to the falsehood spread by these religious leaders.

12. [2:276-280] GOD condemns usury, and blesses charities. GOD dislikes every disbeliever, guilty. O you who believe, you shall observe GOD and refrain from all kinds of usury, if you are believers. If you do not, then expect a war from GOD and His messenger. But if you repent, you may keep your capitals, without inflicting injustice, or incurring injustice. If the debtor is unable to pay, wait for a better time. If you give up the loan as a charity, it would be better for you, if you only knew.

13. [3:130] O you who believe, you shall not take usury, compounded over and over. Observe GOD, that you may succeed.

14. [4:161] And for practicing usury, which was forbidden, and for consuming the people's money illicitly. We have prepared for the disbelievers among them painful retribution.

15. [30:39] The usury that is practiced to increase some people's wealth, does not gain anything at GOD. But if you give to charity, seeking GOD's pleasure, these are the ones who receive their reward manifold.

16. [7:157] "(4) follow the messenger, the gentile prophet (Muhammad), whom they find written in their Torah and Gospel. He exhorts them to be righteous, enjoins them from evil, allows for them all good food, and prohibits that which is bad, and unloads the burdens and the shackles imposed upon them. Those who believe in him, respect him, support him, and follow the light that came with him are the successful ones."

4

Interest Free Financing and Banking

In this section, there are two instances where the author creates confusion. The first instance is when he uses inaccurate definitions, and the second instance occurs when he draws a wrong policy conclusion. He uses the expressions "unearned income" and "fixed rent" in an incorrect context (p. 119). His discussion leaves one with the impression that these two sources of income are completely forbidden in Islam, which is far from the truth. Another instance where he draws a judgmental policy conclusion is when he recommends nationalization of banks on the basis of an undefined, theoretical concept of "social profitability." We find no support from economic theory or the experience of the developing or socialist world to indicate that nationalized banks contribute to social profitability. Instead, banks in the public sector are often found to be economically inefficient, bureaucratic, unresponsive to public needs, and an embodiment of waste and misallocation of economic resources.

Taxation in Islamic Economy

His views about taxation policy in an Islamic state are derived from the application of the same overextended personal logic and individual ijtihad that he has used throughout the book. In order to establish a "basis for a state taxation of income and wealth," he cites two ahadith (p. 168) and then makes the following statement: "Therefore it can be deduced that in the Islamic perspective all forms of income and wealth are taxable whether it is the profit of capital, the wages from labor, the return to entrepreneurship, or the produce of the land, or whether wealth is held as precious metals, bank accounts, real estate, or any other form. This accords with the Shariah's rule of the permissibility of things unless categorically prohibited" (p. 169). It is quite clear that with this statement, the author is not only turning the principle of permissibility upside down, he is also erroneously providing a justification for the government to have a free hand to levy a tax on every imaginable economic resource. The author's conclusions are clearly wrong and untenable for the following reasons: The first hadith is specific to zakah, while the second hadith only mentions a duty on property apart from zakah, which can be met through sadaqah and other extra charity. There is no other hadith that one can quote to justify any mandatory collection of any other tax in Islamic economy. In times of special need, the Prophet used to ask for contributions from the citizens. This practice further proves that in an Islamic state, tax levies are not fixed or mandatory. Rather, they are primarily ad hoc and need based and at times voluntary. Therefore, the clear and unambiguous conclusion from this practice in the context of current economic policy is that the only space- and time-neutral mandatory obligation on all Muslims is to pay zakah. As for other taxes, their collection depends primarily on the needs of the economy and the consensus of the citizens with regards to the amount of services they expect from their government.His views about taxation policy in an Islamic state are derived from the application of the same overextended personal logic and individual ijtihad that he has used throughout the book. In order to establish a "basis for a state taxation of income and wealth," he cites two ahadith (p. 168) and then makes the following statement: "Therefore it can be deduced that in the Islamic perspective all forms of income and wealth are taxable whether it is the profit of capital, the wages from labor, the return to entrepreneurship, or the produce of the land, or whether wealth is held as precious metals, bank accounts, real estate, or any other form. This accords with the Shariah's rule of the permissibility of things unless categorically prohibited" (p. 169). It is quite clear that with this statement, the author is not only turning the principle of permissibility upside down, he is also erroneously providing a justification for the government to have a free hand to levy a tax on every imaginable economic resource. The author's conclusions are clearly wrong and untenable for the following reasons: The first hadith is specific to zakah, while the second hadith only mentions a duty on property apart from zakah, which can be met through sadaqah and other extra charity. There is no other hadith that one can quote to justify any mandatory collection of any other tax in Islamic economy. In times of special need, the Prophet used to ask for contributions from the citizens. This practice further proves that in an Islamic state, tax levies are not fixed or mandatory. Rather, they are primarily ad hoc and need based and at times voluntary. Therefore, the clear and unambiguous conclusion from this practice in the context of current economic policy is that the only space- and time-neutral mandatory obligation on all Muslims is to pay zakah. As for other taxes, their collection depends primarily on the needs of the economy and the consensus of the citizens with regards to the amount of services they expect from their government.

Poverty Employment and Economic Growth

The major problem with the author's presentation throughout the fourth part remains his preoccupation with a big public sector. According to his vision, the government not only acts as "producer and provider of services, as sources of finance, as the maker of rules, but it carries the overall responsibility for planning, coordination, organization, and delivery of goods and services" (p. 216). In his concluding remarks, this vision takes a diametrically opposite turn. He states, "Islam does not envision a welfare state supporting a large class of welfare recipients. On the contrary, it perceives an economy based on the ethics of work and productive economic enterprise" (p. 231). Here again the author fails to recognize that within the framework of rational economic theory, these two visions are inconsistent and incompatible.

In conclusion, I would like to point out that the author has been very successful in effectively presenting an excellent expository analysis of Islamic economic doctrines. His coverage of various economic topics is extensive and his sources are comprehensive. His presentation is clear and succinct and his conclusions are consistent with his economic hypothesis. While allowing for the existence of private enterprise, he perceives the Islamic economic state as an active player in all aspects of a Muslim's life, including production and overall management. It is in this area that I believe that the author's position is inconsistent with the broader economic philosophy of Islam. In my opinion, the state in Islam plays a residual rather than an active role. The policy prescription that he recommends is, therefore, preachy, idealistic, simplistic, and often nonimplementable. Although Dr. Haq alludes to the fact that Islam's emphasis on the establishment of a just, legal, and equitable social and economic order does not presuppose any specific economic policy or operational strategy, his operational economic model presupposes an active and all-engaging public sector as a modus operandi of an Islamic economic system. Finally, throughout his discussion of economic subjects and issues he has exercised too much liberty and personal ijtihad and has relied too heavily on his own deductive reasoning in carrying out interpretative analysis of the Qur'an and the Sunnah. Furthermore, in attempting to portray an idealistic economy, he often starts a discussion of policy prescriptions with a set of unrealistic, simplistic, and untenable assumptions. The result has been that the policy conclusions he draws are neither supportable within the framework of a liberal interpretation of Islamic principles nor consistent with rational economic theory. His major thesis leads to a policy recommendation for the Islamic state to pick up and implement a broad social welfare spending agenda without any concern how these policies will be financed. His advocacy of limiting the size of land ownership without any regard to how the land was accumulated in the first place as well as his recommendation for the Islamic state to follow an open-ended tax policy clearly violates Islam's commitment to private ownership and free enterprise.

5

The Benchmark Issue in the Islamic Financial System

INTRODUCTION

This paper identifies a major lacuna in the conceptual development of Islamic financial market operations. It argues that in the absence of a well developed benchmark that would facilitate macro- and micro-level decision making with regards to cost of capital and opportunity cost of investments in comparative projects of similar risk, Islamic financial institutions are relying on interest rate-based indices such as the London Inter-Bank Offer Rate (LIBOR) to make lending decisions. The author contends that this is clearly unacceptable since Islam disallows a predetermined or fixed rate of capital. The paper then proposes a benchmark based on Tobin's q theory of investment. The author further maintains that unlike existing alternatives which are limited to macro-level applications only, the q-based benchmark would be useful for firms and banks (micro-decisions) as well as governments and institutions (macro-planning).

Background

An Islamic financial system requires elimination of any fixed and pre-determined interest rate and thus closes the door to any form of debt instruments. Instead, it promotes equity participation and direct sharing of risks and rewards. In simple terms, although the system prohibits a fixed and predetermined interest rate on capital, it fully recognizes return on investment. As compared to a conventional debt-based system where capital is rewarded on the basis of a rate fixed ex-ante or determined by the expectations of the future demand and supply of capital, an Islamic system calls for rewarding the capital on the basis of ex-post (actual) return on capital. Whereas market interest rate plays the role of an equilibrium rate for financial intermediation and a benchmark for making efficient investment decisions in a conventional system, so far no equivalent substitute has been available for an equity-based system to determine the internal rate of return or the marginal efficiency of investments.

The Islamic financial system recognizes that investment decision-making will have to be based on the concept of rate of return on capital as it participates in real sector activities and not on the opportunity cost of capital as represented by the interest rate. Though discounting expected future stream of cash flows based on a risk-adjusted expected rate of return does not violate any Islamic principle, and standard techniques for project evaluation are acceptable, the issue is how to determine the so-called "risk-adjusted expected rate of return," or cost of capital, in the absence of a system-wide benchmark or reference rate.

Thus far, the literature on Islamic economics and finance has not developed techniques to determine a rate of return at the firm (micro) or economy (macro) level so that investments can be compared for efficient allocation of capital. In the absence of such a reference rate or benchmark, Islamic financial institutions have resorted to adopting a proxy rate borrowed from their counterparts in the conventional system. It has become a common practice to use the London Inter-Bank Offer Rate (LIBOR) as a reference rate for mark-up instruments or a benchmark to price trade financing instrument and Islamic leasing funds. Without a doubt, this practice is questionable and raises several concerns. Practitioners claim that this arrangement is temporary until a better substitute and viable solution is offered. This paper summarizes the findings of a recent research proposing a model for determining the cost of capital in an economy where debt-instruments are eliminated. This model is based on Tobin's q theory of investment and attempts to devise a benchmark compatible with the Islamic financial system.

Current Practice

Currently, Islamic financial markets are dominated by short-term trade financing instruments. According to some estimates, 80 percent of investment is being channeled through the "cost-plus" (murabaha) mode of financing. The common practice in the market is to use the LIBOR as the reference rate for mark-up.

Similarly, the LIBOR is used for pricing and measuring the performance of Islamic leasing funds. In the absence of LIBOR, the prevailing market interest rate would serve the same purpose. Historically, several factors have contributed to the establishment of this practice. First, Islamic financial institutions required a common reference rate to integrate with international capital markets. Second, as Western banks entered into the Islamic financial markets, they required a comparable benchmark against their cost of funding in the conventional system, which happened to be the LIBOR. These institutions treated the murabaha mode as synonymous with the conventional money market, which was based on the LIBOR. Finally, in those markets where Islamic financial institutions coexisted with conventional banks, the LIBOR became a benchmark for competition in attracting depositors.

The prevalent practice is defended by the arguments that, in the case of the murabaha mode of financing, a practice to charge the LIBOR-based "mark-up" is still Islamic because it is part of the sale agreement price between two parties; and, in case of leasing funds, the LIBOR is used for pricing and performance measurement purposes only and does not influence the actual rate of return on the investment. Further, the LIBOR provides price transparency and global real-time accessibility, which facilitates ease of operation and integration of Islamic and international financial markets. Irrespective of various justifications provided for the practice, obviously the use of any interest rate as part of a mark-up (pricing or performance) is not acceptable because interest rate does not represent real rate of return in the economy as intended by Islamic principles. Although ease of use is the reason cited, the real reason is the lack of a more suitable measure. Finding a practical solution for a benchmark compatible with Islamic principles requires an understanding of the concept of cost of capital in the context of an Islamic financial system. The cost of capital provides a common reference point for comparing heterogenous investments and provides insight into how firms make investment decisions.

Cost of Capital in an Islamic Financial System

By prohibiting interest, Islamic injunctions do not imply that the opportunity cost of capital represented by interest rate in a conventional system is zero. In an Islamic framework, the incentive for the firm to invest will solely depend on prospective profitability. A profit maximizing firm will continue investing until the marginal productivity of capital becomes equal to the opportunity cost of capital; therefore, "cost of capital" in the Islamic system can be represented by the rate of return on alternate opportunities for investment of comparable risk. It has also been demonstrated that there is a rate of return in Islamic capital markets serving opportunity cost of capital, and this rate of return is also closely related to the rate of return in the real sector of the economy.

In the Islamic financial system, determination of prospective profitability and the rate of return on investments of the same risk class plays a pivotal role in determining the relative cost of capital. Tobin's q theory of investment suggests the use of information in asset markets, especially the stock market, in knowing the profitability of investment. The theory relates investment to the ratio of market to replacement value of capital and suggests that when the stock market functions properly, the future profitability of investment will be solely summarized by q. It is a simple arbitrage argument. If the market valuation of capital held by a firm exceeds the cost of capital on the open market, then the firm can increase its value by investing. Tobin argues that if q exceeds unity, the value of capital investment would exceed its costs, and the firm would have incentive to invest.

A recent model presented by Mirakhor utilizes this concept of q in deriving the cost of equity capital of a firm in the Islamic financial system. In its simple form the model states:

$$r = (Y / V)(1 - d + dq)$$

where

r = Firm's cost of capital or shareholder's required rate of return.

Y = Value of expected earnings for the next year.

V = Present value of the firm's stock of capital. Since there is no debt financing in the Islamic system, it is equal to value of the firm.

d = Sum of fraction of expected earnings retained by the firm and the expected rate of stock financing expressed as ratio of firm's expected earnings.

q = Firm's q ratio.

The model implies that a firm's cost of capital (r) is a function of a firm's q ratio and the firm's market value (V), stream of expected future earnings (Y), ratio of retained earnings, and new stock financing. The q ratio can be simply derived by dividing the value of the firm (V) determined by the market price of the firm's stock by the replacement costs of firm's assets such as equipment, land, receivables, and marketable securities.

The cost of capital will fluctuate with the fluctuations in the q ratio, thus signaling the prospects of an investment project. For example, we are interested in finding the cost of capital for a firm with future expected earnings for next year (Y) of \$1,000,000 and equity value of \$10,000,000 (since there is no debt financing, value of the firm is equal to equity value). Based on the historical data, it is known that the firm finances future projects through retained earnings and new equity issues amounting to 20 percent of its earnings (d = .20). If the firm's q ratio is 1, its cost of capital will be 10 percent as the following shows:

$$.1 = \$1,000,000/\$10,000,000\ (\ 1 - .2 + (.2\ .\ 1)\ )$$

The figure below gives a graphical representation of cost of capital for the same firm with varying q ratios. It is obvious from the graph that cost of capital has a linear relationship with q. A firm with q lower than 1 will have a cost of capital lower than the return on equity (10 percent in this case) whereas, firms with q greater than 1 will require higher cost of capital.

A firm's market value reflects the profitability of existing capital. The q ratio is an indication of how much this market value can increase by additional investment, also known as marginal q. Marginal q - the ratio of market value of an additional unit of capital (shadow price of capital) to its replacement cost - is the critical determinant of the firm's investment decision making but is not observable since the shadow price of capital is not observable. Instead, what is observable (in principle) is the average q - ratio of the market value of existing capital to its replacement cost.

Hayashi rigorously proved a relationship of average q with marginal q-based information in stock market valuation.

A relationship of equality between average and marginal q will hold provided conditions of perfect competition in product market and linear function of homogenous technology of production and adjustment costs are satisfied. For competitive firms (price-takers), this relationship is strong because the unobservable shadow price is directly linked to the stock market valuation of existing capital. If one of these conditions is violated, then the average q is no longer equal to the marginal q; however, a relationship may still exist. For example, in firms with monopolistic position (price-makers), average q is higher than marginal q by what is legitimately called the monopoly rent, and it is marginal q that is relevant for investment. Several empirical studies have utilized average q as a proxy for marginal.

Pricing assets using q has several advantages over other methods. First, the market value of the firm is an indicator of future profitability as perceived by investors' expectations rather than the past performance of the firm. Second, since market value is subject to adjustment by variations in expected profits, q incorporates an automatic adjustment for risk independent of any methodology employed by capital markets to determine risk premium. The value of q should be equal to unity only if profits are high enough to compensate for shareholders risks. Finally, as compared to other asset pricing models (capital assets, arbitrage, or option pricing models), a model based on q is subject to less measurement errors.

Implications of Model

Deriving a firm's cost of capital without referring to a fixed and pre-determined rate such as an interest rate has immense implications for Islamic financial markets. Extensive research on q theory of investment suggests that it is possible to determine an industry-wide as well as an economy-wide q ratio. An industry-wide q ratio can very well serve the purpose of establishing the cost of capital for new firms entering the industry and as an indicator of efficiency relative to others in the same industry for existing firms. Similar to the concept of an industry-wide q ratio, an economy-wide q ratio can be used to determine a rate that reflects economy-wide marginal efficiency of capital or internal rate of return for efficient allocation of financial resources. Existence of an economy-wide benchmark has implications at both the micro- and macro-level. At the micro-level, such a benchmark can facilitate the pricing of assets, utilizing an equity-based reference rate. At the macro-level, it will help develop secondary markets, an Islamic money market, and an interbank market and contribute toward financial innovations. All these factors are known to be roadblocks to further development and growth of Islamic financial markets.

Development of a secondary market will enhance liquidity in the market and provide an extended maturity structure to investors. Establishment of a money market and an interbank market will have a great impact on the way Islamic financial institutions operate, since the problem of unavailability of funds at extreme short maturity will be resolved. No doubt, the financial innovations during the 1980s and 1990s changed the international financial markets in a revolutionary fashion. Similarly, financial innovations will introduce new products to Islamic financial markets to equip borrowers and lenders with the tools to better manage business and financial risk.

Another promising arena for applying an economy-wide q is in the way governments in Islamic countries formulate economic policies and raise funds for social sector projects. Central banks can perform monetary operations to achieve economic objectives by influencing q since this ratio is the principal link between the financial and real sector of the economy.

Governments can finance public sector projects by issuing equity-based securities where expected dividend is determined by the market price of government securities (discounted value of streams of expected earnings at a prevailing rate of return) and social rate of return (discounted value of stream of expected earnings derived from government surpluses). Since q is the ratio of the social rate of return to the expected rate of return on financial capital, governments have an incentive to invest only if q exceeds unity. Investors will invest in equity-based government securities provided the rate of return is comparable to the market rate of return.

Concluding Remarks

Despite its considerable theoretical appeal, empirical evidence linking q to investment decision-making of firms has received mixed reviews in the literature. Using Japanese corporate data, a recent time-series study examined the roles of marginal q (based on time-series techniques) and average q (using stock market valuation) in the q-based investment function. Although the study found poor performance of investment function based on average q, it also found, as expected, that entrepreneurs attach much significance to q.

Although the proposed q-based model is theoretically compatible with the Islamic financial system, one reservation about this approach could be that successful application of a model depends on the degree of development and efficiency in existing stock markets.

Since most Islamic countries are developing countries where capital and financial markets are not fully developed and are not integrated with international financial markets, data are subject to noise and distortion, thus contaminating the information content of q and investors' decision making. This reservation is more valid and applicable in determining an economy-wide benchmark based on time series to calculate an average q; however, it is not necessarily a barrier to calculating a q as a benchmark. This is particularly true for firms, banks, and even government projects, thus providing a benchmark conforming to Islamic principals, which excludes the fixed interest rate.

Recently, another model has been presented by Haque and Mirakhor to address the same benchmark issue.

Unlike the q model, the Haque-Mirakhor model attempts to develop an economy-wide index based on major indicators of domestic and international equity market performance to serve as a benchmark for issuing government papers. The suggested index is designed as a weighted average of domestic stock market index, international equity returns, and return on government's development projects. Inclusion of both domestic and international indices make it efficient in terms of its ability to eliminate any arbitrage opportunity and discourages speculative behavior. A similar approach can be taken for determining a benchmark for the private sector. Whereas the Haque-Mirakhor model provides guidelines for a macro-level benchmark, the q-based model can still provide a benchmark at the micro-level.

Nevertheless, the concept of a q-based benchmark is a ground-breaking innovation that requires further refinement. Given the right set of parameters, it may help solve the problem of defining a benchmark for Islamic financial markets.

RESEARCH REPORT ON ISLAMIC BANKING

Islamic banking is a new phenomenon that has taken many observers by surprise. The whole banking system has been islamized in both Iran and Pakistan. In addition, there are some thirty Islamic banks in operation in other parts of the globe, including the Jeddah-based Islamic Development Bank (IDB) but excluding numerous non-bank Islamic financial institutions (see Appendix). What is more, the speed with which Islamic banks have sprung up and the rate at which they have progressed make it worth-while to study them systematically. An attempt is made in this paper (a) to survey the growing literature on Islamic banking, in particular (b) to trace the growth and development of Islamic banking, and (c) to highlight its salient characteristics.

EVOLUTION

The first modern experiment with Islamic banking was undertaken in Egypt under cover, without projecting an Islamic image, for fear of being seen as a manifestation of Islamic fundamentalism which was anathema to the political regime. The pioneering effort, led by Ahmad El Najjar, took the form of a savings bank based on profit-sharing in the Egyptian town of Mit Ghamr in 1963. This experiment lasted until 1967 (Ready 1981), by which time there were nine such banks in the country. These banks, which neither charged nor paid interest, invested mostly by engaging in trade and industry, directly or in partnership with others, and shared the profits with their depositors (Siddiqi 1988). Thus, they functioned essentially as saving- investment institutions rather than as commercial banks. The Nasir Social Bank, established in Egypt in 1971, was declared an interest-free commercial bank, although its charter made no reference to Islam or Shariah (Islamic law).

The IDB was established in 1974 by the Organization of Islamic Countries (OIC), but it was primarily an inter-governmental bank aimed at providing funds for development projects in member countries. The IDB provides fee- based financial services and profit-sharing financial assistance to member countries. The IDB operations are free of interest and are explicitly based on

Shariah Principles

In the seventies, changes took place in the political climate of many Muslim countries so that there was no longer any strong need to establish Islamic financial institutions under cover. A number of Islamic banks, both in letter and spirit, came into existence in the Middle East, e.g., the Dubai Islamic Bank (1975), the Faisal Islamic Bank of Sudan (1977), the Faisal Islamic Bank of Egypt (1977), and the Bahrain Islamic Bank (1979), to mention a few. The Asia-Pacific region was not oblivious to the winds of change. The Philippine Amanah Bank (PAB) was established in 1973 by Presidential Decree as a specialized banking institution without reference to its Islamic character in the bank's charter. The establishment of the PAB was a response by the Philippines Government to the Muslim rebellion in the south, designed to serve the special banking needs of the Muslim community. However, the primary task of the PAB was to assist rehabilitation and reconstruction in Mindanao, Sulu and Palawan in the south (Mastura 1988). The PAB has eight branches located in the major cities of the southern Muslim provinces, including one in Makati (Metro Manila), in addition to the head office located at Zamboanga City in Mindanao. The PAB, however, is not strictly an Islamic bank, since interest-based operations continue to coexist with the Islamic modes of financing. It is indeed fascinating to observe that the PAB operates two 'windows' for deposit transactions, i.e., conventional and Islamic. Nevertheless, efforts are underway to convert the PAB into a full-fledged Islamic bank (Mastura 1988).

Islamic banking made its debut in Malaysia in 1983, but not without antecedents. The first Islamic financial institution in Malaysia was the Muslim Pilgrims Savings Corporation set up in 1963 to help people save for performing hajj (pilgrimage to Mecca and Medina). In 1969, this body evolved into the Pilgrims Management and Fund Board or the Tabung Haji as it is now popularly known. The Tabung Haji has been acting as a finance company that invests the savings of would-be pilgrims in accordance with Shariah, but its role is rather limited, as it is a non-bank financial institution. The success of the Tabung Haji, however, provided the main impetus for establishing Bank Islam Malaysia Berhad (BIMB) which represents a full- fledged Islamic commercial bank in Malaysia. The Tabung Haji also contributed 12.5 per cent of BIMB's initial capital of M$80 million. BIMB has a complement of fourteen branches in several parts of the country. Plans are afoot to open six new branches a year so that by 1990 the branch network of BIMB will total thirty-three (Man 1988).

Reference should also be made to some Islamic financial institutions established in countries where Muslims are a minority. There was a proliferation of interest-free savings and loan societies in India during the seventies (Siddiqi 1988). The Islamic Banking System (now called Islamic Finance House), established in Luxembourg in 1978, represents the first attempt at Islamic bankir g in the Western world. There is also an Islamic Bank International of Denmark, in Copenhagen, and the Islamic Investment Company has been set up in Melbourne, Australia.

Rationale

The essential feature of Islamic banking is that it is interest-free. Although it is often claimed that there is more to Islamic banking, such as contributions towards a more equitable distribution of income and wealth, and increased equity participation in the economy (Chapra 1982), it nevertheless derives its specific rationale from the fact that there is no place for the institution of interest in the Islamic order.

Islam prohibits Muslims from taking or giving interest (riba) regardless of the purpose for which such loans are made and regardless of the rates at which interest is charged. To be sure, there have been attempts to distinguish between usury and interest and between loans for consumption and for production. It has also been argued that riba refers to usury practiced by petty money-lenders and not to interest charged by modern banks and that no riba is involved when interest is imposed on productive loans, but these arguments have not won acceptance. Apart from a few dissenting opinions, he general consensus among Muslim scholars clearly is that there is no difference between riba and interest. In what follows, these two terms are used interchangeably.

The prohibition of riba is mentioned in four different revelations in the Qur'an. The first revelation emphasizes that interest deprives wealth of God's blessings. The second revelation condemns it, placing interest in juxtaposition with wrongful appropriation of property belonging to others. The third revelation enjoins Muslims to stay clear of interest for the sake of their own welfare. The fourth revelation establishes a clear distinction between interest and trade, urging Muslims to take only the principal sum and to forgo even this sum if the borrower is unable to repay. It is further declared in the Qur'an that those who disregard the prohibition of interest are at war with God and His Prophet. The prohibition of interest is also cited in no uncertain terms in the Hadith (sayings of the Prophet). The Prophet condemned not only those who take interest but also those who give interest and those who record or witness the transaction, saying that they are all alike in guilt.

It may be mentioned in passing that similar prohibitions are to be found in the pre-Qur'anic scriptures, although the 'People of the Book', as the Qur'an refers to them, had chosen to rationalize them. It is amazing that Islam has successfully warded off various subsequent rationalization attempts aimed at legitimizing the institution of interest.

Some scholars have put forward economic reasons to explain why interest is banned in Islam. It has been argued, for instance, that interest, being a pre- determined cost of production, tends to prevent full employment (Khan 1968; Ahmad n.d.; Mannan 1970). In the same vein, it has been contended that international monetary crises are largely due to the institution of interest (Khan, n.d), and that trade cycles are in no small measure attributable to the phenomenon of interest (Ahmad 1952; Su'ud n.d.). None of these studies, however, has really succeeded in establishing a causal link between interest, on the one hand, and employment and trade cycles, on the other. Others, anxious to vindicate the Islamic position on interest, have argued that interest is not very effective as a monetary policy instrument even in capitalist economies and have questioned the efficacy of the rate of interest as a determinant of saving and investment (Ariff 1982). A common thread running through all these discussions is the exploitative character of the institution of interest, although some have pointed out that profit (which is lawful in Islam) can also be exploitative. One response to this is that one must distinguish between profit and profiteering, and Islam has prohibited the latter as well.

Some writings have alluded to the 'unearned income' aspect of interest payments as a possible explanation for the Islamic doctrine. The objection that rent on property is considered halal (lawful) is then answered by rejecting the analogy between rent on property and interest on loans, since the benefit to the tenant is certain, while the productivity of the borrowed capital is uncertain. Besides, property rented out is subject to physical wear and tear, while money lent out is not. The question of erosion in the value of money and hence the need for indexation is an interesting one. But the Islamic jurists have ruled out compensation for erosion in the value of money, or, according to Hadith, a fungible good must be returned by its like (mithl): 'gold for gold, silver for silver, wheat for wheat, barley for barley, dates for dates, salt for salt, like for like, equal for equal, and hand to hand ...'.

The bottom line is that Muslims need no 'proofs' before they reject the institution of interest: no human explanation for a divine injunction is necessary for them to accept a dictum, as they recognize the limits to human reasoning. No human mind can fathom a divine order; therefore it is a matter of faith (iman).

The Islamic ban on interest does not mean that capital is costless in an Islamic system. Islam recognizes capital as a factor of production but it does not allow the factor to make a prior or pre-determined claim on the productive surplus in the form of interest. This obviously poses the question as to what will then replace the interest rate mechanism in an Islamic framework. There have been suggestions that profit-sharing can be a viable alternative (Kahf 1982a and 1982b). In Islam, the owner of capital can legitimately share the profits made by the entrepreneur. What makes profit- sharing permissible in Islam, while interest is not, is that in the case of the former it is only the profit-sharing ratio, not the rate of return itself that is predetermined.

It has been argued that profit-sharing can help allocate resources efficiently, as the profit-sharing ratio can be influenced by market forces so that capital will flow into those sectors which offer the highest profit- sharing ratio to the investor, other things being equal. One dissenting view is that the substitution of profit-sharing for interest as a resource allocating mechanism is crude and imperfect and that the institution of interest should therefore be retained as a necessary evil (Naqvi 1982). However, mainstream Islamic thinking on this subject clearly points to the need to replace interest with something else, although there is no clear consensus on what form the alternative to the interest rate mechanism should take. The issue is not resolved and the search for an alternative continues, but it has not detracted from efforts to experiment with Islamic banking without interest.

Anatomy

As mentioned earlier, Islam does not deny that capital, as a factor of production, deserves to be rewarded. Islam allows the owners of capital a share in a surplus which is uncertain. To put it differently, investors in the Islamic order have no right to demand a fixed rate of return. No one is entitled to any addition to the principal sum if he does not share in the risks involved. The owner of capital (rabbul-mal) may 'invest' by allowing an entrepreneur with ideas and expertise to use the capital for productive purposes and he may share the profits, if any, with the entrepreneur- borrower (mudarib); losses, if any, however, will be borne wholly by the rabbul-mal. This mode of financing, termed mudaraba in the Islamic literature, was in practice even in the pre-Qur'anic days and, according to jurists, it was approved by the Prophet.

Another legitimate mode of financing recognized in Islam is one based on equity participation (musharaka) in which the partners use their capital jointly to generate a surplus. Profits or losses will be shared between the partners according to some agreed formula depending on the equity ratio. Mudaraba and musharaka constitute, at least in principle if not in practice, the twin pillars of Islamic banking. The musharaka principle is invoked in the equity structure of Islamic banks and is similar to the modern concepts of partnership and joint stock ownership. In so far as the depositors are concerned, an Islamic bank acts as a mudarib which manages the funds of the depositors to generate profits subject to the rules of mudaraba as outlined above. The bank may in turn use the depositors' funds on a mudaraba basis in addition to other lawful modes of financing. In other words, the bank operates a two-tier mudaraba system in which it acts both as the mudarib on the saving side of the equation and as the rabbul-mal on the investment portfolio side. The bank may also enter into musharaka contracts with the users of the funds, sharing profits and losses, as mentioned above. At the deposit end of the scale, Islamic banks normally operate three broad categories of account, mainly current, savings, and investment accounts. The current account, as in the case of conventional banks, gives no return to the depositors. It is essentially a safe-keeping (al-wadiah) arrangement between the depositors and the bank, which allows the depositors to withdraw their money at any time and permits the bank to use the depositors' money. As in the case of conventional banks, cheque books are issued to the current account deposit holders and the Islamic banks provide the broad range of payment facilities - clearing mechanisms, bank drafts, bills of exchange, travellers cheques, etc. (but not yet, it seems, credit cards or bank cards). More often than not, no service charges are made by the banks in this regard.

The savings account is also operated on an al-wadiah basis, but the bank may at its absolute discretion pay the depositors a positive return periodically, depending on its own profitability. Such payment is considered lawful in Islam since it is not a condition for lending by the depositors to the bank, nor is it pre-determined. The savings account holders are issued with savings books and are allowed to withdraw their money as and when they please. The investment account is based on the mudaraba principle, and the deposits are term deposits which cannot be withdrawn before maturity. The profit- sharing ratio varies from bank to bank and from time to time depending on supply and demand conditions.4 In theory, the rate of return could be positive or negative, but in practice the returns have always been positive and quite comparable to rates conventional banks offer on their term deposits.

At the investment portfolio end of the scale, Islamic banks employ a variety of instruments. The mudaraba and musharaka modes, referred to earlier, are supposedly the main conduits for the outflow of funds from the banks. In practice, however, Islamic banks have shown a strong preference for other modes which are less risky.

The most commonly used mode of financing seems to be the 'mark-up' device which is termed murabaha. In a murabaha transaction, the bank finances the purchase of a good or asset by buying it on behalf of its client and adding a mark-up before re-selling it to the client on a 'cost-plus' basis. It may appear at first glance that the mark-up is just another term for interest as charged by conventional banks, interest thus being admitted through the back door. What makes the murabaha transaction Islamically legitimate is that the bank first acquires the asset and in the process it assumes certain risks between purchase and resale. The bank takes responsibility for the good before it is safely delivered to the client. The services rendered by the Islamic bank are therefore regarded as quite different from those of a conventional bank which simply lends money to the client to buy the good.

Islamic banks have also been resorting to purchase and resale of properties on a deferred payment basis, which is termed bai' muajjal. It is considered lawful in fiqh (jurisprudence) to charge a higher price for a good if payments are to be made at a later date. According to fiqh, this does not amount to charging interest, since it is not a lending transaction but a trading one.

Leasing or ijara is also frequently practised by Islamic banks. Under this mode, the banks would buy the equipment or machinery and lease it out to their clients who may opt to buy the items eventually, in which case the monthly payments will consist of two components, i.e., rental for the use of the equipment and instalment towards the purchase price.

Reference must also be made to pre-paid purchase of goods, which is termed bai'salam, as a means used by Islamic banks to finance production. Here the price is paid at the time of the contract but the delivery would take place at a future date. This mode enables an entrepreneur to sell his output to the bank at a price determined in advance. Islamic banks, in keeping with modern times, have extended this facility to manufactures as well.

It is clear from the above sketch that Islamic banking goes beyond the pure financing activities of conventional banks. Islamic banks engage in equity financing and trade financing. By its very nature, Islamic banking is a risky business compared with conventional banking, for risk-sharing forms the very basis of all Islamic financial transactions. To minimize risks, however, Islamic banks have taken pains to distribute the eggs over many baskets and have established reserve funds out of past profits which they can fall back on in the event of any major loss.

LITERATURE: THEORY

It is not possible to cover in this survey all the publications which have appeared on Islamic banking. There are numerous publications in Arabic and Urdu which have made significant contributions to the theoretical discussion. A brief description of these in English can be found in the Appendix to Siddiqi's book on Banking without Interest (Siddiqi 1983a). The early contributions on the subject of Islamic banking were somewhat casual in the sense that only passing references were made to it in the discussion of wider issues relating to the Islamic economic system as a whole. In other words, the early writers had been simply thinking aloud rather than presenting well-thought-out ideas. Thus, for example, the book by Qureshi on Islam and the Theory of Interest (Qureshi 1946) looked upon banking as a social service that should be sponsored by the government like public health and education. Qureshi took this point of view since the bank could neither pay any interest to account holders nor charge any interest on loans advanced. Qureshi also spoke of partnerships between banks and businessmen as a possible alternative, sharing losses if any. No mention was made of profit-sharing.

Ahmad, in Chapter VII of his book Economics of Islam (Ahmad 1952), envisaged the establishment of Islamic banks on the basis of a joint stock company with limited liability. In his scheme, in addition to current accounts, on which no dividend or interest should be paid, there was an account in which people could deposit their capital on the basis of partnership, with shareholders receiving higher dividends than the account holders from the profits made. Like Qureshi, above, Ahmad also spoke of possible partnership arrangements with the businessmen who seek capital from the banks. However, the partnership principle was left undefined, nor was it clear who would bear the loss if any. It was suggested that banks should cash bills of trade without charging interest, using the current account funds.

The principle of mudaraba based on Shariah was invoked systematically by Uzair (1955). His principal contribution lay in suggesting mudaraba as the main premise for 'interestless banking'. However, his argument that the bank should not make any capital investment with its own deposits rendered his analysis somewhat impractical.

Al-Arabi (1966) envisaged a banking system with mudaraba as the main pivot. He was actually advancing the idea of a two-tier mudaraba which would enable the bank to mobilize savings on a mudaraba basis, allocating the funds so mobilized also on a mudaraba basis. In other words the bank would act as a mudarib in so far as the depositors were concerned, while the 'borrowers' would act as mudaribs in so far as the bank was concerned. In his scheme, the bank could advance not only the capital procured through deposits but also the capital of its own shareholders. It is also of interest to note that his position with regard to the distribution of profits and the responsibility for losses was strictly in accordance with the Shariah.6 Irshad (1964) also spoke of mudaraba as the basis of Islamic banking, but his concept of mudaraba was quite different from the traditional one in that he thought of capital and labour (including entrepreneurship) as having equal shares in output, thus sharing the losses and profits equally. This actually means that the owner of capital and the entrepreneur have a fifty-fifty share in the profit or loss as the case may be, which runs counter to the Shariah position. Irshad envisaged two kinds of deposit accounts. The first sounded like current deposits in the sense that it would be payable on demand, but the money kept in this deposit would be used for social welfare projects, as the depositors would get zero return. The second one amounted to term deposits which would entitle the depositors to a share in the profits at the end of the year proportionately to the size and duration of the deposits. He recommended the setting up of a Reserve Fund which would absorb all losses so that no depositor would have to bear any loss. According to Irshad, all losses would be either recovered from the Reserve Fund or borne by the shareholders of the bank.

A pioneering attempt at providing a fairly detailed outline of Islamic banking was made in Urdu by Siddiqi in 1968. (The English version was not published until 1983.) His Islamic banking model was based on mudaraba and shirka (partnership or musharaka as it is now usually called). His model was essentially one based on a two-tier mudaraba financier-entrepreneur relationship, but he took pains to describe the mechanics of such transactions in considerable detail with numerous hypothetical and arithmetic examples. He classified the operations of an Islamic bank into three categories: services based on fees, commissions or other fixed charges; financing on the basis of mudaraba and partnership; and services provided free of charge. His thesis was that such interest-free banks could be a viable alternative to interest-based conventional banks.

The issue of loans for consumption clearly presents a problem, as there is no profit to be shared. Siddiqi addressed this problem, but he managed only to scratch the surface. While recognizing the need for such interest-free loans (qard hasan), especially for meeting basic needs, he seemed to think it was the duty of the community and the State (through its baitul mal or treasury) to cater to those needs; the Islamic bank's primary objective, like that of any other business unit, is to earn profit. He therefore tended to downplay the role of Islamic banks in providing consumption loans, but he suggested limited overdraft facilities without interest. He even considered a portion of the fund being set aside for consumption loans, repayment being guaranteed by the State. He also suggested that consumers buying durables on credit would issue 'certificates of sale' which could be encashed by the seller at the bank for a fee. It was then the seller not the buyer who would be liable as far as the bank was concerned. However, the principles of murabaha and bai' muajjal were not invoked.

Strangely, Siddiqi favoured keeping the number of shareholders to the minimum, without advancing any strong reasons. This is contrary to the general consensus which now seems to have emerged with reference to Islamic banks operating on a joint stock company basis, a consensus which incidentally is also in line with the Islamic value attached to a broad equity base as against heavy concentration of equity and wealth. Ironically, Siddiqi thought that interest-free banking could operate successfully 'only in a country where interest is legally prohibited and any transaction based upon interest is declared a punishable offense' (1983b:13). He also thought it important to have Islamic laws enforced before interest-free banking could operate well. This view has not gained acceptance, as demonstrated by the many Islamic banks which operate profitably in 'hostile' environments, as noted earlier.

Chapra's model of Islamic banking (Chapra 1982), like Siddiqi's, was based on the mudaraba principle. His main concern, however, centered on the role of artificial purchasing power through credit creation. He even suggested that 'seigniorage' resulting from it should be transferred to the public exchequer, for the sake of equity and justice. Al-Jarhi (1983) went so far as to favor the imposition of a 100 per cent reserve requirement on commercial banks. Chapra was also much concerned about the concentration of economic power private banks might enjoy in a system based on equity financing. He therefore preferred medium-sized banks which are neither so large as to wield excessive power nor so small as to be uneconomical. Chapra's scheme also contained proposals for loss-compensating reserves and loss-absorbing insurance facilities. He also spoke of non-bank financial institutions, which specialize in bringing financiers and entrepreneurs together and act as investment trusts.

Mohsin (1982) has presented a detailed and elaborate framework of Islamic banking in a modern setting. His model incorporates the characteristics of commercial, merchant, and development banks, blending them in novel fashion. It adds various non-banking services such as trust business, factoring, real estate, and consultancy, as though interest-free banks could not survive by banking business alone. Many of the activities listed certainly go beyond the realm of commercial banking and are of so sophisticated and specialized a nature that they may be thought irrelevant to most Muslim countries at their present stage of development. Mohsin's model clearly was designed to fit into a capitalist environment; indeed he explicitly stated that riba-free banks could coexist with interest-based banks. The point that there is more to Islamic banking than mere abolition of interest was driven home strongly by Chapra (1985). He envisaged Islamic banks whose nature, outlook and operations could be distinctly different from those of conventional banks. Besides the outlawing of riba, he considered it essential that Islamic banks should, since they handle public funds, serve the public interest rather than individual or group interests. In other words, they should play a social-welfare-oriented rather than a profit-maximizing role. He conceived of Islamic banks as a cross-breed of commercial and merchant banks, investment trusts and investment-management institutions that would offer a wide spectrum of services to their customers. Unlike conventional banks which depend heavily on the 'crutches of collateral and of non-participation in risk' (p. 155), Islamic banks would have to rely heavily on project evaluation, especially for equity-oriented financing. Thanks to the profit-and-loss sharing nature of the operations, bank-customer relations would be much closer and more cordial than is possible under conventional banking. Finally, the problems of liquidity shortage or surplus would have to be handled differently in Islamic banking, since the ban on interest rules out resort to the money market and the central bank. Chapra suggested alternatives such as reciprocal accommodation among banks without interest payments and creation of a common fund at the central bank into which surpluses would flow and from which shortages could be met without any interest charges.

The literature also discusses the question of central banking in an Islamic framework. The general opinion seems to be that the basic functions of a modern central bank are relevant also for an Islamic monetary system, although the mechanisms may have to be different. Thus, for example, the bank rate instrument cannot be used as it entails interest. Uzair (1982) has suggested adjustments in profit-sharing ratios as a substitute for bank rate manipulations by the central bank. Thus, credit can be tightened by reducing the share accruing to the businessmen and eased by increasing it. Siddiqi (1982) has suggested that variations in the so-called 'refinance ratio' (which refers to the central bank refinancing of a part of the interest-free loans provided by the commercial banks) would influence the quantum of short-term credit extended. Siddiqi has also proposed a prescribed 'lending ratio' (i.e., the proportion of demand deposits that commercial banks are obliged to lend out as interest-free loans) that can be adjusted by the central bank according to changing circumstances. In this context, reference may also be made to a proposal by Uzair (1982) that the central bank should acquire an equity stake in commercial banking by holding, say, 25 per cent of the capital stock of the commercial banks. The rationale behind this proposal was that it would give the central bank access to a permanent source of income so that it could effectively act as lender of last resort. The discussion of central banking in an Islamic context is somewhat scanty, presumably because Islamic central banking is viewed as too far-fetched an idea, except in Iran and Pakistan.

It emerges from all this that Islamic banking has three distinguishing features: (a) it is interest-free, (b) it is multi-purpose and not purely commercial, and (c) it is strongly equity-oriented. The literature contains hardly any serious criticism of the interest-free character of the operation, since this is taken for granted, although concerns have been expressed about the lack of adequate interest-free instruments. There is a near-consensus that Islamic banks can function well without interest. A recent International Monetary Fund study by Iqbal and Mirakhor (1987) has found Islamic banking to be a viable proposition that can result in efficient resource allocation. The study suggests that banks in an Islamic system face fewer solvency and liquidity risks than their conventional counterparts. The multi-purpose and extra-commercial nature of the Islamic banking operation does not seem to pose intractable problems. The abolition of interest makes it imperative for Islamic banks to look for other instruments, which renders operations outside the periphery of commercial banking unavoidable. Such operations may yield economies of scope. But it is undeniable that the multipurpose character of Islamic banking poses serious practical problems, especially in relation to the skills needed to handle such diverse and complex transactions (Iqbal and Mirakhor 1987).

The stress on equity-oriented transactions in Islamic banking, especially the mudaraba mode, has been criticized. It has been argued that the replacement of pre-determined interest by uncertain profits is not enough to render a transaction Islamic, since profit can be just as exploitative as interest is, if it is 'excessive' (Naqvi 1981).

Naqvi has also pointed out that there is nothing sacrosanct about the institution of mudaraba in Islam. Naqvi maintains that mudaraba is not based on the Qur'an or the Hadith but was a custom of the pre-Islamic Arabs. Historically, mudaraba, he contends, enabled the aged, women, and children with capital to engage in trade through merchants for a share in the profit, all losses being borne by the owners of capital, and therefore it cannot claim any sanctity. The fact remains that the Prophet raised no objection to mudaraba, so that it was at least not considered un-Islamic.

The distribution of profit in mudaraba transactions presents practical difficulties, especially where there are multiple providers of capital, but these difficulties are not regarded as insurmountable. The Report of Pakistan's Council of Islamic Ideology (CII 1983) has suggested that the respective capital contributions of parties can be converted to a common denominator by multiplying the amounts provided with the number of days during which each component, such as the firm's own equity capital, its current cash surplus and suppliers' credit was actually deployed in the business, i.e., on a daily product basis. As for deposits, profits (net of administrative expenses, taxes, and appropriation for reserves) would be divided between the shareholders of the bank and the holders of deposits, again on a daily product basis.

LITERATURE: PRACTICE

Recent years have brought an increasing flow of empirical studies of Islamic banking. The earliest systematic empirical work was undertaken by Khan (1983). His observations covered Islamic banks operating in Sudan, United Arab Emirates, Kuwait, Bahrain, Jordan, and Egypt. Khan's study showed that these banks had little difficulty in devising practices in conformity with Shariah.

He identified two types of investment accounts: one where the depositor authorized the banks to invest the money in any project and the other where the depositor had a say in the choice of project to be financed. On the asset side, the banks under investigation had been resorting to mudaraba, musharaka and murabaha modes. Khan's study reported profit rates ranging from 9 to 20 per cent which were competitive with conventional banks in the corresponding areas. The rates of return to depositors varied between 8 and 15 per cent, which were quite comparable with the rates of return offered by conventional banks.

Khan's study revealed that Islamic banks had a preference for trade finance and real estate investments. The study also revealed a strong preference for quick returns, which is understandable in view of the fact that these newly established institutions were anxious to report positive results even in the early years of operation. Nienhaus (1988) suggests that the relative profitability of Islamic banks, especially in the Middle East in recent years, was to a large extent due to the property (real estate) boom. He has cited cases of heavy losses which came with the crash of the property sector.

The IMF study referred to earlier by Iqbal and Mirakhor (1987) also contains extremely interesting empirical observations, although these are confined to the experience of Iran and Pakistan, both of which have attempted to islamize the entire banking system on a comprehensive basis. Iran switched to Islamic banking in August 1983 with a three-year transition period. The Iranian system allows banks to accept current and savings deposits without having to pay any return, but it permits the banks to offer incentives such as variable prizes or bonuses in cash or kind on these deposits. Term deposits (both short-term and long-term) earn a rate of return based on the bank's profits and on the deposit maturity. No empirical evidence is as yet available on the interesting question as to whether interest or a profit-share provides the more effective incentive to depositors for the mobilization of private saving. Where Islamic and conventional banks exist side by side, central bank control of bank interest rates is liable to be circumvented by shifts of funds to the Islamic banks.

Iqbal and Mirakhor have noted that the conversion to Islamic modes has been much slower on the asset than on the deposit side. It appears that the Islamic banking system in Iran was able to use less than half of its resources for credit to the private sector, mostly in the form of short-term facilities, i.e., commercial and trade transactions. The slower pace of conversion on the asset side was attributed by the authors to the inadequate supply of personnel trained in long-term financing. The authors, however, found no evidence to show that the effectiveness of monetary policy in Iran, broadly speaking, was altered by the conversion.

The Pakistani experience differs from the Iranian one in that Pakistan had opted for a gradual islamization process which began in 1979. In the first phase, which ended on 1 January 1985, domestic banks operated both interest- free and interest-based 'windows'. In the second phase of the transformation process, the banking system was geared to operate all transactions on the basis of no interest, the only exceptions being foreign currency deposits, foreign loans and government debts. The Pakistani model took care to ensure that the new modes of financing did not upset the basic functioning and structure of the banking system. This and the gradual pace of transition, according to the authors, made it easier for the Pakistani banks to adapt to the new system. The rate of return on profit-and-loss sharing (PLS) deposits appears not only to have been in general higher than the interest rate before islamization but also to have varied between banks, the differential indicating the degree of competition in the banking industry. The authors noted that the PLS system and the new modes of financing had accorded considerable flexibility to banks and their clients. Once again the study concluded that the effectiveness of monetary policy in Pakistan was not impaired by the changeover.

The IMF study, however, expressed considerable uneasiness about the concentration of bank assets on short-term trade credits rather than on long-term financing. This the authors found undesirable, not only because it is inconsistent with the intentions of the new system, but also because the heavy concentration on a few assets might increase risks and destabilize the asset portfolios. The study also drew attention to the difficulty experienced in both Iran and Pakistan in financing budget deficits under a non-interest system and underscored the urgent need to devise suitable interest-free instruments. Iran has, however, decreed that government borrowing on the basis of a fixed rate of return from the nationalized banking system would not amount to interest and would hence be permissible. The official rationalization is that, since all banks are nationalized, interest rates and payments among banks will cancel out in the consolidated accounts. (This, of course, abstracts from the banks' business with non-bank customers.) There are also some small case studies of Islamic banks operating in Bangladesh (Huq 1986), Egypt (Mohammad 1986), Malaysia (Halim 1988b), Pakistan (Khan 1986), and Sudan (Salama 1988b). These studies reveal interesting similarities and differences. The current accounts in all cases are operated on the principles of al-wadiah. Savings deposits, too, are accepted on the basis of al-wadiah, but 'gifts' to depositors are given entirely at the discretion of the Islamic banks on the minimum balance, so that the depositors also share in profits. Investment deposits are invariably based on the mudaraba principle, but there are considerable variations. Thus, for example, the Islamic Bank of Bangladesh has been offering PLS Deposit Accounts, PLS Special Notice Deposit Accounts, and PLS Term Deposit Accounts, while Bank Islam Malaysia has been operating two kinds of investment deposits, one for the general public and the other for institutional clients.

The studies also show that the profit-sharing ratios and the modes of payment vary from place to place and from time to time. Thus, for example, profits are provisionally declared on a monthly basis in Malaysia, on a quarterly basis in Egypt, on a half-yearly basis in Bangladesh and Pakistan, and on an annual basis in Sudan.

A striking common feature of all these banks is that even their investment deposits are mostly short-term, reflecting the depositors' preference for assets in as liquid a form as possible. Even in Malaysia, where investment deposits have accounted for a much larger proportion of the total, the bulk of them were made for a period of less than two years. By contrast, in Sudan most of the deposits have consisted of current and savings deposits, apparently because of the ceiling imposed by the Sudanese monetary authorities on investment deposits which in turn was influenced by limited investment opportunities in the domestic economy. There are also interesting variations in the pattern of resource utilization by the Islamic banks. For example, musharaka has been far more important than murabaha as an investment mode in Sudan, while the reverse has been the case in Malaysia. On the average, however, murabaha, bai'muajjal and ijara, rather than musharaka represent the most commonly used modes of financing. The case studies also show that the structure of the clientele has been skewed in favor of the more affluent segment of society, no doubt because the banks are located mainly in metropolitan centres with small branch networks.

The two main problems identified by the case studies are the absence of suitable non-interest-based financial instruments for money and capital market transactions and the high rate of borrower delinquency. The former problem has been partially redressed by Islamic banks resorting to mutual inter-bank arrangements and central bank cooperation, as mentioned earlier. The Bank Islam Malaysia, for instance, has been placing its excess liquidity with the central bank which usually exercises its discretionary powers to give some returns. The delinquency problem appears to be real and serious. Murabaha payments have often been held up because late payments cannot be penalized, in contrast to the interest system in which delayed payments would automatically mean increased interest payments. To overcome this problem, the Pakistani banks have resorted to what is called 'mark-down' which is the opposite of 'mark-up' (i.e., the profit margin in the cost-plus approach of murabaha transactions). 'Mark-down' amounts to giving rebates as an incentive for early payments. But the legitimacy of this 'mark-down' practice is questionable on Shariah grounds, since it is time- based and therefore smacks of interest.

In the Southeast Asian context, two recent studies on the Bank Islam Malaysia by Man (1988) and the Philippine Amanah Bank by Mastura (1988) deserve special mention. The Malaysian experience in Islamic banking has been encouraging. Man's study shows that the average return to depositors has been quite competitive with that offered by conventional banks. By the end of 1986, after three years of operation, the bank had a network of fourteen branches. However, 90 per cent of its deposits had maturities of two years or less, and non-Muslim depositors accounted for only 2 per cent of the total. Man is particularly critical of the fact that the mudaraba and musharaka modes of operation, which are considered most meaningful by Islamic scholars, accounted for a very small proportion of the total investment portfolio, while bai'muajjal and ijara formed the bulk of the total. It is evident from Mastura's analysis that the Philippine Amanah Bank is, strictly speaking, not an Islamic bank, as interest-based operations continue to coexist with Islamic modes of financing. Thus, the PAB has been operating both interest and Islamic 'windows' for deposits. Mastura's study has produced evidence to show that the PAB has been concentrating on murabaha transactions, paying hardly any attention to the mudaraba and musharaka means of financing. The PAB has also been adopting unorthodox approaches in dealing with excess liquidity by making use of interest- bearing treasury bills. Nonetheless, the PAB has also been invoking some Islamic modes in several major investment activities. Mastura has made special references to the qirad principle adopted by the PAB in the Kilu-sang Kabuhayan at Kaunlaran (KKK) movement launched under Marcos and to the ijara financing for the acquisition of farm implements and supplies in the Quedon food production program undertaken by the present regime. So far no reference has been made to Indonesia, the largest Muslim country in the world, with Muslims accounting for 90 per cent of a population of some 165 million. The explanation is that a substantial proportion, especially in Java, are arguably nominal Muslims. Indonesians by and large subscribe to the Pancasila ideology which is essentially secular in character. The present regime seems to associate Islamic banking with Islamic fundamentalism to which the regime is not at all sympathetic. Besides, the intellectual tradition in Indonesia in modern times has not been conducive to the idea of interest-free banking. There were several well respected Indonesian intellectuals including Hatta (the former Vice President) who had argued that riba prohibited in Islam was not the same as interest charged or offered by modern commercial banks, although Islamic jurists in Indonesia hold the opposite view. The Muslim public seems somewhat indifferent to all this. This, however, does not mean that there are no interest-free financial institutions operating in Indonesia. One form of traditional interest-free borrowing is the still widely prevalent form of informal rural credit known as ijon (green) because the loan is secured on the standing crop as described by Partadireja (1974). Another is the arisan system practiced among consumers and small craftsmen and traders. In this system, each member contributes regularly a certain sum and obtains interest-free loans from the pool by drawing lots. The chances of an Islamic bank being established in Indonesia seem at present remote (cf. Rahardjo 1988).

Finally, in the most recent contribution to the growing Islamic banking literature, Nien-haus (1988) concludes that Islamic banking is viable at the microeconomic level but dismisses the proponents' ideological claims for superiority of Islamic banking as 'unfounded'. Nienhaus points out that there are some failure stories. Examples cited include the Kuwait Finance House which had its fingers burned by investing heavily in the Kuwaiti real estate and construction sector in 1984, and the Islamic Bank International of Denmark which suffered heavy losses in 1985 and 1986 to the tune of more than 30 per cent of its paid-up capital. But then, as Nienhaus himself has noted, the quoted troubles of individual banks had specific causes and it would be inappropriate to draw general conclusions from particular cases. Nienhaus notes that the high growth rates of the initial years have been falling off, but he rejects the thesis that the Islamic banks have reached their 'limits of growth' after filling a market gap. The falling growth rates might well be due to the bigger base values, and the growth performance of Islamic banks has been relatively better in most cases than that of conventional banks in recent years.

According to Nienhaus, the market shares of many Islamic banks have increased over time, notwithstanding the deceleration in the growth of deposits. The only exception was the Faisal Islamic Bank of Sudan (FIBS) whose market share had shrunk from 15 per cent in 1982 to 7 per cent in 1986, but Nien-haus claims that the market shares lost by FIBS were won not by conventional banks but by newer Islamic banks in Sudan. Short-term trade financing has clearly been dominant in most Islamic banks regardless of size. This is contrary to the expectation that the Islamic banks would be active mainly in the field of corporate financing on a participation basis. Nien-haus attributes this not only to insufficient supply by the banks but also to weak demand by entrepreneurs who may prefer fixed interest cost to sharing their profits with the banks.

CONCLUSION

The preceding discussion makes it clear that Islamic banking is not a negligible or merely temporary phenomenon. Islamic banks are here to stay and there are signs that they will continue to grow and expand. Even if one does not subscribe to the Islamic injunction against the institution of interest, one may find in Islamic banking some innovative ideas which could add more variety to the existing financial network.

One of the main selling points of Islamic banking, at least in theory, is that, unlike conventional banking, it is concerned about the viability of the project and the profitability of the operation but not the size of the collateral. Good projects which might be turned down by conventional banks for lack of collateral would be financed by Islamic banks on a profit-sharing basis. It is especially in this sense that Islamic banks can play a catalytic role in stimulating economic development. In many developing countries, of course, development banks are supposed to perform this function. Islamic banks are expected to be more enterprising than their conventional counterparts. In practice, however, Islamic banks have been concentrating on short-term trade finance which is the least risky.

Part of the explanation is that long-term financing requires expertise which is not always available. Another reason is that there are no back-up institutional structures such as secondary capital markets for Islamic financial instruments. It is possible also that the tendency to concentrate on short-term financing reflects the early years of operation: it is easier to administer, less risky, and the returns are quicker. The banks may learn to pay more attention to equity financing as they grow older.

It is sometimes suggested that Islamic banks are rather complacent. They tend to behave as though they had a captive market in the Muslim masses who will come to them on religious grounds. This complacency seems more pronounced in countries with only one Islamic bank. Many Muslims find it more convenient to deal with conventional banks and have no qualms about shifting their deposits between Islamic banks and conventional ones depending on which bank offers a better return. This might suggest a case for more Islamic banks in those countries as it would force the banks to be more innovative and competitive. Another solution would be to allow the conventional banks to undertake equity financing and/or to operate Islamic 'counters' or 'windows', subject to strict compliance with the Shariah rules. It is perhaps not too wild a proposition to suggest that there is a need for specialized Islamic financial institutions such as mudaraba banks, murabaha banks and musharaka banks which would compete with one another to provide the best possible services.

6

Banking in Retrospect

The word "Bank" is of a European origin and is derived from the Italian word "BANCO", which means a table or a counter. In the opinion of the eminent scholars of banking, the reason why this word was given to the banking business was the then prevailing traditions of Lombardian money changers. It was at the end of the middle ages when the trade and the business of exchange of money was flourishing in the Northern cities of Italy and the money changers used the wooden benches to carry out their business in the markets of buying and selling of various currencies.

It will be no use to involve the origin of the word "BANK". It, however, found its way through the passage of various conditions prevailing at various stages. Banking, however, did not become a coordinated and systematized business. It has evolved and developed according to the conditions and requirements ever since. A through study of subject will reveal that modern banking is not very much different with its past, and therefore, it would, no doubt, be useful to have a general comprehension of the methods which were practiced in this field in the ancient days. What we would like to derive from the discussion and the historical review of the subject is to try to unveil certain aspects which may be useful while comparing the current banking business with the era of evolution of banking.

It is a difficult task to establish the first starting point of the banking business, but one thing is clear that the money as means of exchange at the beginning of organized agriculture, industry and trade gave birth to the banking transaction first and then converted the scattered money transaction into an organized shape. The conditions needed for the growth of the system are the development of civilization, its stability and the environment in which the confidence grows and trade flourishes. The first were the cultures of Sumerians and Babylonians under which the various activities were quite different in the form and appearances, were introduced in the banking system.

The Greeks, in the early stages, had almost the similar banking activities to that of Babylonians. At that time the sacred temples were the most popular place of banking operations but did not monopolize it totally. The financial activities like accepting deposits giving loans, checking and exchanging money and making remittances between different cities, to minimize the risk of carrying money were being carried out during 4th Century B.C.

The Romans, when appeared on the horizon of a new civilization, served their apprenticeship in the art of banking under the Greeks and altogether changed the banking procedure in most of the ancient world along with the expansion of their influence. After the fall of Roman Empire till the dawn of Islam the world passed through the darkest period and faced the most corrupt and unsettled conditions known in the history of Banking.

With the dawn of Islam, the darkness was removed from the face of life and the environment of security and stability re-established in the areas which came under the influence of Islam. Islam came as a religion for the guidance of the misled humanity and to rectify the deviation of belief, to establish justice and to guide life to righteousness and goodness. For a better understanding of the above principles the ban on usury (RIBA) was necessary for the way of life. Islam introduced in the society which was aimed to honor and provide protection from being ether the oppressor or the oppressed.

MODERN BANKING

The banking which was known in various forms and guises in the ancient civilization in various parts of the world did not coincide with the emergence of the modern Banks. The banking which had its roots in the flourished culture and had lost its required effectiveness regained the strength with the development of the modern banking.

The development of modern banking operations began when the trade in the cities of North Italy flourished due to the advantage of their locations, as they were situated near the passes of Alps and were being used as trade routes. Thus the birth of the modern banking took place in the same area which had witnessed the burial of the ancient relations of cultures of this field. Probably this might be the reason the name of first bank was given as "BANCO" which means the wooden desks.

The money changers of Lombardia used to sit behind their wooden desks and, therefore, the place became known as Banco. At a later stage, this word became closely connected with banking title in the current age. Lombardia, Geneva and Milano became famous but Florence and Venice excelled. The various conditions and factors which were responsible for the slow beginning in the development of banking in the early period had a significant effect on giving banking operations a form which was pragmatic. It was because of the various laws which remained inconsistent, reflecting the difference and disparity of the points of view of the various legislation on this subjects.

FACTORS

The increase in the quantum of the commercial dealing led to the re-emergence of banking operations at the end of Medieval ages. The banking business, therefore, started flourishing in the cities of the Northern Italy, where a section of people emerged who indulged in the exchange, verification and the ascertainment of various kinds of metal currencies having different weights, types and purifies. The widespread commercial transaction, due to the increase in the trade, gave birth to the traders in money who were given the name of money exchangers. The banking operation thus became dependent on these professionals. The money changers gradually linked the banking operations with commercial operations which paved the ground for the prosperity of the banking subsequently. With the passage of time the relationship of banking operations with the commercial operations developed to the extent that the survival of these two operations became interdependent on each other for subsequent centuries. This dependency of the banking activities gave commercial prosperity to the European countries one after another. Moving from Italy it entered into Spain and Holland, until it settled in England. The stability and the isolation of this country became the nursery of the newly-born banking system and provided the opportunity to play the role of being the pioneer of the modern banking in the new era.

BANKING ORGANIZATION IN PAKISTAN

Pakistan's financial sector consists of Scheduled Commercial Banks which include nationalized, foreign, and private banks; and Non-banking Financial Institutions (NBFIs) which include Development Finance Institutions (DFIs), Investment Banks, leasing companies, modarabas, and housing finance companies.

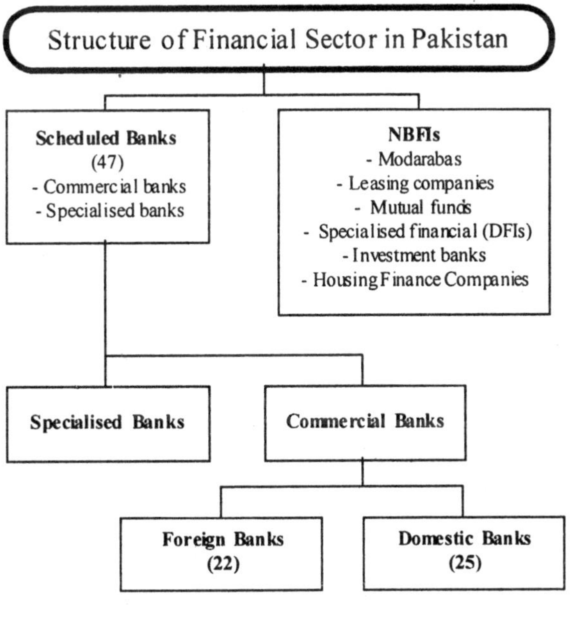

Scheduled Banks and NBFIs (excluding modaraba and leasing companies) are both regulated by the State Bank of Pakistan's Prudential Regulations, albeit through different wings, and are subject to different SBP regulatory requirements such as capital and liquidity reserve requirements. Modaraba and leasing companies are being regulated by the Securities and Exchange Commission of Pakistan (formerly Corporate Law Authority), which is a body corporate. Compared to commercial banks which cater mostly to short term working capital requirements, NBFIs cater to medium and long term financing needs and, thus, are barred from engaging in any commercial banking activities including trade business and issuing cheques. However, the SBP allowed commercial banks to undertake long term project lending. Among the scheduled banks, only Pakistani commercial banks are listed.

BRIEF HISTORY

Prior to partition in 1947, banking in Pakistan was dominated by branches of British banks. The State Bank of Pakistan, the central bank, was formed after partition in 1948. It assumed the supervisory and monetary policy powers of the State Bank of India. In the period of 60s to 70s the emergence of a number of specialized development finance institutions (DFIs) such as Industrial Development Bank of Pakistan (IDBP) and the Agricultural Development Bank (ADB). These DFIs were either controlled directly by the state or through the SBP, and were intended to concentrate on specific priority sector lending. In 1974 all domestic commercial banks were nationalized by the Government.

The Pakistan Banking Council was established, which assumed the role of a banking holding company but with limited supervisory powers. However, PBC was dissolved in 1997, leaving the SBP as the sole regulatory authority for banks and financial institutions in Pakistan. Nationalization of the banking sector led to pet projects. The branch network of NCBs also proliferated in an effort to provide banking services to all regions/territories of the country, often with disregard to the viability or feasibility of such expansion.

CHANGES INTRODUCED IN BANKING SYSTEM

It should be kept in mind that Pakistan despite formulating good policies has not been able to attain the desired results mainly due to poor implementation of the polices.

- Deregulation of the financial sector and capital markets led to mushrooming growth of banking companies in the private sector. Several big industrial groups set up their own banks, which to date remain relatively small compared to the NCBs and other larger foreign banks. The new banking sector reforms have also stripped the government of its powers to interfere in a bank's operations. e.g., by issuing SROs and/or by influencing appointment of directors and other higher level management officers. All such powers now rest with the SBP only, thereby significantly reducing political influence/intervention in financial institutions and, hence, credit quality.

- After the change the SBP has taken a number of steps to introduce professional management in the nationalized banks. The strategy of the SBP is to, first improve the quality of new loans and then to tackle the non-performing loans problems. All nationalized banks have been asked to curtail their overheads, especially the head counts. Professionals from the private sector have been appointed as Presidents to improve the health of nationalized banks and make them more attractive for privatization.
- The SBP has completely revamped the disclosure laws and introduced a highly informative new format for presenting annual accounts of banks. Under the new format, banks would now have to provide details about bad loans, the level of provisioning held, maturity profile as well as the currency breakdown of both assets and liabilities, and details of transactions with associated companies.
- Interest rate has been under pressure since 1997. The SBP has been coercing banks, specially nationalized commercial banks to lower their mark-up rates. A number of NCBs have announced a reduction in maximum mark-up rates, ranging from 2% to over 5%. Yield on government securities have also been driven down to just over 16% to 17.5%.
- The new military coup's government seems to be relying on a lower interest rate environment to spur domestic industrial activity. The intention is to cut mark-up rates, to make working capital more affordable. Banks have been straining under the burden of non-performing loans and low capitalization, and unable to step up lending activities in the recent past. Banks have concentrated on building up provisions. However, the weakness in interest rates is expected to continue. With interest rates set to weaken further the spreads is likely to improve. Large banks with widespread networks would be ideally suited to leverage-off their traditional cost advantage to capture cheap deposits. Profitability is expected to improve dramatically for the banking sector.

The banking sector in Pakistan has been going through a comprehensive but complex and painful process of restructuring since 1997. It is aimed at making these institutions financially sound and forging their links firmly with the real sector for promotion of savings, investment and growth. Although a complete turnaround in banking sector performance is not expected till the completion of reforms, signs of improvement are visible. The almost simultaneous nature of various factors makes it difficult to disentangle signs of improvement and deterioration.

Commercial banks have been exposed and withstood several types of pressure since 1997. Some of these are: **1)** multipronged reforms introduced by thje central bank, **2)** freezing of foreign currency accounts, **3)** continued stagnation in economic activities and low growth and **4)** drive for accountability and loan recovery. All these have brought a behavioral change both among the borrowers as well as the lenders. The risk aversion has been more pronounced than warranted.

Commercial banks operating in Pakistan can be divided into four categories: **1)** Nationalized Commercial Banks (NCBs), **2)** Privatized Banks, **3)** Private Banks and **4)** Foreign Banks. While preparing this report efforts have been made to evaluate the performance of each group which enjoy certain strengths and weaknesses as per procedure followed by State Bank of Pakistan (SBP). The central bank has been following a supervisory framework, CAMEL, which involves the analysis of six indicators which reflect the financial health of financial institutions. These are: **1)** Capital Adequacy, **2)** Asset Quality, **3)** Management Soundness, **4)** Earnings and Profitability, **5)** Liquidity and **6)** Sensitivity to Market Risk.

Capital Adequacy

To protect the interest of depositors as well as shareholders, SBP introduced the risk based system for capital adequacy in late 1998. Banks are required to maintain 8 per cent capital to Risk Weighted Assets (CRWA) ratio. Banks were required to achieve a minimum paid-up capital to Rs. 500 million by December 31, 1998. This requirement has been raised to one billion rupee and banks have been given a deadline up to January 1, 2003 to comply with this.

The ratio has deteriorated after 1998. However, it was fallout of economic sanctions imposed on Pakistan after it conducted nuclear tests. The shift in SBP policy regarding investment in securities also led to a fall in ratio. However, most of the banks have been able to maintain above the desired ratio as well as direct their investment towards more productive private sector advances. Higher provisioning against non-performing loans (NPLs) has also contributed to this decline. However, this is considered a positive development.

Asset Quality

Asset quality is generally measured in relation to the level and severity of non-performing assets, recoveries, adequacy of provisions and distribution of assetsj. Although, the banking system is infected with large volume of NPLs, its severity has stabilized to some extent. The rise over the years was due to increase in volume of NPLs following enforcement of more vigorous standards for classifying loans, improved reporting and disclosure requirements adopted by the SBP.

In case of NCBs this improvement is much more pronounced given their share in total NPLs. In case of privatized and private banks, this ratio went up considerably and become a cause of concern. However, the level of infection in foreign banks is not only the lowest but also close to constant.

The ratio of net NPLs to net advances, another indicator of asset quality, for all banks has declined. Marked improvement is viable in recovery efforts of banks. This has been remarkable in the case of NCBs, in terms of reduction in the ratio of loan defaults to gross advances. Although, privatized banks do not show significant improvement, their ratio is much lower than that of NCBs. Only exception is the group of private banks for which the ratio has gone up due to bad performance of some of the banks in the group. However, it is still the lower, except when compared with that of foreign banks.

Management Soundness

Given the qualitative nature of management, it is difficult to judge its soundness just by looking at financial accounts of the banks. Nevertheless, total expenditure to total income and operating expenses to total expenses help in gauging the management quality of any commercial bank.

Pressure on earnings and profitability of foreign and private banks caused their expenditure to income ratio to rise in 1998. However, it started tapering down as they adjusted their portfolios. An across the board increase in administrative expenses to total expenditure is visible from the year 1999. The worst performers in this regard are the privatized banks, mostly because of high salaries and allowances.

Earnings and Profitability

Strong earnings and profitability profile of banks reflects the ability to support present and future operations. More specifically, this determines the capacity to absorb losses, finance its expansion programme, pay dividend to its shareholders and build up adequate level of capital. Being front line of defense against erosion of capital base from losses, the need for high earnings and profitability can hardly be overemphasized. Although different indicators are used to serve the purpose, the best and most widely used indicator is return on assets (ROA). Net interest margin is also used. Since NCBs have significantly large share in the banking sector, their performance overshadows the other banks. However, profit earned by this group resulted in positive value of ROA of banking sector during 2000, despite losses suffered by ABL.

Pressure on earnings was most visible in case of foreign banks in 1998. The stress on earnings and profitability was inevitable despite the steps taken by the SBP to improve liquidity. Not only did liquid assets to total assets ratio declined sharply, earning assets to total assets also fell. T-Bill portfolio of banks declined considerably, as they were less remunerative. Foreign currency deposits became less attractive due to the rise in forward cover charged by the SBP. Banks reduced return on deposits to maintain their spread. However, they were not able to contain the decline in ROA due to declining stock and remuneration of their earning assets.

Liquidity

Movement in liquidity indicators since 1997 indicates the painful process of adjustments. Ratio of liquid assets to total assets has been on a constant decline. This was consciously brought about by the monetary policy changes by the SBP to manage the crisis-like situation created after 1998. Both the cash reserve requirement ((CRR) and the statutory liquidity requirement (SLR) were reduced in 1999. These steps were reinforced by declines in SBP's discount rate and T-Bill yields to help banks manage rupee withdrawals and still meet the credit requirement of the private sector.

Foreign banks have gone through this adjustment much more quickly than other banks. Their decline in liquid assets to total assets ratio, as well as the rise in loan to deposit ratio, are much steeper than other groups. Trend in growth of deposits shows that most painful part of the adjustment is over. This is reflected in the reversal of decelerating deposit growth into accelerating one in year 2000.

Sensitivity to Market Risk

Rate sensitive assets have diverged from rate sensitive liabilities in absolute terms since 1997. The negative gap has widened. Negative value indicates comparatively higher risk sensitivity towards liability side, while decline in interest rates may prove beneficial.

Deposit Mobilization

Deposit mobilization has dwindled considerably after 1997. Deposits as a proportion of GDP have been going down. Growth rate of overall deposits of banks has gone down. However, the slow down seems to have been arrested and reversed in year 2000.

Group-wise performance of deposit mobilization is the reflection of the varying degree with which each group has been affected since 1998. Foreign banks were affected the most due to their heavy reliance of foreign currency deposits. They experience 14 per cent erosion in 1999. However, they were able to achieve over 2 per cent growth in year 2000. Similar recovery was shown by private banks.

Deposit mobilization by NCBs seems to be waning after discontinuation of their rupee deposit schemes linked with lottery prizes. Growths in their deposits were on the decline. Despite the decline NCBs control a large share in total deposits. Aggressive posture of private banks in mobilizing more deposits in year 2000 is clearly reflected in their deposit growth, from 1.9 per cent in year 1999 to 21.7 per cent in year 2000. This has also helped them in increasing their share in total deposits to over 14 per cent in year 2000.

Due to the shift in policy, now banks are neither required nor have the option to place their foreign currency deposits with the SBP. Although, the growth in foreign currency deposits increases the deposit base, it does not add to their rupee liquidity. The increasing share of foreign currency deposits in total base is a worrying development. In order to check this trend, SBP made it compulsory for the banks not to allow foreign currency deposits to exceed 20 per cent of their rupee deposits effective from January 1, 2002.

Credit Extension

Bulk of the advances extended by banks is for working capital which is self-liquidating in nature. However, due to an easing in SBP's policy, credit extension has exceeded deposit mobilization. This is reflected in advances growing at 12.3 per cent in year 1j999 and 14 per cent in year 2000.

Group-wise performance of banks in credit extension reveals three distinct features. 1) Foreign banks curtailed their lending, 2) continued dominance by NCBs and 3) aggressive approach being followed by private banks. Private Banks were the only group that not only maintained their growth in double-digit but also pushed it to over 31 per cent in year 2000. With this high growth, they have surpassed foreign banks, in terms of their share in total advances in year 2000.

Banking Spreads

Over the years there has been a declining trend both in lending and deposit rates. Downward trend in lending rates was due to SBP policy. The realized trend in lending rates was in line with monetary objectives of SBP, though achieved with lags following the sharp reduction in T-Bill yields in year 1999, needed to induce required change in investment portfolio of banks.

Downward trend in deposit rates was almost inevitable. One can argue that banks should have maintained, if not increased, their deposit rates to arrest declining growth in total deposits. However, this was not possible at times of eroding balance sheet; steady earnings were of prime importance. Consequently banks tried to find creative ways of mobilizing deposits at low rates. However, due to inefficiencies of the large banks, the spread has remained high.

Asset Composition

Assets of banking sector, as per cent of GDP, have been on the decline. Slowdown in asset growth was also accompanied by changing share of different groups. Negative growth in the assets of foreign banks during 1998 and 1999 was the prime reason behind declining growth in overall assets of the banking sector. Share of NCBs have been decreasing since private banks were allowed to operate in 1992. In terms of asset share, private banks are now as large as foreign banks.

Problem Bank Management

The central bank is the sole authority to supervise, monitor and regulate financial institutions. It is also responsible to safeguard the interest of depositors and shareholders of these institutions. Lately, SBP took actions against two private banks which became a threat to viability of the financial system in the country. These were Indus Bank and Prudential Commercial Bank. On the basis of detailed investigations, the license of Indus Bank was cancelled on September 11, 2000. After successful negotiations, management and control of Prudential Bank handed over to Saudi-Pak group.

Outlook

Commercial banks have been going through the process of restructuring. There are efforts to reduce lending rates. The SBP has been successful in implementing its policies. Most of the banks have been able to adjust to new working environment. The proposed increase in capital base will provide further impetus to financial system in the country.

In the post September 11 era, the GoP borrowing from SBP and commercial banks is expected to come down substantially and private sector borrowing to increase. However, a temporary decline in repayment ability of borrowers may increase provisioning for the year 2001. The situation is expected to improve in year 2002.

Unless efforts are made by banks to shrink spread, depositors will not be able to get return which corresponds with the rate of inflation in the country.

Privatization of NCBs is expected to be delayed due to external factors. However, it is an opportunity for the banks to further clean their slate.

FUNCTIONS OF COMMERCIAL BANKING

Scheduled commercial banks in Pakistan which include nationalized, foreign, and private banks are operating in accordance with the provision of the Banking Companies Ordinance, 1962. Under the Banking Companies Ordinance, the legislators tried to classify the functions of commercial banks as:

(i) Development of resources which include accepting the deposits in various types of account whether they are demand or time deposits;

(ii) Credits and investments operations. In this group we include the loans given to the clients of the bank on short and long term. The investment operations means where the bank invests part of its own assets or of deposits of its clients in buying securities which are often in the form of Bonds, Certificates of Bills issued mostly by the State. Though not in the strict sense, this also includes the guarantees of various types which sometimes end in financial transactions; and

(iii) Ancillary operations which consist of collecting of cheques, handling of negotiable instruments, transfer of money from one place to another whether within or outside the country, opening of letters of credit, local or international, and leasing out the safe deposit lockers.

(iv) Other several aspects of banking operations are accepting of deposits, transactions relating to transfer of funds, various types of collections and many others.

Subsequently, the banking operations are classified into three groups:

- Commercial operations took the first place which is further divided into several divisions.
- Financial operations which are relevant to long or short term investment such as participation in industrial projects, issue of shares, debentures and other instruments of companies.
- Service and commission operations which cover a variety of operations among which are:

- Safekeeping operations i.e., safe deposits lockers.
- Management of service operations of the customers.
- Providing the financial information to the clients.
- Creating a link between the stock exchanges and the customers for exchange operations.

THE BANKER'S FUND

The funds available to a banker for the purpose of his business comprises of the following:

1 Banker's own paid up capital, the reserve fund and liquid assets.

2 Money received from depositors in current, fixed and term deposits.

Bank's Capital

The amount with which a banking company in Pakistan has been registered is called the nominal or authorized capital. It is further divided into paid up and subscribed capital. Banking company's ordinance 1962, further lays down that no banking company shall carry on business in Pakistan unless it satisfied the following conditions:

i The subscribed capital of the company is not less than one half of the authorized capital and the paid up capital is not less than one half of the subscribed capital.

ii The capital of the company should consist of ordinary shares only.

iii The voting right of the shares holders should be strictly in proportion with the share holders contributions to the paid up capital of the company.

The Reserve Fund

This fund consists of accumulated undivided trading profits set aside for contingencies and any un usual call upon the bank's resources. In the case of many Pakistani banks the reserve fund has approached in amount more than the paid-up capital.

Section 21 of the Banking Companies Ordinance, 1962, has made it obligatory for the every banking company incorporated in Pakistan to create a reserve fund.

Liquid Assets

According to Section 29 (1) of the Banking Companies Ordinance, 1962, every bank in Pakistan is under legal obligation to maintain liquid in Pakistan. This amount should be such percentage of the total demand and time liabilities of the bank as may be notified by the State bank of Pakistan from time to time. These liquids assets should be maintained in Pakistan in cash-on-hand and balances with the State bank of Pakistan, money at call and short notice, bill discounted, gold and billion, debentures, securities issued by the semi Govt. agencies, guaranteed by the Federal or Provincial Governments in Pakistan as also approved foreign exchange.

Deposits: The Life-Blood of a Bank

In modern times, very few business enterprises are carried out solely with the capital of owners. Borrowing funds from different sources has become an essential feature of today's business enterprise. But in the case of a bank, borrowing funds from outside parties is all the more vital because of the entire banking system is based on it. The borrowed capital of a bank is much greater than their own capital. Bank's borrowing is mostly in the form of deposits. These deposits are lent out to different parties. The larger are difference between the rate at which these deposits are borrowed and the rate at which they are lent out, the greater will be the profit margin of the bank. Furthermore, the larger the deposits the larger will be the funds available for employment; larger the funds lent out the greater will be the profits of the bank. It is because of this inter-related relationship that deposits are referred to as the "life blood" of a bank.

To receive deposits is one of the basic functions of all Commercial banks. Commercial banks do not receive these deposits for safe-keeping purpose only, but they accept deposits as debts. When a bank receives a deposit from a customer, the relationship of a debtor and creditor is established whereby the customer becomes the creditor, and the bank a debtor. When the bank receives the amount of deposit as a debtor, it becomes the owner of it. It may, therefore, use it as it deems appropriate. Bur there is an implicit agreement that the amount owned will be paid back by the bank to the depositor on demand or after a specified time.

Nature of Deposits

Bank deposits can be broadly classified as Current Deposits, Fixed Deposits or Term Deposits and Saving Deposits.

This classification is based on the duration and purpose for which the deposits are to kept at the bank before they can withdrawn by the depositors.

Current Deposits

These are payable to the customer whenever they are demanded. When a banker accepts a demand deposit, he incurs the obligation of paying all cheques etc. drawn against him to the extent of the balance in the account. Because of their nature, these deposits are treated as current liabilities by the banks. Bankers in Pakistan do not allow any profit on these deposits, and customers are required to maintain a minimum balance, failing which, incidental charges are deducted from such accounts. This is because Current Deposits may be withdrawn by the depositors at any time, and as such the bank is not entirely free to employ such deposits.

Until a few decades back, the proportion of Current Deposits in relation to Term Deposits was very small. In recent years, however, the position has changed remarkably. Now, the Current Deposits have become very important; but still the proportion of Current Deposits and Term Deposits varies from bank to bank, branch to branch, and from time to time.

Fixed or Term Deposits

The deposits that can be withdrawn after a specified period of time are referred to as Fixed or Term Deposits. The period for which these deposits are kept by the bank ordinarily varies from three months to five years in accordance with the agreement made between the customer and the banker. Profit/Return is paid to the depositors on all Fixed or Time Deposits, and the rate of profit/return varies with the duration for which the amount is kept with the banker. In Pearce *v* Creswick (1843), it was held that a banker continuous to be a debtor even after expiry of the fixed time. Many depositors keep their money in Term Deposits with banks as an investment because of the profit/return paid on them. The depositors are issued a receipt, usually an instrument marked "Not Negotiable" but it was never been recognized as negotiable.

Since Fixed or Term Deposits remain with the bank for a specified period, they can be profitably employed. By lending out or investing these funds, the bank earns more than the profit/return that it has to pay on them to the depositors.

Payment of Fixed/Term Deposits before Maturity

Sometimes the bankers oblige the customers by allowing the withdrawal of Fixed/Term Deposits before their due date; but it is not a good practice and impairs the banker's own cash resources. In such situations the customers forego the interest/return accrued on their Fixed/Term Deposits at the rate of service charge which is generally very nominal. However, in the Interest Free Banking (PLS) this is changed, and the depositor is paid the return at the rate prescribed for the lower period for which the deposit has remained with the bank.

In re-Dillion (1890) and in re-Madrid (1880), it was held that since the Fixed/Term Deposit receipt is not a negotiable instrument, it can be transferred by way of assignment to a third party, but the transferee gets no right to the bank in his own name.

Law of Limitation

As long as the profit/return is being paid or the receipt is being renewed, the law of limitation does not apply to Fixed/Term Deposits, it begins to run form the expiry of fixed period.

Attachment by Court

In Rogers *v* Whitelay (1892. A.C. 118) it was held that "when money lying in the credit of a customer is attached by an order of a court, it will depend on the terms of the order of attachment whether the entire balance standing to the credit of the customer is to be attached, or only such part of it as is necessary to satisfy the decree in execution whereof the order of attachment is made."

A *Garnishee Order* is an order issued by a court to a judgment creditor to attach the funds in the hands of a third person who owes money to the judgment debtor. The *garnishee order* warns the third person, called '*garnishee*' against releasing the money attached until directed by the court to do so.

According to Lord Watson, "The effect of an order attaching 'all debts' owing are accruing due by him to judgment debtor is to make the *garnishee* custodian for the court of whole funds attached; and he cannot expect at his own peril, part with any of those funds without the sanction of the court"

A *garnishee* order may be '*nisi*' or '*absolute*'; '*nisi*' means 'unless', and such a *garnishee* order takes effect at a certain date unless in the meantime something occurs to prevent it from becoming 'absolute'. Thus an order *nisi* gives the judgment creditor an equitable charge upon the debt and a *garnishee* cannot obtain a discharge by payment before the order *nisi* is made '*absolute.*'

A *garnishee* order '*absolute*' directs the *garnishee* to pay the money due or accruing due in satisfaction of the judgment debt; thus the judgment creditor has the power to realize that charge.

Attachment of particular deposit by *garnishee order* depends on the terms of the order as attachable.

TERM DEPOSITS ACCOUNT IN JOINT NAMES

Term Deposits Account may be in the joint names of two or more persons. The payment to either of them will not discharge the banker, unless authorized by all the joint depositors. In Innes *v* Stephenson (1-Moore, Role) it was ruled by Lord Tenterden (1851) that "Where money is paid into a bank on the joint account of persons not partners in trade, the bank is not discharged by payments to one of those persons, without the authority of the others".

In case of death of one or more of the persons the deposit passes on to the survivors, whom the banker can safely pay.

Term Deposits accounts may be opened in the names of minors and they can give a valid discharge for deposited amount repaid to them.

Savings Deposits

Savings Deposits Accounts were introduced in England by the Trustee Savings Banks which were established under Trustee Savings Bank Act, 1963, for receipt of money from depositors without any benefit to the trustees or organizers. The main object of the savings deposits was to encourage thrift among people of small means like children, married and household women, who could deposit only a very small amount at a time.

Savings Deposits Accounts in India were first started in Presidency towns of Bombay, Calcutta and Madras during 1833 and 1835. Their success encouraged the opening of District Savings Banks in 1870 in certain selected district treasuries. By 1882, Post Office Savings Bank also started functioning in all the principal Post Offices in India. The simplicity of the procedure and nearness of the Post Office to the intending depositor made Post Office Bank very popular within a short span of time.

When commercial banks found that it was a paying business, they also started accepting savings deposits. Upto recent past the depositor was not allowed to withdraw more than a fixed amount from deposits in a month; and if he desired to withdraw a large sum, he had to give a prior notice of 10-15 day. Thus the bankers did not need large sums in reserves to meet the demand on them; while in the other hand some money was always available for still more expansion of the banker's business.

In Pakistan a savings Deposits Account can be opened with a very small amount of money, and the depositor is issued a cheque book for withdrawals. Profit is paid at a flexible rate calculated in six-monthly basis under the Interest Free Banking System. There is no restriction in the withdrawals from the deposit accounts but the amount of money withdrawn is deleted from the to be taken for calculation of products for assessment of profit to be paid to the account holder. It discourages unnecessary withdrawals from the deposits.

In order to popularize this scheme the State Bank of Pakistan has allowed the Saving Scheme for school and college students and industrial labor also. The purpose of these accounts is to inculcate the habit of savings in the constituents. As such, the initial deposits required for opening these accounts is very nominal.

Pak Rupee Non-Resident Accounts

Accounts in Pak Rupees of individuals, firms or companies residing in countries outside Pakistan are known as 'Non-Resident Accounts'. The State Bank Notification has categorized the following accounts as 'N.R.A.'

(i) Accounts of Pakistan nationals, permanently resident and domiciled abroad. However, accounts of Pakistan nationals holding office in the service of Pakistan in a foreign country are exempted.

(ii) Accounts of Pakistan nationals who go out of Pakistan for a short duration in connection with study, business tour or pleasure trip etc.

(iii) Accounts of foreign nationals ordinarily residing in Pakistan but go abroad for a short duration.

(iv) Accounts of foreign nationals residing abroad.

ACCOUNTS OF FOREIGN NATIONALS RESIDENT IN PAKISTAN

The accounts of all foreign nationals, who are resident in Pakistan and the accounts of companies or firms (other than banks) whose head offices or controlling offices are abroad but the accounts are operated on by persons in Pakistan are treated as non-resident accounts.

Debits from Accounts

(i) Payment on behalf of the account holder direct to the institutions concerned in respect of insurance premium, club bills or other payments of a regular nature. These payments must be supported by receipts and bills, vouchers etc.

(ii) Payments of Government and Municipal dues supported by official claims and documents of receipt.

(iii) Disbursement in Pakistan from the amount received from abroad in the account through banking channel.

(iv) Amount representing payments through cheques direct to the carrier or the travel agent for travel within country by train, sea or air for self, wife, children and parents. Travel abroad after approval of P-Form is also included.

(v) Amount needed for purchase of shares of public limited companies, securities of the Government of Pakistan, N.I.T. Units, Prize Bond, Defence Savings Certificates etc. However, the purchase of these shares and securities etc. is to be made by the bank itself on the behalf of the Non-Resident Account holder.

(vi) Payments against bills for hotel expense in Pakistan, of the account holder and his family members. This payment is permissible only to hotels of the category of three stars and above.

(vii) Cheques drawn for self or in favour of his dependants residing in Pakistan for their maintenance.

(viii) Amount to reserve previous credits.

(ix) Amount in respect of approved remittances in foreign exchange.

(x) Payments of loan installments direct to the financial institutions from whom the account holder had obtained loan.

Credits into the Accounts

(i) Receipt on account salary, allowances, bonus, commission etc. direct from the employer by cheque.

(ii) Divided and interest income on investment in shares and securities from the company by cheque etc.

(iii) Income from landed property and agricultural rent against identity of depositor.

(iv) Credit of remittances received from abroad through banking channel

(v) Return/Interest accrued on the amount lying in the Non-resident accounts.

(vi) Sale proceeds of landed property as supported by a registered sale deed.

(vii) Amount representing the maturity proceeds/surrender or paid-up value of insurance policies and sale proceeds of the shares of the public limited companies and/or securities of Government of Pakistan purchased earlier.

(viii) Refund of amounts previously debited or over-charged.

Foreign Currency Accounts

Government of Pakistan has introduced many important reforms in Foreign Exchange Control in the country since February, 1990, for the purpose of strengthening the Foreign Exchange Reserve. One of these reforms relates to Foreign Currency Accounts, which can be opened in United States Dollars, Pound Sterling, Euro and Japanese Yen in any of the authorized branches of commercial banks throughout the country.

Any individual, firm and company, whether Pakistani or foreigner, and whether a resident or non-resident in Pakistan, can open the Current, Saving Bank, Special Notice and Term Deposits Accounts in any of the above mentioned foreign currencies.

Inquiries are made about the sources of fund for these Foreign Currency Accounts, and the State Bank of Pakistan has asked the banks to be vigilant to avoid the use of these accounts for money laundering and other illegal purposes.

Moreover, State Bank of Pakistan regularly monitors the satisfactory operations of these accounts and issues guide-lines and instruction for this purpose, periodically.

WAYS TO IMPROVE COMMERCIAL BANKING IN PAKISTAN

Nationalized Commercial Banks (NCBs)

NCBs are still the market's dominant players, controlling about 51% of the entire banking sector deposits and 50% of advances. NCBs have the most extensive branch network with deep penetration in both urban and rural Pakistan - a major competitive advantage over their more urban - oriented Newly Established Private Banks and foreign banks. This extensive network has allowed NCBs to tap into a lucrative base of low cost and stable deposits. However, this has come at the expense of high operational costs and a large number of loss making branches. Most of the loss making branches must be shut down. NCBs have also been victims of political interference, which is reflected by their high share (roughly 58%) of total loan defaults. Operational inefficiencies and unusually high loan defaults have resulted in huge losses, decline in shareholders equity and low yield on earning assets. To overcome these and to restructure the NCBs it is essential to appoint professionals from the private sector in the management.

Denationalized Banks (DNB)

Of the DNBs, both MCB and Allied Bank have managed to show strong performance after privatization. To reduce costs, it is also required to decide for closing down of its unprofitable branches and redundant workers must be offered "golden hand-shakes".

Newly established private Banks (NEPB)- Foreign Banks (FB)

Most NEPBs restrict operations to short term trade-related financing, with the exception of the larger private banks such as Askari, Faysal and MCB that have limited long term exposure. Increased competition in the banking sector will force smaller banks to either sell out to other larger banks or merge. A small capital base will also restrict branch expansion of smaller banks, forcing them to focus on relatively smaller retail clients. Hence, it is foreseen that a major merger/ acquisition potential in the banking sector. Competition would also spill over to other customer services such as provision of ATM machines and better banking facilities. Again, only the larger banks would be able to invest in automation technology and branch expansion necessary to improve efficiencies and mobilize cheaper funds. FB comprise 24% of total advances and deposits within the banking system, but as a percentage of total profitability they are far ahead. A major constraint for foreign banks is the restrictions placed on branch expansion by the SBP. This should be according to liberalization policy to relax restrictions on foreign banks in emerging economies.

ROLE OF DEVELOPMENT FINANCIAL INSTITUTIONS

Development Financial Institutions in Pakistan are mainly involved to perform developmental roles through the provisions of credit to the agricultural and industrial sector. Many of the DFIs are heavily dependent on SBP funding. These are:

- PICIC
- IDBP
- ADBP
- NIT
- ICP
- HBFC
- NDFC
- BEL
- Equity Participation Fund

NDFC can be ranked first in the DFIs. It was set up by the Federal Government in 1973 for the purpose of lending to the public sector and since 1980 also to the private sector. Apart from its traditional activities of providing loans, advances and lease financing on a short, medium and long-term basis and accepting deposits of fixed maturities, the NDFC is now engaged in bridge financing, trade financing and , through its merchant banking division, in underwriting, equity investment, bond floatation and financial advisory services. With the Government's assistance, it is also involved in raising loans in foreign currency for infrastructural and developmental projects./ NDFC continues to play a leading role in development and the financing of infrastructure to facilitate industrial development (e.g. in the oil and gas sectors, under the private energy financing initiatives). PICIC was incorporated in 1957 as a medium through which financial and other assistance could be provided to the private industrial sector of Pakistan. Its objectives are:

- to stimulate the development of the country by providing finance for the establishment of new industries as well as for the balancing, modernization and expansion of existing industries in the private sector;
- to assist in broadening the base of industrial ownership in the country, thereby developing the stock market; and
- to encourage the establishment of viable projects in under-developed regions of the country.

Preference is given to the financing of industries which are based on local raw materials and which are either export-oriented or would result in import saving.

The current activities of PICIC comprise: medium and long term lending, in both domestic and foreign currencies, generally for the acquisition of fixed assets; the provision of loans for working capital; the provisions of underwriting assistance; equity finance; industrial promotion; the provision of guidance and counseling service to clients.

IDBP succeeded the Pakistan Industrial Finance Corporation in 1961 to promote small and medium-sized industrial enterprises in the private sector by way of providing term loans for the establishment of new industrial units and to meet the expansion, modernization and replacement needs to existing industrial units. Today nearly 90% share capital is held by the Federal Government and the balance by government-controlled financial institutions or Provincial Governments. IDBP give priority to the financing of small projects, especially agricultural, export-based or engineering. The dispersal of industrial in less-developed regions, and the promotion of new industrial capacity consistent with the financial targets and socio-economic objective established in the five year plans.

BEL established in 1980 with the principal objective of accelerating the pace of industrial development, primarily in the private and mixed sectors of the economy. It was first sponsored by the SBP and in 1996 government privatized it by selling its 26% shareholding to LTV Consortium. New management of a privatized financial institution ensuring to provide financial facilities to enterprises in the private sector through equity participation, and profit and loss shares modes of financing.

D.F.I. SHOULD BE CURTAILED TO SAVE OVERHEAD EXPENSES? WHY OR WHY NOT

The role of specialized development financial institutions has been slowly diminishing in Pakistan. Total advances of scheduled banks (which include both commercial banks and specialized institutions such as IDBP and ADBP) have been increased. The share of specialized DFIs in total advances has declined. Thus commercial banks are likely to be the private beneficiaries of the less restrictive monetary and credit policy. In the past, DFIs were involved in influence/ intervention of politicians This act lost their credit quality and caused increase in overhead and head counts.

DFIs play vital role in the economy of any country. Under the new policy SBP is maintaining strategy to improve the quality of new loans and then to tackle the non-performing loans problem. DFIs have been asked to curtail their overheads, especially the head counts. Professionals from the private sector have been appointed. All these measures are likely to improve the health of DFIs to come back on the track.

There are two prospects of international banking (i) International Financial Institution which are engaged with the scope of solving the economic problems of the world; (ii) International Banking providing financial system - shifting of funds, foreign exchange, etc. as well as foreign commercial banking. These are discussed in detail as under:

INTERNATIONAL FINANCIAL INSTITUTIONS

With the end of the World War II, keeping in view the broken economics of the world and taking responsibility of rebuilding, world financial experts and leaders of the world met in Breton Woods, USA to find ways and means of solving the economic problems. This was a conference which looked at some of the financial problems which the world will be facing after the War and in view of these, decided to set up both the World Bank and the International Monetary Fund (IMF). Whereas the World Bank was to focus on development loans to the developing countries, the IMF was particularly concerned with minimizing exchange disorders in the post-war period, which turned out to have larger payment deficits, inconvertible currencies and persistent inflation. In 1950, an International Finance Corporation was set up to supplement the World Bank by participating in equity financing in member countries and in 1960 a third organization International Development Association was created to complete the World Bank group. In 1966 Asian Development Bank was established by the Asian countries and raised funds from the private and governmental sources in the region and have aim to provide project aid to member countries. In 1974, more than 42 member states, established Islamic Development Bank with the principles declared by the Organization of Islamic Countries to promote cooperation and strengthen ties between member countries in all aspects of life, with special emphasis on economic development and financing.

For example, now-a-days Pakistan's economy is mainly depending upon the IMF, World Bank, ADB and IDB loans programmes. Recently Asian Development Bank (ADB) has extended a Capital Market Development Programme Loan (CMDPL) of US $ 250 million for balance of payment support to Pakistan. Loan negotiations were held with ADB in September 1997 and the Loan Agreement was signed on January 5, 1998. Export-Import (EXIM) Bank of Japan had indicated its willingness to provide additional US $ 250 million through co-financing arrangement. Apart from the above, ADB has also extended a loan of US $ 5 million from the Bank's Special Funds resources for technical assistance for the following areas:

- Institutional strengthening of regulators of Securities Market:
- Development of a self-regulatory frame-work.
- Development of National Clearing and Settlement System:
- Development of secondary debt market:

INTERNATIONAL BANKING - FINANCIAL SYSTEM

New York, London, Tokyo, Singapore, Hong Kong and many other cities constitute important financial centres which linked by close communications, enable nations and the overall world economy to function around the clock to serve people. The massive shifting of funds for oil payments and the subsequent investment of oil revenues, for example, have involved a great deal of financial recycling through the complex, far-flung, and effective international monetary, financial, and banking system. Commercial banks have carried a very large proportion of these recycling operations and also play a role in helping some countries to meet their balance of payments adjustment problems.

The global money system is now dominated by the United States dollar, The German mark, Japanese Yen, etc. A number of other money units play important roles in specific local markets. They physical transfer of actual paper money, coins, gold and silver bullion and travelers cheques among nations is small as compared with the massive volume of credit, deposits and investment funds moving daily across boundaries.

In international bank, an elaborate global system of foreign exchange trading provides the mechanism by which individual currency value are continually determined for transaction purposes. Ordinarily, governments will intervene through purchases or sales in foreign exchange markets to seek to stabilize the value of their currency.

FOREIGN BANKING

Traditionally, the forcign banking focused on short term trade finance, targeting mainly low risk blue chip clients and high net worth individuals. More recently, foreign banks have also expanded into merchant banking, capital market operations, and consumer/retail banking. Foreign banks have been extremely successful in capturing a major market share of consumer banking business, especially that of credit cards. Head office support in terms of international network and technology has enabled the foreign banks to become important players in the corporate and consumer banking arena. If you're like most people, you've heard a lot about online banking but probably haven't tried it yourself. You still pay your bills by mail and deposit checks at your bank branch, much the way your parents did. You might shop online for a loan, life insurance or a home mortgage, but when it comes time to commit, you feel more comfortable working with your banker or an agent you know and trust.

Online banking isn't out to change your money habits. Instead, it uses today's computer technology to give you the option of bypassing the time-consuming, paper-based aspects of traditional banking in order to manage your finances more quickly and efficiently.

Origin of Online Banking

The advent of the Internet and the popularity of personal computers presented both an opportunity and a challenge for the banking industry.

For years, financial institutions have used powerful computer networks to automate millions of daily transactions; today, often the only paper record is the customer's receipt at the point of sale. Now that its customers are connected to the Internet via personal computers, banks envision similar economic advantages by adapting those same internal electronic processes to home use.

Banks view online banking as a powerful "value added" tool to attract and retain new customers while helping to eliminate costly paper handling and teller interactions in an increasingly competitive banking environment.

Brick-to-click Banks

Today, most large national banks, many regional banks and even smaller banks and credit unions offer some form of online banking, variously known as PC banking, home banking, electronic banking or Internet banking. Those that do are sometimes referred to as "brick-to-click" banks, both to distinguish them from brick-and-mortar banks that have yet to offer online banking, as well as from online or "virtual" banks that have no physical branches or tellers whatsoever. The challenge for the banking industry has been to design this new service channel in such a way that its customers will readily learn to use and trust it. After all, banks have spent generations earning our trust; they aren't about to risk that on a Web site that is frustrating, confusing or less than secure.

Most of the large banks now offer fully secure, fully functional online banking for free or for a small fee. Some smaller banks offer limited access or functionality; for instance, you may be able to view your account balance and history but not initiate transactions online. As more banks succeed online and more customers use their sites, fully functional online banking likely will become as commonplace as automated teller machines.

Virtual Banks

If you don't mind foregoing the teller window, lobby cookie and kindly bank president, a "virtual" or e-bank may save you very real money. Virtual banks are banks without bricks; from the customer's perspective, they exist entirely on the Internet, where they offer pretty much the same range of services and adhere to the same federal regulations as your corner bank.

Virtual banks pass the money they save on overhead like buildings and tellers along to you in the form of higher yields, lower fees and more generous account thresholds.

The major disadvantage of virtual banks revolves around ATMs. Because they have no ATM machines, virtual banks typically charge the same surcharge that your brick-and-mortar bank would if you used another bank's automated teller. Likewise, many virtual banks won't accept deposits via ATM; you'll have to either deposit the check by mail or transfer money from another account.

Advantages of Online Banking

- Convenience: Unlike your corner bank, online banking sites never close; they're available 24 hours a day, seven days a week, and they're only a mouse click away.
- Ubiquity: If you're out of state or even out of the country when a money problem arises, you can log on instantly to your online bank and take care of business, 24/7.
- Transaction speed: Online bank sites generally execute and confirm transactions at or quicker than ATM processing speeds.
- Efficiency: You can access and manage all of your bank accounts, including IRAs, CDs, even securities, from one secure site.
- Effectiveness: Many online banking sites now offer sophisticated tools, including account aggregation, stock quotes, rate alerts and portfolio managing programs to help you manage all of your assets more effectively. Most are also compatible with money managing programs such as Quicken and Microsoft Money.

Disadvantages of Online Banking

- Start-up may take time: In order to register for your bank's online program, you will probably have to provide ID and sign a form at a bank branch. If you and your spouse wish to view and manage your assets together online, one of you may have to sign a durable power of attorney before the bank will display all of your holdings together.
- Learning curve: Banking sites can be difficult to navigate at first. Plan to invest some time and/or read the tutorials in order to become comfortable in your virtual lobby.
- Bank site changes: Even the largest banks periodically upgrade their online programs, adding new features in unfamiliar places. In some cases, you may have to re-enter account information.
- The trust thing: For many people, the biggest hurdle to online banking is learning to trust it. Did my transaction go through? Did I push the transfer button once or twice? Best

bet: always print the transaction receipt and keep it with your bank records until it shows up on your personal site and/or your bank statement.

ONLINE BANKING

Online banking isn't out to change your money habits. It simply uses today's technology to give you the option of bypassing the time-consuming, paper-based aspects of traditional banking in order to manage your finances more quickly and efficiently.

It is almost certainly the way most banking will be conducted in the not-too-distant future.

Whether your bank is a traditional brick and mortar institution or a Web-only bank with no brick and mortar branches, online banking lets you connect to your bank through the Internet and do things such as view your accounts, transfer money between accounts, view images of cancelled checks, print copies of those checks and pay bills online. You'll find that it's common for online banking sites to be compatible with money managing programs such as Quicken and Microsoft Money.

Many banks make it easier to manage your checking account by allowing you set up e-mail alerts so you can be notified when checks clear or when your balance slips below a certain level. There is also a detailed listing of your cancelled checks.

If you'd like to eliminate paper checks from your life, you'll find that a growing number of companies allow you to make automatic payments through your online banking account.

Getting started is easy. The bank's Web site will walk you through the steps of registering the bills you want to pay and the accounts you want to use to pay them. You'll only have to enter the information once. You can always make changes and add or subtract bills.

If a monthly bill is for the same amount each month, you might want to schedule a recurring payment. If the amount varies from month to month you can pay the bill each month on a "one time" basis.

Once you have registered the accounts you wish to pay online, the next step is to schedule payments. Your creditors receive your online payment in one of two ways: electronic payment or check. If the company is set up to accept electronic payments, your payment is automatically debited from your account and deposited electronically into their account. If the company can't accept electronic payments, your bank issues a check based on your online payment instructions.

Most bill payment sites include a payment activity page that lists all of your payments and their status — scheduled, pending or processed.

Be aware that companies sometimes change the billing address or your account number without warning. It's important to check your statement each month to verify those details as well as your transactions.

You'll have a user name and password to access your online account. Just as with any information used to access any other financial account, you should keep these codes secret. Your bank will tell you what to look for — usually an icon of a locked padlock — to ensure you're accessing your account over a secure line.

You should also beware of a scam called phishing where crooks send an e-mail that may look exactly like e-mails from your bank. These e-mails often claim that some account or personal information is needed. You're asked to click on a link and fill in the information. As a hard-and-fast rule, never click on a link in an e-mail and then divulge account information. Call your bank — don't use a phone number supplied in the e-mail — and ask if the e-mail is legitimate.

Whether you bank online or prefer the old fashioned way, you receive a statement every month that details transactions and account status. In the next section, you'll see why you should take time each month to carefully review your statement.

7

Modern Islamic Banking

INTRODUCTION

Modern banking system was introduced into the Muslim countries at a time when they were politically and economically at a low ebb, in the late 19th century. The main banks in the home countries of the imperial powers established local branches in the capitals of the subject countries and they catered mainly to the import export requirements of the foreign businesses. The banks were generally confined to the capital cities and the local population remained largely untouched by the banking system. The local trading community avoided the "foreign" banks both for nationalistic as well as religious reasons. However, as time went on it became difficult to engage in trade and other activities without making use of commercial banks. Even then many confined their involvement to transaction activities such as current accounts and money transfers. Borrowing from the banks and depositing their savings with the bank were strictly avoided in order to keep away from dealing in interest which is prohibited by religion.

With the passage of time, however, and other socio-economic forces demanding more involvement in national economic and financial activities, avoiding the interaction with the banks became impossible. Local banks were established on the same lines as the interest-based foreign banks for want of another system and they began to expand within the country bringing the banking system to more local people.

As countries became independent the need to engage in banking activities became unavoidable and urgent. Governments, businesses and individuals began to transact business with the banks, with or without liking it. This state of affairs drew the attention and concern of Muslim intellectuals. The story of interest-free or Islamic banking begins here. In the following paragraphs we will trace this story to date and examine how far and how su cessfully their concerns have been addressed.

Historical Development

It seems that the history of interest-free banking could be divided into two parts. First, when it still remained an idea; second, when it became a reality — by private initiative in some countries and by law in others. We will discuss the two periods separately. The last decade has seen a marked decline in the establishment of new Islamic banks and the established banks seem to have failed to live up to the expectations. The literature of the period begins with evaluations and ends with attempts at finding ways and means of correcting and overcoming the problems encouutered by the existing banks.

Interest-free banking as an idea

Interest-free banking seems to be of very recent origin. The earliest references to the reorganisation of banking on the basis of profit sharing rather than interest are found in Anwar Qureshi (1946), Naiem Siddiqi (1948) and Mahmud Ahmad (1952) in the late forties, followed by a more elaborate exposition by Mawdudi in 1950 (1961). Muhammad Hamidullah's 1944, 1955, 1957 and 1962 writings too should be included in this category. They have all recognised the need for commercial banks and the evil of interest in that enterprise, and have proposed a banking system based on the concept of *Mudarabha* - profit and loss sharing.

In the next two decades interest-free banking attracted more attention, partly because of the political interest it created in Pakistan and partly because of the emergence of young Muslim economists. Works specifically devoted to this subject began to appear in this period. The first such work is that of Muhammad Uzair (1955). Another set of works emerged in the late sixties and early seventies. Abdullah al-Araby (1967), Nejatullah Siddiqi (1961, 1969), al-Najjar (1971) and Baqir al-Sadr (1961, 1974) were the main contributors.

Early seventies saw the institutional involvement. Conference of the Finance Ministers of the Islamic Countries held in Karachi in 1970, the Egyptian study in 1972, First International Conference on Islamic Economics in Mecca in 1976, International Economic Conference in London in 1977 were the result of such involvement. The involvement of institutions and governments led to the application of theory to practice and resulted in the establishment of the first interest-free banks. The Islamic Development Bank, an inter-governmental bank established in 1975, was born of this process.

The coming into being of interest-free banks

The first private interest-free bank, the Dubai Islamic Bank, was also set up in 1975 by a group of Muslim businessmen from several countries. Two more private banks were founded in 1977 under the name of Faisal Islamic Bank in Egypt and the Sudan. In the same year the Kuwaiti government set up the Kuwait Finance House. However, small scale limited scope interest-free banks have been tried before. One in Malaysia in the mid-forties and another in Pakistan in the late-fifties. Neither survived. In 1962 the Malaysian government set up the

"Pilgrim's Management Fund" to help prospective pilgrims to save and profit. The savings bank established in 1963 at Mit-Ghamr in Egypt was very popular and prospered initially and then closed down for various reasons. However this experiment led to the creation of the Nasser Social Bank in 1972. Though the bank is still active, its objectives are more social than commercial.

In the ten years since the establishment of the first private commercial bank in Dubai, more than 50 interest-free banks have come into being. Though nearly all of them are in Muslim countries, there are some in Western Europe as well: in Denmark, Luxembourg , Switzerland and the UK. Many banks were established in 1983 (11) and 1984 (13). The numbers have declined considerably in the following years.

In most countries the establishment of interest-free banking had been by private initiative and were confined to that bank. In Iran and Pakistan, however, it was by government initiative and covered all banks in the country. The governments in both these countries took steps in 1981 to introduce interest-free banking. In Pakistan, effective 1 January 1981 all domestic commercial banks were permitted to accept deposits on the basis of profit-and-loss sharing (PLS). New steps were introduced on 1 January 1985 to formally transform the banking system over the next six months to one based on no interest. From 1 July 1985 no banks could accept any interest bearing deposits, and all existing deposits became subject to PLS rules. Yet some operations were still allowed to continue on the old basis. In Iran, certain administrative steps were taken in February 1981 to eliminate interest from banking operations. Interest on all assets was replaced by a 4 percent maximum service charge and by a 4 to 8 percent 'profit' rate depending on the type of economic activity. Interest on deposits was also converted into a 'guaranteed minimum profit.' In August 1983 the Usury-free Banking Law was introduced and a fourteen-month change over period began in January 1984. The whole system was converted to an interest-free one in March 1985.

The last decade

The subject matter of writings and conferences in the eighties have changed from the concepts and possibilities of interest-free banking to the evaluation of their performance and their impact on the rest of the economy and the world. Their very titles bear testimony to this and the places indicate the world-wide interest in the subject. Conference on Islamic Banking: Its impact on world financial and commercial practices held in London in September 1984, Workshop on Industrial Financing Activities of Islamic Banks held in Vienna in June 1986, International Conference on Islamic Banking held in Tehran in June 1986, International Conference on Islamic Banking and Finance: Current issues and future prospects held in Washington, D.C. in September 1986, Islamic Banking Conference held in Geneva in October 1986, and Conference 'Into the 1990's with Islamic Banking' held in London in 1988 belong to this category. The most recent one is the Workshop on the Elimination of *Riba* from the Economy held in Islamabad in April 1992.

Several articles, books and PhD theses have been written on Islamic Banking during this period. Special mention must be made of the work by M. Akram Khan in preparing annotated bibliographies of all published (and some unpublished) works on Islamic Economics (including Islamic Banking) from 1940 and before. It is very useful to students of Islamic Economics and Banking, especially since both English and Urdu works are included (1983, 1991, 1992). M.N. Siddiqi's bibliographies include early works in Arabic, English and Urdu (1980, 1988). Turkish literature is found in Sabahuddin Zaim (1980).

Current Practices

Generally speaking, all interest-free banks agree on the basic principles. However, individual banks differ in their application. These differences are due to several reasons including the laws of the country, objectives of the different banks, individual bank's circumstances and experiences, the need to interact with other interest-based banks, etc. In the following paragraphs, we will describe the salient features common to all banks.

Deposit accounts

All the Islamic banks have three kinds of deposit accounts: current, savings and investment.

Current accounts

Current or demand deposit accounts are virtually the same as in all conventional banks. Deposit is guaranteed.

Savings accounts

Savings deposit accounts operate in different ways. In some banks, the depositors allow the banks to use their money but they obtain a guarantee of getting the full amount back from the bank. Banks adopt several methods of inducing their clients to deposit with them, but no profit is promised. In others, savings accounts are treated as investment accounts but with less stringent conditions as to withdrawals and minimum balance. Capital is not guaranteed but the banks take care to invest money from such accounts in relatively risk-free short-term projects. As such lower profit rates are expected and that too only on a portion of the average minimum balance on the ground that a high level of reserves needs to be kept at all times to meet withdrawal demands.

Investment account

Investment deposits are accepted for a fixed or unlimited period of time and the investors agree in advance to share the profit (or loss) in a given proportion with the bank. Capital is not guaranteed.

Modes of financing

Banks adopt several modes of acquiring assets or financing projects. But they can be broadly categorised into three areas: investment, trade and lending.

Investment financing

This is done in three main ways: (a) *Musharaka* where a bank may join another entity to set up a joint venture, both parties participating in the various aspects of the project in varying degrees. Profit and loss are shared in a pre-arranged fashion. This is not very different from the joint venture concept. The venture is an independent legal entity and the bank may withdraw gradually after an initial period. (b) *Mudarabha* where the bank contributes the finance and the client provides the expertise, management and labour. Profits are shared by both the partners in a pre-arranged proportion, but when a loss occurs the total loss is borne by the bank. (c) Financing on the basis of an *estimated rate of return*. Under this scheme, the bank estimates the expected rate of return on the specific project it is asked to finance and provides financing on the understanding that at least that rate is payable to the bank. (Perhaps this rate is negotiable.) If the project ends up in a profit more than the estimated rate the excess goes to the client. If the profit is less than the estimate the bank will accept the lower rate. In case a loss is suffered the bank will take a share in it.

Trade financing

This is also done in several ways. The main ones are: (a) *Mark-up* where the bank buys an item for a client and the client agrees to repay the bank the price and an agreed profit later on. (b) *Leasing* where the bank buys an item for a client and leases it to him for an agreed period and at the end of that period the lessee pays the balance on the price agreed at the beginning an becomes the owner of the item. (c) *Hire-purchase* where the bank buys an item for the client and hires it to him for an agreed rent and period, and at the end of that period the client automatically becomes the owner of the item. (d) *Sell-and-buy-back* where a client sells one of his properties to the bank for an agreed price payable now on condition that he will buy the property back after certain time for an agreed price. (e) *Letters of credit* where the bank guarantees the import of an item using its own funds for a client, on the basis of sharing the profit from the sale of this item or on a mark-up basis.

Lending

Main forms of Lending are: (a) *Loans with a service charge* where the bank lends money without interest but they cover their expenses by levying a service charge. This charge may be subject to a maximum set by the authorities. (b) *No-cost loans* where each bank is expected to set aside a part of their funds to grant no-cost loans to needy persons such as small farmers, entrepreneurs, producers, etc. and to needy consumers. (c) *Overdrafts* also are to be provided, subject to a certain maximum, free of charge.

Services

Other banking services such as money transfers, bill collections, trade in foreign currencies at spot rate etc. where the bank's own money is not involved are provided on a commission or charges basis.

Shortcomings in current practices

In the previous section we listed the current practices under three categories: deposits, modes of financing (or acquiring assets) and services. There seems to be no problems as far as banking services are concerned. Islamic banks are able to provide nearly all the services that are available in the conventional banks. The only exception seems to be in the case of letters of credit where there is a possibility for interest involvement. However some solutions have been found for this problem — mainly by having excess liquidity with the foreign bank. On the deposit side, judging by the volume of deposits both in the countries where both systems are available and in countries where law prohibits any dealing in interest, the non-payment of interest on deposit accounts seems to be no serious problem. Customers still seem to deposit their money with interest-free banks.

The main problem, both for the banks and for the customers, seem to be in the area of financing. Bank lending is still practised but that is limited to either no-cost loans (mainly consumer loans) including overdrafts, or loans with service charges only. Both these types of loans bring no income to the banks and therefore naturally they are not that keen to engage in this activity much. That leaves us with investment financing and trade financing. Islamic banks are expected to engage in these activities only on a profit and loss sharing (PLS) basis. This is where the banks' main income is to come from and this is also from where the investment account holders are expected to derive their profits from. And the latter is supposed to be the incentive for people to deposit their money with the Islamic banks. And it is precisely in this PLS scheme that the main problems of the Islamic banks lie. Therefore we will look at this system more carefully in the following section.

Problems in Implementing the PLS Scheme

Several writers have attempted to show, with varying degrees of success, that Islamic Banking based on the concept of profit and loss sharing (PLS) is theoretically superior to conventional banking from different angles. See, for example, Khan and Mirakhor (1987). However from the practical point of view things do not seem that rosy. Our concern here is this latter aspect. In the over half-a-decade of full-scale experience in implementing the PLS scheme the problems have begun to show up. If one goes by the experience of Pakistan as portrayed in the papers presented at the conference held in Islamabad in 1992, the situation is very serious and no satisfactory remedy seems to emerge. In the following paragraphs we will try to set down some of the major difficulties.

Financing

There are four main areas where the Islamic banks find it difficult to finance under the PLS scheme: (a) participating in long-term low-yield projects, (b) financing the small businessman, (c) granting non-participating loans to running businesses, and (d) financing government borrowing. Let us examine them in turn.

Long-term projects

Table below shows the term structure of investment by 20 Islamic Banks in 1988. It is clear that less than 10 percent of the total assets goes into medium- and long-term investment. Admittedly, the banks are unable or unwilling to participate in long-term projects. This is a very unsatisfactory situation.

Table: Term Structure of Investment by 20 Islamic Banks, 1988

Type of Investment	Amount*	% of Total
Short-term	4,909.8	68.4
Social lending	64.2	0.9
Real-estate investment	1,498.2	20.9
Medium- and long-term investment	707.7	9.8

Source: Aggregate balance sheets prepared by the International Association of Islamic Banks, Bahrain, 1988. Quoted in: Ausaf Ahmed (1994). * Unit of currency not given.

The main reason of course is the need to participate in the enterprise on a PLS basis which involves time consuming complicated assessment procedures and negotiations, requiring expertise and experience. The banks do not seem to have developed the latter and they seem to be averse to the former. There are no commonly accepted criteria for project evaluation based on PLS partnerships. Each single case has to be treated separately with utmost care and each has to be assessed and negotiated on its own merits. Other obvious reasons are: (a) such investments tie up capital for very long periods, unlike in conventional banking where the capital is recovered in regular instalments almost right from the beginning, and the uncertainty and risk are that much higher, (b) the longer the maturity of the project the longer it takes to realise the returns and the banks therefore cannot pay a return to their depositors as quick as the conventional banks can. Thus it is no wonder that the banks are averse to such investments.

Small businesses

Small scale businesses form a major part of a country's productive sector. Besides, they form a greater number of the bank's clientele. Yet it seems difficult to provide them with the necessary financing under the PLS scheme, even though there is excess liquidity in the banks. The observations of Iqbal and Mirakhor is revealing:

Given the comprehensive criteria to be followed in granting loans and monitoring their use by banks, small-scale enterprises have, in general encountered greater difficulties in obtaining financing than their large-scale counterparts in the Islamic Republic of Iran. This has been particularly relevant for the construction and service sectors, which have large share in the gross domestic product (GDP). The service sector is made up of many small producers for whom the banking sector has not been able to provide sufficient financing. Many of these small producers, who traditionally were able to obtain interest-based credit facilities on the basis of collateral, are now finding it difficult to raise funds for their operations.

Running businesses

Running businesses frequently need short-term capital as well as working capital and ready cash for miscellaneous on-the-spot purchases and sundry expenses. This is the daily reality in the business world. Very little thought seems to have been given to this important aspect of the business world's requirement. The PLS scheme is not geared to cater to this need. Even if there is complete trust and exchange of information between the bank and the business it is nearly impossible or prohibitively costly to estimate the contribution of such short-term financing on the return of a given business. Neither is the much used mark-up system suitable in this case. It looks unlikely to be able to arrive at general rules to cover all the different situations.

Added to this is the delays involved in authorising emergency loans. One staff member of the Bank of Industry and Mines of Iran has commented:

Often the clients need to have quick access to fresh funds for the immediate needs to prevent possible delays in the project's implementation schedule. According to the set regulations, it is not possible to bridge-finance such requirements and any grant of financial assistance must be made on the basis of the project's appraisal to determine type and terms and conditions of the scheme of financing.

The enormity of the damage or hindrance caused by the inability to provide financing to this sector will become clear if we realise that running businesses and enterprises are the mainstay of the country's very economic survival.

Government borrowing

In all countries the Government accounts for a major component of the demand for credit — both short-term and long-term. Unlike business loans these borrowings are not always for investment purposes, nor for investment in productive enterprises. Even when invested in productive enterprises they are generally of a longer-term type and of low yield. This latter only multiplies the difficulties in estimating a rate of return on these loans if they are granted under the PLS scheme. In Iran, ... it has been decreed that financial transactions between and among the elements of the public sector, including Bank Markazi [the central bank] and commercial banks that are wholly nationalised, can take place on the basis of a fixed rate of return; such a fixed rate is not viewed as interest. Therefore the Government can borrow from the nationalised banking system without violating the Law.

While the last claim may be subject to question, there is another serious consequence:

Continued borrowing on a fixed rate basis by the Government would inevitably index bank charges to this rate than to the actual profits of borrowing entities.

Legislation

Existing banking laws do not permit banks to engage directly in business enterprises using depositors' funds. But this is the basic asset acquiring method of Islamic banks. Therefore new legislation and/or government authorisation are necessary to establish such banks. In Iran a comprehensive legislation was passed to establish Islamic banks. In Pakistan the Central Bank was authorised to take the necessary steps. In other countries either the banks found ways of using existing regulations or were given special accommodation. In all cases government intervention or active support was necessary to establish Islamic banks working under the PLS scheme.

In spite of this, there is still need for further auxiliary legislation in order to fully realise the goals of Islamic banking. For example, in Pakistan,

... the new law has been introduced without fundamental changes in the existing laws governing contracts, mortgages, and pledges. Similarly no law has been introduced to define modes of participatory financing, that is *Musharakah* and PTCs. It is presumed that whenever there is a conflict between the Islamic banking framework and the existing law, the latter will prevail. In essence, therefore, the relationship between the bank and the client, that of creditor and debtor is left unchanged as specified by the existing law. .... The existing banking law was developed to protect mainly the credit transactions; its application to other modes of financing results in the treatment of those modes as credit transactions also. Banks doubt whether some contracts, though consistent with the Islamic banking framework, would be acceptable in the courts. Hence, incentives exist for default and abuse.

In Iran, although the law establishing interest-free banking :

... is comprehensive, the lack of proper definitions of property rights may have constrained bank lending. Thus far there has been no precise legislative and legal expression of what is viewed as "lawful and conditional" private property rights. This may also have militated against investment lending in agricultural and industrial sectors and thus encouraged increased concentration of assets in short-term trade financing instruments.

Iran and Pakistan are countries committed to ridding their economies of *riba* and have made immense strides in towards achieving it. Yet there are many legal difficulties still to be solved as we have seen above. In other Muslim countries the authorities actively or passively participate in the establishment of Islamic banks on account of their religious persuasion. Such is not the case in non-Muslim countries. Here establishing Islamic banks involves conformation to the existing laws of the concerned country which generally are not conducive to PLS type of financing in the banking sector.

Involvement in specialised non-bank activities

Dr Hasanuz-Zaman, lists the traditional tasks of the bank and then questions its ability to take on the additional functions it is called upon to perform under the PLS scheme:

It is due to historical reasons that banks have evolved purely as a financial institution. They are suited to attract money, keep it in safe custody, lend it under safety, invest it profitably and enjoy the capacity to create the means of payment. A bank has to maintain a balance between income, liquidity and flexibility. While allocating its funds it has to be meticulously sensitive about the factors like capital position and rate of profitability of various types of loans, stability of deposit, economic conditions, influence of monetary and fiscal policy, ability and experience of bank's personnel and credit needs of the area. So far these banks thrive on a fixed rate of return a portion of which is passed on by them to the depositor. Thus the entire effort of a bank is directed towards money management and it is not geared to act as an entrepreneur, trader, industrialist, contractor or caterer.

The question arises: with all these limitations can a bank claim any competence in trading or entrepreneurship which is necessary for *musharakah* or *mudarba* contract, or can it act as an owner of a large variety of heavy machinery, transport vehicles or real estate to take the position of a lessor or, can it act as a stockist to buy and resell the entire stock of imports and exports that are needed by genuine traders?

Then he raises the even more serious question:

In case the bank is historically and practically not competent to do all these jobs its claim to share a portion of profits as a working partner, trader or lessor becomes questionable.

Traditional banks do perform a certain amount of project evaluation when granting large medium- and long-term loans. But doing such detailed evaluation as would be required to embark on a PLS scheme, such as determining the rates of return and their time schedule, is beyond the scope of conventional banks. So is the detailed accounting and monitoring necessary to determine the actual performance.

Under Islamic banking these exercises are not limited to relatively few large loans but need to be carried out on nearly all the advances made by the bank. Yet, widely acceptable and reliable techniques are yet to be devised. This is confounded by the fact that no consensus has yet been reached on the principles. Both the unprecedented nature of the task as well as the huge amount of work that need be done and the trained and experienced personnel needed to carry them out seems a daunting prospect.

Re-training of staff

As was seen in the previous section, the bank staff will have to acquire many new skills and learn new procedures to operate the Islamic banking system. This is a time consuming process which is aggravated by two other factors. One, the sheer number of persons that need to be re-trained and, two, the additional staff that need to be recruited and trained to carry out the increased work. Principles are still to be laid down and techniques and procedures evolved to carry them out. It is only after the satisfactory achievement of these that proper training can begin. This delay and the resulting confusion appears to be among the main reasons for the banks to stick to modes of financing that are close to the familiar interest-based modes.

Other disincentives

Among the other disincentives from the borrower's point of view are the need to disclose his accounts to the bank if he were to borrow on the PLS basis, and the fear that eventually the tax authorities will become wise to the extent of his business and the profits. Several writers have lashed out at the lack of business ethics among the business community, but that is a fact of life at least for the foreseeable future. There is a paucity of survey or case studies of clients to see their reaction to current modes of financing. As such we are not aware of further disincentives that might be there.

Accounts

When a business is financed under the PLS scheme it is necessary that the actual profit/loss made using that money be calculated. Though no satisfactory methods have yet been devised, the first requirement for any such activity is to have the necessary accounts. On the borrowers' side there are two difficulties: one, many small-time businessmen do not keep any accounts, leave alone proper accounts. The time and money costs will cut into his profits. Larger businesses do not like to disclose their real accounts to anybody. On the banks' side the effort and expense involved in checking the accounts of many small accounts is prohibitive and will again cut into their own share of the profits. Thus both sides would prefer to avoid having to calculate the actually realised profit/loss. To quote Iqbal and Mirakhor: .... the commercial banks do face an element of moral hazard owing to the non-existence of systematic book-keeping in this sector. Additionally the reluctance of small producers to submit their operations to bank audits and the perceived enormous cost of auditing and monitoring relative to the small size of the potential credits makes banks unwilling to extend credit on the basis of new modes of financing to these small producers. These reduced lending to small producers may also explain the existence of excess liquidity in the banking system.

Tax

The bank is a big business and it has to declare its profit and loss and is legally required to present an audited account of its operations. Once the bank's accounts are known it doesn't take much for the tax collectors to figure out the share of the businesses financed by the bank under the PLS scheme. Thus it's no surprise that businesses are not too very happy about the situation. The fact that suggestions have been made to use the banks to collect taxes due has not helped the matter either.

Excess liquidity

Presence of excess liquidity is reported in nearly all Islamic banks. This is not due to reduced demand for credit but the due to the inability of the banks to find clients willing to be funded under the new modes of financing. Financing. Here we have a situation where there is money available on the one hand and there is need for it on the other but the new rules stand in the way of bringing them together! This is a very strange situation — specially in the developing Muslim countries where money is at a premium even for ordinary economic activities, leave alone development efforts. Removal of riba was expected to ease such difficulties, not to aggravate the already existing ones!

Uneasy questions of morality

The practices in use by the Islamic banks have evoked questions of morality. Do the practices adopted to avoid interest really do their job or is it simply a change of name? It suffices to quote a few authors.

The Economist writes:

> ..... *Muslim theoreticians and bankers have between them devised ingenious ways of coping with the interest problem. One is* murabaha. *The Koran says you cannot borrow $100m from the bank for a year, at 5% interest, to buy the new machinery your factory needs? Fine. You get the bank to buy the machinery for you — cost, $100m — and then you buy the stuff from the bank, paying it $105m a year from now. The difference is that the extra $5m is not interest on loan, which the Koran (perhaps) forbids, but your thanks to the bank for the risk it takes of losing money while it is the owner of the machinery: this is honest trading, okay with the Koran. Since with modern communications the bank's ownership may last about half a second, its risk is not great, but the transaction is pure. It is not surprising that* some Muslims uneasily sniff logic-chopping here.

Dr Ghulam Qadir says of practices in Pakistan:

> *Two of the modes of financing prescribed by the State Bank, namely financing through the purchase of client's property with a buy-back agreement and sale of goods to clients on a mark-up, involved the least risk and were closest to the old interest-based operations. Hence the banks confined their operations mostly to these modes, particularly the former, after changing the simple buy-back agreement (prescribed by the State Bank) to buy-back agreement with a mark-up, as otherwise there was no incentive for them to extend any finances. The banks also reduced their mark-up-based financing, whether through the purchase of client's property or through the sale of goods to clients, to mere paper work, instead of actual buying of goods (property), taking their possession and then selling (back) to the client. As a result, there was no difference between the mark-up as practised by the banks and the conventional interest rate, and hence it was judged repugnant to Islam in the recent decision of the Federal Shari'ah court.*

As banks are essentially financial institutions and not trading houses, requiring them to undertake trading in the form of buy-back arrangements and sale on mark-up amounts to imposing on them a function for which they are not well equipped. Therefore, *banks in Pakistan made such modifications in the prescribed modes which defeated the very purpose of interest-free financing.* Furthermore, as these two minimum-risk modes of financing were kept open to banks, they never tried to devise innovative and imaginative modes of financing within the framework of musharakah and mudarba.

Prof. Khurshid Ahmad says:

> Murabaha *(cost-plus financing) and* bai' mu'ajjal *(sale with deferred payment) are permitted in the Shari'ah under certain conditions. Technically, it is not a form of financial mediation but a kind of business participation. The Shari'ah assumes that the financier actually buys the goods and then sells them to the client. Unfortunately, the current practice of "buy-back on mark-up" is not in keeping with the conditions on which* murabaha *or* bai' mu'ajjal *are permitted. What is being done is* a fictitious deal which ensures a predetermined profit to the bank without actually dealing in goods or sharing any real risk. This is against the letter and spirit of Shari'ah injunctions.

While I would not venture a *fatwa*, as I do not qualify for that function, yet as a student of economics and Shari'ah I regard this practice of "buy-back on mark-up" very similar to *riba* and would suggest its discontinuation. I understand that the Council of Islamic Ideology has also expressed a similar opinion.

Dr Hasanuz Zaman is more scathing in his condemnation:

> *It emerges that practically it is impossible for large banks or the banking system to practise the modes like mark-up,* bai' salam, *buy-back,* murabaha, *etc. in a way that fulfils the Shari'ah conditions. But in order to make themselves eligible to a return on their operations, the banks are compelled to* play tricks with the letters of the law. *They actually do not buy, do not posses, do not actually sell and deliver the goods; but the transition is assumed to have taken place. By signing a number of documents of purchase, sale and transfer they might fulfil a legal requirement but* it is by violating the spirit of prohibition.

Again,

> *It seems that in large number of cases* the ghost of interest is haunting them *to calculate a fixed rate percent per annum even in* musharakah, mudarba, *leasing, hire-purchase, rent sharing,* murabaha, (bai' mu'ajjal, *mark-up), PTC, TFC, etc. The spirit behind all these contracts seems to make a sure earning comparable with the prevalent rate of interest and, as far as possible, avoid losses which otherwise could occur.*

To sum up, in Dr Hasanuz Zaman's words:

> *... many techniques that the interest-free banks are practising are not either in full conformity with the spirit of Shari'ah or practicable in the case of large banks or the entire banking system. Moreover,* they have failed to do away with undesirable aspects of interest. Thus, they have retained what an Islamic bank should eliminate.

Islamic Banking in Non-Muslim Countries

The modern commercial banking system in nearly all countries of the world is mainly evolved from and modelled on the practices in Europe, especially that in the United Kingdom. The philosophical roots of this system revolves around the basic principles of capital certainty for depositors and certainty as to the rate of return on deposits. In order to enforce these principles for the sake of the depositors and to ensure the smooth functioning of the banking system Central Banks have been vested with powers of supervision and control.

All banks have to submit to the Central Bank rules. Islamic banks which wish to operate in non-Muslim countries have some difficulties in complying with these rules. We will examine below the salient features.

Certainty of capital and return

While the conventional banks guarantee the capital and rate of return, the Islamic banking system, working on the principle of profit and loss sharing, cannot, by definition, guarantee any fixed rate of return on deposits. Many Islamic banks do not guarantee the capital either, because if there is a loss it has to be deducted from the capital. Thus the basic difference lies in the very roots of the two systems. Consequently countries working under conventional laws are unable to grant permission to institutions which wish to operate under the PLS scheme to functions as commercial banks. Two official comments, one from the UK an the other from the USA suffice to illustrate this.

Sir Leigh Pemberton, the Governor of the Bank of England, told the Arab Bankers' Association in London that:

- o It is important not to risk misleading and confusing the general public by allowing two essentially different banking systems to operate in parallel;
- o A central feature of the banking system of the United Kingdom as enshrined in the legal framework is capital certainty for depositors. It is the most important feature which distinguished the banking sector from the other segments of the financial system;
- o Islamic banking is a perfectly acceptable mode of financing but it does not fall within the definition of what constitutes banking in the UK;
- o The Bank of England is not legally able to authorise under the Banking Act, an institution which does not take deposits as defined under that Act;
- o The Islamic facilities might be provided within other areas of the financial system without using a banking name.

In the United States, Mr Charles Schotte, the US Treasury Department specialist in regulatory issues has remarked:

There has never been an application for an Islamic establishment to set up either as a bank or as anything else. So there is no precedent to guide us. Any institution that wishes to use the word 'bank' in its title has to guarantee at least a zero rate of interest — and even that might contravene Islamic laws.

Supervision and control

Besides these, there are other concerns as well. One is the Central Bank supervision and control. This mainly relates to liquidity requirements and adequacy of capital. These in turn depend on an assessment of the value of assets of the Islamic banks. A financial advisor has this to say:

The bank of England, under the 1979 Act, would have great difficulty in putting a value on the assets of an Islamic institution which wanted to operate as a bank in the UK. The traditional banking system has much of its assets in fixed interest instruments and it is comparatively easy to value that. For example, if they are British Government instruments they will have a quoted market value; and there are recognised methods for valuing traditional banking assets when they become non-productive. But it is very difficult indeed to value an Islamic asset such as a share in a joint venture; and the Bank of England would have to send a team of experienced accountants into every Islamic bank operating in the UK as a bank under the 1979 Act, to try to put a proper and cautious value on its assets.

Another financial analyst states:

Even if a method could be found for assessing the risks to calculate the capital necessary, little comfort could be taken from the profitability which is usually relied upon to cover day-to-day losses arising from the bank's business, because a substantial part of an Islamic bank's portfolio is venture capital without any guaranteed return.

It is evident then that even if there is a desire to accommodate the Islamic system, the new procedures that need be developed and the modifications that need be made to existing procedures are so large that the chances of such accommodation in a cautious sector such as banking is very remote indeed. Any relaxation of strict supervision is precluded because should an Islamic bank fail it would undermine the confidence in the whole financial system, with which it is inevitably identified. As Suratgar puts it:

There could be potential dangers for the international system, where the failure of such an institution could bring with it the failure of other associated institutions, or of all the Western banking institutions which come closely tied to with such an operation.

The question has engaged the attention of Central Banks in Muslim countries as well. But reliable satisfactory methods are still to developed.

Tax regulations

Another important consideration is the tax procedures in non-Muslim countries. While interest is a 'passive' income, profit is an earned income which is treated differently. In addition, in trade financing there are title transfers twice — once from seller to bank and then from bank to buyer — and therefore twice taxed on this account decreasing the profitability of the venture.

The Director of the International Islamic Bank of Denmark says: Tax laws are against the Islamic philosophy and pose the greatest difficulty. In most OECD countries Mudarabha is constrained by fiscal acts which define profits as an after tax item for the profit creator and a fully taxable item for the profit receiver.

Discussion and Suggestions

People have needs — food, clothes, houses, machinery, services; the list is endless. Entrepreneurs perceive these needs and develop ways and means of catering to them. They advertise their products and services, peoples expectations are raised and people become customers of the entrepreneur. If the customers' needs are fulfilled according to their expectations they continue to patronise the entrepreneur and his enterprise flourishes. Otherwise his enterprise fails and people take to other entrepreneurs.

Banks too are enterprises; they cater to peoples' needs connected with money — safe-keeping, acquiring capital, transferring funds etc. The fact that they existed for centuries and continue to exist and prosper is proof that their methods are good and they fulfil the customers' needs and expectations. Conventional commercial banking system as it operates today is accepted in all countries except the Islamic world where it is received with some reservation. The reservation is on account of the fact that the banking operations involve dealing in interest which is prohibited in Islam. Conventional banks have ignored this concern on the part of their Muslim clientele. Muslims patronised the conventional banks out of necessity and, when another entrepreneur — the Islamic banker — offered to address their concern many Muslims turned to him. The question is: has the new entrepreneur successfully met their concerns, needs and expectations? If not he may have to put up his shutters!

Broadly speaking, banks have three types of different customers: depositors, borrowers and seekers of bank's other services such as money transfer. Since services do not generally involve dealing in interest Muslims have no problem transacting such businesses with conventional banks; neither do Islamic banks experience any problems in providing these services. Among the depositors there are current account holders who too, similarly, have no problems. It is the savings account holders and the borrowers who have reservations in dealing with the conventional banks. In the following paragraphs we will see how well the Islamic banks have succeeded in addressing their customers' special concern.

Savings accounts and capital guarantee

As pointed out earlier, our concern here is the savings account holders. As the name itself indicates the primary aim of the saving account depositor is the safe-keeping of his savings. It is correctly perceived by the conventional banker and he guarantees the return of the deposit in toto. The banker also assumes that the depositor will prefer to keep his money with him in preference to another who might also provide the same guarantee if the depositor is provided an incentive. This incentive is called interest, and this interest is made proportional to the amount and length of time it is left with the bank in order to encourage more money brought into the bank and left there for longer periods of time. In addition, the interest rate is fixed in advance so that the depositor and the banker are fully aware of their respective rights and obligations from the beginning. And laws have been enacted to guarantee their enforcement. In Economic theory the interest is often taken to be the "compensation" the depositors demand and receive for parting with their savings. The fact that the depositors accept the paid interest and that, given other things being equal, they prefer the bank or the scheme which offers the highest interest proves the banker's assumption correct.

The scheme is simple, transparent and seems to have satisfied the requirements of all types of savers — from teenagers to old-age pensioners, from individuals to large institutions, pension funds and endowments, from small amounts to millions, and from a few weeks or months to years — that it has survived over centuries and operates across national, cultural and religious borders.

The situation is very different in the Islamic banks. Here too the depositor's first aim is to keep his savings in safe custody. Islamic bankers divide the conventional savings account into two categories (alternatively, create a new kind of account): savings account and investment account. The investment accounts operate fully under the PLS scheme — capital is not guaranteed, neither is there any pre-fixed return. Under the savings account the nominal value of the deposit is guaranteed, but they receive no further guaranteed returns. Banks may consider funds under the savings accounts too as part of their resources and use it to create assets. This is theory. In practice, however, the banks prefer, encourage and emphasise the investment accounts. This is because since their assets operate under the PLS scheme they might incur losses on these assets which losses they cannot pass onto the savings accounts depositors on account of the capital guarantee on these accounts. In the process the first aim of the depositor is pushed aside and the basic rule of commercial banking —capital guarantee— is broken.

It is suggested that all Islamic banks guarantee the capital under their savings accounts. This will satisfy the primary need and expectation of an important section of the depositors and, in Muslim countries where both Islamic and conventional banks co-exist, will induce more depositors to bank with the Islamic banks. At the same time, it will remove the major objection to establishing Islamic banks in non-Muslim countries.

But the question is how does the bank make an income from these deposits? We will examine this in the next section.

Loans with a service charge

We have already seen that all the problems of the Islamic banks arise from their need to acquire their assets under the PLS scheme. A simple solution does, in fact, already exist in the current theories of Islamic banking. It need only be pointed out and acted upon. We will examine the provisions in the Iranian, Pakistani and the Siddiqi models.

All three models provide for loans with a service charge. Though the specific rules are not identical, the principle is the same. We suggest that the funds in the deposit accounts (current and savings) be used to grant loans (short- and long-term) with a service charge. By doing this the Islamic banks will be able to provide all the loan facilities that conventional banks provide while giving capital guarantee for depositors and earning an income for themselves. This would also remove the rest of the obstacles in opening and operating Islamic banks in non-Muslim countries. The bonus for the borrowers is that the service charge levied by the Islamic banks will necessarily be less than the interest charged by conventional banks.

Let us now look at the existing relevant rules in the three models. The Iranian model provides for *Gharz-al hasaneh* whose definition, purpose and operation are given in Articles 15, 16 and 17 of Regulations relating to the granting of banking facilities:

Article 15

Gharz-al-hasaneh is a contract in which one (the lender) of the two parties relinquishes a specific portion of his possessions to the other party (the borrower) which the borrower is obliged to return to the lender in kind or, where not possible, its cash value.

Article 16

... the banks ... shall set aside a part of their resources and provide Gharz-al-hasaneh for the following purposes:

(a) to provide equipment, tools and other necessary resources so as to enable the creation of employment, in the form of co-operative bodies, for those who lack the necessary means;

(b) to enable expansion in production, with particular emphasis on agricultural, livestock and industrial products;

(c) to meet essential needs.

Article 17

The expenses incurred in the provision of Gharz-al-hasaneh shall be, in each case, calculated on the basis of the directives issued by Bank Markazi Jomhouri Islami Iran and collected from the borrower.

In Pakistan, permissible modes of financing include:

Financing by lending:

(i) Loans not carrying any interest on which the banks may recover a service charge not exceeding the proportionate cost of the operation, excluding the cost of funds and provisions for bad and doubtful debts. The maximum service charge permissible to each bank will be determined by the State Bank from time to time.

(ii) Qard-e-hasana loans given on compassionate grounds free of any interest or service charge and repayable if and when the borrower is able to pay.

Siddiqi has suggested that 50 percent of the funds in the 'loan' (i.e. current and savings) accounts be used to grant short-term loans. A fee is to be charged for providing these loans:

An appropriate way of levying such a fee would be to require prospective borrowers to pay a fixed amount on each application, regardless of the amount required, the term of the loan or whether the application is granted or rejected. Then the applicants to whom a loan is granted may be required to pay an additional prescribed fee for all the entries made in the banks registers. The criterion for fixing the fees must be the actual expenditure which the banks have incurred in scrutinising the applications and making decisions, and in maintaining accounts until loans are repaid. These fees should not be made a source of income for the banks, but regarded solely as a means of maintaining and managing the interest-free loans.

It is clear from the above that all three models agree on the need for having cash loans as one mode of financing, and that this service should be paid for by the borrower. Though the details may vary, all seem to suggest that the charge should be the absolute cost only. We suggest that a percentage of this absolute cost be added to the charge as a payment to the bank for providing this service. This should enable an Islamic bank to exist and function independently of its performance in its PLS operations.

Investment under PLS scheme

The idea of participatory financing introduced by the Islamic banking movement is a unique and positive contribution to modern banking. However, as we saw earlier, by making the PLS mode of financing the main (often almost the only) mode of financing the Islamic banks have run into several difficulties. If, as suggested in the previous section, the Islamic banks would provide all the conventional financing through lending from their deposit accounts (current and savings), it will leave their hands free to engage in this responsible form of financing innovatively, using the funds in their investment accounts. They could then engage in genuine *Mudaraba* financing. Being partners in an enterprise they will have access to its accounts, and the problems associated with the non-availability of accounts will not arise.

Commenting on *Mudaraba* financing, *The Economist* says:

.... some people in the West have begun to find the idea attractive. It gives the provider of money a strong incentive to be sure he is doing something sensible with it. What a pity the West's banks did not have that incentive in so many of their lending decisions in the 1970s and 1980s. It also emphasises the sharing of responsibility, by all the users of money. That helps to make the free-market system more open; you might say more democratic.

CONCLUSIONS

Islamic banking is a very young concept. Yet it has already been implemented as the only system in two Muslim countries; there are Islamic banks in many Muslim countries, and a few in non-Muslim countries as well. Despite the successful acceptance there are problems. These problems are mainly in the area of financing.

With only minor changes in their practices, Islamic banks can get rid of all their cumbersome, burdensome and sometimes doubtful forms of financing and offer a clean and efficient interest-free banking. All the necessary ingredients are already there. The modified system will make use of only two forms of financing — loans with a service charge and *Mudaraba* participatory financing — both of which are fully accepted by all Muslim writers on the subject.

Such a system will offer an effective banking system where Islamic banking is obligatory and a powerful alternative to conventional banking where both co-exist. Additionally, such a system will have no problem in obtaining authorisation to operate in non-Muslim countries.

Participatory financing is a unique feature of Islamic banking, and can offer responsible financing to socially and economically relevant development projects. This is an additional service Islamic banks offer over and above the traditional services provided by conventional commercial banks.

8

Islamic Banking and Finance: Another Approach

In recent years a series of three books has been published on the above subject.Each book is self-contained, treats a specific topic, and presents a new methodology.However, taken together, they provide a comprehensive banking system that addresses the needs and concerns of Muslims today.Their titles speak for themselves: *Interest-free Commercial Banking, Participatory Financing through Investment Banks and Commercial Banks,* and *Commercial Banking in the presence of Inflation.*In this article we propose to give an overview of this new approach.

MAIN FEATURES

The salient features of the proposed system are: (1) There is no interest on deposits, but capital is guaranteed. (2) Lending and investing are treated differently; loans are interest-free but carry a service charge, while investing is on a profit-and-loss-sharing (*mudaraba*) basis.Commercial banks will grant loans but they will not engage in investment-financing.Investment-financing will be done through investment banks and investment companies. (3) Value erosion of capital due to inflation is compensated. With these features the proposed system simply *avoids* the many problems faced by Islamic banking as practised today, including its inability to set up and operate interest-free banks in most countries of the world.The problem of inflation is not explicitly treated by any system of banking, but it is a general problem and is treated as such in the third book.The system can be considered as consisting of several independent modules.And, one or more could be implemented at a time, according to the requirements of a given situation.We will expand on these topics in the following sections.

As far as commercial banking is concerned, there are two major departures from the traditional approaches (conventional or Islamic), and these are very important developments.One is that this system considers commercial banks as service providers, instead of as "money lenders" (conventional) or "investment-partners" (Islamic).Two, the books present a general model of commercial bank lending process, and interest-free banking is derived as a sub-model; the conventional banking is seen as an "inflation-free" sub-model of the general model.These departures enable one to eliminate *riba* from the system without resorting to drastic measures, and still have a fully viable system compatible with the conventional one.In turn, this compatibility makes the new system easy to understand and to explain, and therefore easy to implement in all countries.The philosophical re-orientation, procedural adjustments, and the re-training of staff required for the change over from the conventional to the proposed system are also minimal.More importantly, the new approach makes commercial banking transparent, interest-free or not.

ZERO INTEREST AND CAPITAL GUARANTEE

Muslims are prohibited by their religion to deal in interest (*riba*) in any way.Giving and receiving as well as witnessing are all prohibited.Thus an Islamic banking system cannot pay any interest to its depositors; neither can it demand or receive any interest from the borrowers.Nor could the banks witness or keep accounts of these transactions.But the lender is entitled to the return of his capital in full.This is a Qur'anic injunction.The proposed system complies with these fundamental Islamic requirements.

A basic tenet of commercial banking is capital guarantee.The capital entrusted to the bank by a depositor must be returned to him in full.The proposed system fully complies with this requirement.Islamic banking as practised today does not provide capital guarantee in all its deposit accounts.In many countries, this is one of the two main objections to permitting the establishment of Islamic banks.There is no objection to paying zero interest on deposits.

Thus, by paying zero interest and guaranteeing capital, the proposed system satisfies both the *riba*-prohibition rule of Islam and the capital guarantee requirement of conventional Banking Acts.This enables it to obtain permission to set up and operate as a deposit bank in all countries of the world, while obeying the *riba*-prohibition rule and qualifying to be an "Islamic" bank.This is of paramount importance to Muslim minorities living in non-Muslim countries.Furthermore, the existence of interest-free banks in all countries will also remove the many difficulties faced today by Islamic banks in transacting international business.

LENDING AND INVESTING

In conventional banking, depositing is a form of investment for the savers where the capital remains intact while a known income (in the form of interest) is promised.To the banks lending is a form of investment where the capital and a known return are assured; the return will also cover all their costs.Since Islam prohibits dealing in interest in any form this type of banking is not acceptable to the Muslims.

In Islam, there is a clear difference between lending and investing — lending can be done only on the basis of zero interest and capital guarantee, and investing only on the basis of *mudaraba* (profit-and-loss-sharing).Conventional banking does not — and need not — make this differentiation.But an Islamic bank has to take this into consideration in devising a system to cater to the Muslims.Therefore such a system has to provide for two sub-systems — one to cater to those who would "lend" and another for those who wish to invest.

In the proposed system, the depositors are considered as lenders to the bank and, since a Muslim lender cannot receive any interest, he lends without interest but with the assurance that his capital will be returned in full.This applies to demand (current account) deposits as well as to savings deposits.The bank, in turn, lends (the depositors' funds) to the borrower who should return the capital in full plus the costs of the bank's services and a remuneration (or profit) to the bank for providing these services.This suits some depositors and some borrowers.The first book — *Interest-free Commercial Banking* — is concerned with this group of people.The theory and method are fully explained in the book.

The second objection to Islamic banks as they operate today is that their assets are not readily assessable (since they are tied up in equity-type investments where neither capital nor return are guaranteed), and to put a reasonable value on these assets will require enormous amounts of effort and experience.In the proposed system, the depositors' capital and return (*albeit* zero) are guaranteed; and the bank's assets are also guaranteed and their costs are fully covered; and the accounting procedures are well defined and uncomplicated.As such the bank's assets are assessable. Therefore the proposed method should attract no objection from any banking authority, thereby enabling interest-free (or Islamic) banks to be set up in all countries of the world.

In conventional banking those who wish to earn an income using their savings do so by putting their capital in savings deposits or time (fixed) deposits and receive an interest payment.A Muslim cannot earn an income by this means.He has to *participate* in a project by financing it and by sharing in its loss or profit.The participatory financing described in the next section is devised to cater to this group.

PARTICIPATORY FINANCING

The second book, *Participatory Financing through Investment Banks and Commercial Banks,* provides the mechanics of a financing scheme that would cater to the needs of those Muslim capital-holders who wish to earn an income using their capital without involving themselves in *riba.*The Islamic option for this group is the concept called *mudaraba,* which is usually translated as profit-and-loss-sharing but is in fact profit-sharing-and-loss-absorbing, and in this book it is named as participatory financing.The basic idea is that two parties, one with capital and the other with know-how, get together to carry out a project.If the project ends in profit they share the profit in a pre-arranged proportion; if it results in loss the entire loss is borne by the financier.There are many variations of this simple model but this is the basic concept. The book provides a general mechanism for the implementation of this concept, examines various different situations that occur in real life, and shows how the same mechanism can be modified to suit each situation.The situations range from the simple two-person model and the slightly more complex one-project-many-investors case, to one where an intermediary comes in, to accept capital from several investors for investing in many different enterprises and then to collect and distribute the profit/loss to the investors.The intermediaries may range from small local investment companies to large-scale multinationals, and from investment banks to commercial banks.And the investors may range from small-time individual savers to institutional savers and millionaires.The projects too may vary from small one-person enterprises to multimillion projects by very large companies.And the projects may last for a short limited period or continue for a very long time.

The investor is essentially a sleeping partner.He provides the financing and then shares the profit or absorbs the loss.It is the responsibility of the entrepreneur to present a good project proposal, convince the financier that it is viable and profitable, and provide proof that he is able, qualified and experienced to carry out the project successfully.The intermediary is at once both an entrepreneur and a financier.When he accepts funds from an investor, he is an entrepreneur; and when he finances a project submitted by an entrepreneur, he is a financier.

The function of the intermediary is very important.He is responsible for identifying good projects for financing as well as for monitoring its progress and ensuring its proper accounting and auditing.But he (the intermediary) plays no part in managing the project or in making policy decisions — that is the exclusive domain of the entrepreneur.The intermediary is a separate physical and legal entity, independent of both the investors and the entrepreneurs.But he (she/it) is an equal partner in every project he finances so that he has full legal right to the physical and financial assets of all the projects and has full access to all the books.This is very important, and it is here that participatory financing differs from conventional financing practices; in this respect it differs from the current practices of Islamic banks too.It allows the intermediary to have a true picture of the health of the project at all times.He can then take any preventive or corrective action (in extreme cases), and, in the event of the failure of a project, he can recover whatever is left of it.This arrangement assures the investors that their investment is safe and that the profit and loss account given to them are reliable and transparent.The fact that the investors' confidence and the intermediary's own profit depends on the number and size of the successful projects should ensure that the intermediary seeks out good projects and closely monitors their progress.

The proposed scheme provides for two types of investments: one called Participatory Financing (PF) stocks and the other PF shares.These are essentially stocks and shares in the intermediary's PF scheme (which is a collection of all (or a group of) the projects financed by the intermediary), and they roughly correspond to short- and long-term fixed deposit accounts.The main difference is that the return is computed from the profit and loss statements of all the projects in the PF scheme (and the profit/loss shared among the participants) at the end of the accounting period.Therefore the profit/loss is a *realised* one, and not an anticipated or a pre-fixed one.Thus neither speculation, nor uncertainty, nor *riba* is involved in the operation.

Islamic Banking actually took root in 1975 with the establishment of the Islamic Development Bank, an inter-governmental bank; and the Dubai Islamic Bank, a private one.The question of establishing interest-free banks and thus freeing the Islamic economies from *riba* had exercised the minds of Muslim thinkers for the better part of this century.But the immediate impetus for their establishment was the excess cash the oil-rich middle-eastern countries earned following the 1973 oil-price hike.Thus the primary need for these banks was the investment aspect of banking, and not the transaction (i.e. current account operations) aspect.The author believes that an Islamic banking system should separate these two aspects of banking and devise two separate schemes appropriate to the different requirements.It is the failure to do so that has resulted in Islamic banking facing the problems it faces today.The second book —*Participatory Financing through Investment Banks and Commercial Banks*— provides for the needs of this group of people — those who posses capital and wish to use it to earn an income, but without involving in *riba.*

There are Muslim capital-owners in all countries, ranging from those in the oil-rich countries and the very rich in all countries, possessing millions and billions, to the small timers in every country and those in the rich non-Muslim countries living in small communities.Each will find a suitable spot in this participatory financing scheme, which spans a large spectrum of different situations.One end of this spectrum is really micro-level financing and the other end encompasses international financing.

One important feature of participatory financing is that the entrepreneur need not provide security for the financing he receives.The project itself is the security, and the intermediary, being an equal partner in the enterprise, is its guardian.This should play a very constructive role in discovering and developing new entrepreneurial and other talents in the society, especially at the micro level.

Financing by lending

Traditionally, commercial banks performed two functions: money transfer services, including all current account operations, and money lending.The latter brought in the major part of the bank's income while the former enabled it to "create" money and to lend more money than it actually possessed.The primary concerns of the bank were the security of its capital and the ability of the borrower to pay the interest — not the end use of the lent money.Whether it was intended for establishing a new enterprise, to expand an existing one, to bridge a cash flow problem of a running concern, or to be used by a small business, by a sole-owner enterprise, or for consumption purposes, etc. was not the prime concern of the bank.Neither did it matter whether or how the borrower kept his accounts.The borrower must pay back all the capital and the pre-fixed amount of interest, no matter how he achieved that.In the case of Islamic banks, however, the end use mattered because the return on their "investment" (they do not lend) depended on how the profit/loss was achieved and how it was computed.The questions of true and proper bookkeeping by the borrowers (or entrepreneurs) and the auditing of these accounts, and that of determining the actual profit/loss directly attributable to the investment by the bank are still being debated.The inherent inability to resolve these questions is at the bottom of many of the problems faced by Islamic banks.Devices adopted to overcome these problems have only led to uneasy questions of morality.

In the proposed system, only the financing of *new* enterprises is recognised as amenable to *mudaraba*-type financing.The fact that the intermediary becomes an equal partner in the new enterprise avoids the difficulties caused by the above questions.All other types of end uses must be financed by loans from commercial banks, which would recover their costs and profit from the borrowers.We will look at some features of this "Islamic" or interest-free commercial banking in the next section.

INTEREST-FREE COMMERCIAL BANKING

As we saw earlier, commercial banks performed two functions: money transfer services (including all current account operations) and money lending.In general, the former does not involve any interest.On the other side of the balance sheet, we have two types of deposits: current account (demand) deposits and savings deposits.Here too, the former generally does not involve any interest.Therefore current account operations and money transfer operations are free of *riba* on both sides of the balance sheet.As such all commercial banks are interest-free banks with respect to these operations.

The problem, then, arises only in respect of savings deposits on the one side and loans on the other, because both incur interest.The question of lending and accepting savings deposits, without dealing in interest (*riba*), is dealt with in the first book — *Interest-free Commercial banking*.In this section we will give an overview of the approach.Details are to be found in the book.The book, however, takes it for granted that Muslims *do* wish to avoid dealing in interest in order to comply with their religious belief, and limits itself to finding a simple, logical and easily executable methodology of achieving this objective.It does not concern itself with providing a justification or philosophy for the prohibition.Nor with the subtle differences and related discussions regarding the correct definition of *riba*.It simply accepts the commonly understood meaning of it — that any money demanded or received by the lender in addition to his original capital is *riba* — and proceeds from there.The resulting system, therefore, is practicable irrespective of why one wishes to avoid dealing in interest.For there are also people who are convinced for various reasons that demanding or receiving interest is bad.

The approach adopted is to "first take a closer look at modern banking practices and find out whether and where the prohibited *riba* (interest) occurred and then to see whether it could be eliminated from the existing practices and then to check if the resulting system was still viable."

On the deposit side, what the depositor receives in addition to his capital is the interest.This is *riba* (pure interest) by definition.If a Muslim refuses this interest because it is prohibited by his religion, then this side of the balance sheet is free of *riba*.On the other side of the balance sheet, we have the "interest" collected by the bank from the borrower.Ideally, the bank uses the funds it receives from depositors to grant loans to clients.But the "interest" it charges the borrowers is more than the interest it pays the depositors.This is because the former should also cover, besides the interest paid to the depositor, the costs the bank incurs in collecting and disbursing the funds as well as in accounting, administration, safekeeping, etc.

A model is constructed where the "interest" charged by the bank is split into several components.Then each of these components is studied to see if it contained the prohibited *riba*.The idea is that if any one component contained such *riba* then to see if it could be removed.If some components are free of *riba*, and others containing *riba* can be removed, then we have an "interest" which is free of *riba*.If this can be achieved and if the resulting system is viable, then we have a *riba*-free system that is also viable.And, since it was originally derived from the conventional model it should also be compatible with it.

This "interest" collected by the bank from the borrower is a cost to the borrower, of obtaining this amount of financing.Therefore, it is named the Cost of Borrowing (CoB) and is considered as consisting of six components: interest (paid to the depositor), services cost, overheads cost, risk premium, profit, and compensation for the value erosion of capital due to inflation.It is shown that only the first component falls under the definition of *riba* and all others are free of it.Since the population the book is concerned with refuse to accept any interest paid by the bank (on religious or other grounds) the bank need not collect this component from the borrower.Thus this CoB is free of interest, despite the fact that it looks like the conventional "interest".Consequently, the whole commercial banking system becomes *riba*-free.

This is the essence of the thesis presented in the book.A description of each of the components, the method of their computation, how to implement the system, the advantages and consequences, and a whole lot of other necessary details are given in the book.It also provides an analytical method that can be used to test any lending scheme to see if it is *riba*-free or not.

In countries such as Pakistan, Iran and the Sudan where interest-free banking is mandatory, the system described in this section will be immediately relevant and will overcome all the problems the current practices in these countries find it difficult to solve.All that an existing bank has to do to change over to this system is to adopt the accounting system proposed in the book. We have already seen that this system should face no objection from banking authorities in non-Muslim countries, and since it is compatible with the conventional system it is easy to set up and operate such banks with the minimum of delay and difficulties (including staff training). Furthermore, unlike the conventional system, this system is transparent, rests on a firm theoretical foundation, and provides management information that is very useful for effective monitoring and control.The last is a very useful tool both to the concerned bank's internal management and to the Central Bank authorities.

Loan Default Insurance

The risk premium is one of the six components of the cost of borrowing.In conventional banking, the risk premium against default and delays is included in the interest and the bank bears the risk.The interest rate increases as the probability of risk increases; high-risk advances (such as unsecured loans) bearing a higher interest rate than low-risk ones.The model used in this book separates out this component, and proposes that it be a premium contribution to a *collective* insurance scheme, administered by a separate entity.Every borrower in any bank (in the scheme) is a member of this scheme for the duration of his loan.The premium depends on the amount of the loan, and not on the repayment period.The premiums paid by the members go into a collective fund.Any loss suffered by a member-bank due to bad loans is made good from this fund.On complete repayment of a loan the borrower will be paid part of his premium, after allowing for the administrative costs of the scheme and reimbursements to the banks (which depends on the number and size of defaults) during the period of his membership in the scheme, and proportionate to his contribution to the fund.

This is a novel proposal, and has three main beneficial consequences.One, this takes away any risk the bank runs due to non-payment of loans; thus making the bank a pure service provider.Then commercial banking becomes a service industry in the true sense.And, the burden of repayment is justifiably shifted to the borrower.Two, since the recovery of the loans are guaranteed the depositors are automatically assured of their capital.This obviates the need for deposit insurance.Three, there is an ongoing debate among Islamic scholars about the propriety of imposing a fine on a defaulting or delaying borrower, by the bank, fearing that it may amount to *riba*.In such cases the banks are expected to resort to the courts, which have powers to recover the amount due and/or impose a fine.But this is a costly and time-consuming process that can be misused.The new suggestion shifts that burden to the insurance company.They may have a credit-rating scheme, and each applicant for a loan may be assigned a premium depending on his past record.Defaulters may even be refused cover.

PARTICIPATORY FINANCING THROUGH COMMERCIAL BANKS

Commercial banks enjoy a privilege that investment banks and investment companies do not.They are able to "create" money which privilege they acquire through their current account operations.The process, called credit creation, is explained in the second book in an appendix.Briefly, it means that commercial banks can lend more money than they actually have in their custody.How much more depends on the particular circumstances of the concerned bank, but it can be anywhere from five to nine times.This is also called financing with bank money.A methodology has been developed in this book, where this ability is combined with the concepts of investment accounts (introduced by Islamic banks) and the *mudaraba* participation, to produce participatory financing through commercial banks.This will enable commercial banks to participate-finance many more projects than investment banks or investment companies could do with the same amount of money.But this is a new concept traditional banks are not equipped for.Bankers who wish to engage in this activity will have to have entrepreneurial talents and they have to acquire the necessary skills and cultivate suitable attitudes.

The concept, mechanism and application as well as concerns and cautions are extensively discussed in the book.But what is appropriate to say here is that this will allow low-yield and/ or long-duration projects, which will be unattractive to investment banks and companies, also to be commercially financed.A two-percent return on a 100,000 project is not very attractive.It is even less attractive if the profit is to be shared by three participants.But a commercial bank can finance this on the strength of a 20,000 deposit in the investment account, if it had a credit creation factor of 5.So, even if the project made only a two percent profit on the investment of 100,000, the resulting 2000 would still be a 10 percent profit on the original 20,000 deposit.On a factor of nine it would be a staggering 18 percent.Suppose the three participants — the investor, the bank and the entrepreneur — had originally agreed on an equal share of the profit, the investor would then receive a six-percent return on his investment.Thus an unattractive 2-percent-yield project can be made a very profitable one if financed through a commercial bank.

Such (unattractive) enterprises are socially and economically the most necessary ones, especially at the micro level; ones that bring direct benefit to people at the periphery — in the villages, in the small towns, and in the slums of large cities.This is an instrument that can be used to *commercially* finance social and economic development where it is most needed and will be most appreciated — at the grass roots level.

However, introducing participatory financing into commercial banking is asking it to shoulder extra burdens, including specialised staff training and additional risks.Conventional commercial banks are prohibited from directly investing in commercial enterprises, and hence they will not be able to offer participatory financing.In countries where Islamic banks are permitted to operate this should be no problem, provided the banks are prepared to take on the extra burdens, which of course, will bring them extra profits.They may consider setting up investment companies as fully owned subsidiaries of local branches.

COMPENSATION FOR INFLATION

In the last few decades, inflation seems to have become a permanent feature of all economies, especially of developing economies.This has a devastating effect on those who save money.If they keep it at home as cash, its value is eroded daily by inflation.If a friend borrowed it, its purchasing power is reduced when he returns it. If they deposit their savings with a bank, its value, when they withdraw it after some time, is much reduced.Sometimes the interest rate payable to the depositors lacks so behind the inflation rate that the combined purchasing power of the capital and interest is less than that of the original deposit!On the other hand, the bank's capital also loses value in the hands of the borrowers.Yet the banking system does not seem to specifically address this problem.For, legally speaking, the problem does not exist — one thousand today of any currency is legally one thousand tomorrow or ten years later, irrespective of any change in its purchasing power.But, admitting the reality, the banks do accommodate a compensation for the loss by adjusting the interest rate.The adjustment, however, is generally always in favour of the bank.This is unfair to both the depositor and the borrower.

In the case of a (Muslim) depositor who eschews interest, in rejecting the paid interest he also rejects the little compensation for inflation contained therein.This is as if he is being punished for his religious (or other) conviction, and for his desire to act on it.This is unfair.Therefore the third book —*Commercial Banking in the presence of Inflation*— addresses the problem explicitly so that neither the banks nor the clients are dealt an unfair deal.

The book begins by asking simple questions such as what is inflation and how it is measured.It explains the relation between price, inflation and money — when the price of a product increases your money buys less of that product; inflation has eaten the value of your money.But since there are several products (and services), each with its own price, and since all prices do not vary at the same speed, there are innumerable rates of inflation.Again, since all people do not spend their money on the same things or to the same extent, different people experience inflation to different degrees.It concludes its second extensive chapter by saying, "... the common perception that there exists a single rate of inflation, and an appropriate method of measuring it, is not correct."

Measuring inflation on capital

Price indexes are constructed to indicate average price changes among a group of related products or services.The groupings may relate to specific industries, to those used by a specific group of people, to a specific geographical area, etc.These price indexes are then used as indicators (or measures) of inflation.Price indexes can also be constructed by the purposes for which people spend their money.The money people earn or posses are also used for different purposes — a portion of it (in many cases, all of it or most it) is used for daily consumption expenses; what is left over is saved for future use, or is invested.The popular price index called the cost of living index (also called consumer price index) measures the inflation on the former type of money.But the concern in this study is the other two types of money — that is, money that one may consider his savings, wealth or capital.After studying several popular measures of inflation and showing that each one was constructed for a specific purpose, the third chapter concludes by saying that none of those measures are appropriate for the purpose at hand, i.e. as a measure of inflation on capital.The study also brings out other essential characteristics, besides appropriateness, that any measure should posses in order to meet the requirements of the present purpose.These include uniqueness; consistency, continuity and reliability; timeliness; and legal and popular acceptance.None of the existing measures of inflation posses these qualities.

Historically people have stored their wealth in gold and silver.Banks, including the central banks and the IMF, too hold a major portion of their reserves in gold.In fact, until recent times gold and silver coins were used as medium of exchange — that is, as money.The British Pound and the US Dollar owe the prestige of their use as reserve currencies to their (now historical) guaranteed equivalence to a certain amount of gold, as much as to any other new cause.Even today, when people's trust ebbed as to the ability of the banking system to return their deposits or as to that of the government to guarantee the value of the currency, people resorted to gold to hold their wealth in, if it was possible.In times and places of high inflation, gold is seen as a good hedge against erosion of the value of wealth.The book cites several recent examples from different countries.At the end of a series of arguments, gold is found to be the best *store of wealth* when there is inflation.Consequently the *market price* of gold can be used as a *measure of inflation on wealth* (or capital).In Chapter 4, a measure specific to this purpose is designed, and its characteristics examined to see if it satisfied all the specified criteria.It does satisfy all the criteria.Furthermore, the effort and expenses necessary to set up this new measure is almost negligible, on account of the fact that only one commodity and its price need be monitored; all other measures involve hundreds of prices.The interested reader may refer the book for details.

The new measure has been defined as the 13-week moving average of the previous 13 weekly average prices of a specified quality of gold at the local (meaning national) gold market, as determined by the country's Central Bank.This is the standard price of wealth for the current week.Its rate of change is the rate of inflation (or simply inflation) with respect to wealth (or capital).This measure, however, has a major hurdle to overcome if it is to be valid and useful in banking and financial transactions.That is, it needs to be legally recognised.This will need parliamentary legislation.If and when that happens it will be the legally accepted common measure of the rate of inflation on capital for the whole country, and one can use it straight away, both in official and private transactions.

Application to Commercial Banking

Inflation is a slow process that eats into capital imperceptibly.The damage occurs gradually over time, and the damage done during a short period of time is not worth bothering about.Therefore, in computing the compensation for capital erosion, one has to make a choice as to the time limit beyond which this damage requires attention.One month may be too short for inflation to make any substantial impact, and one year too long for someone to put his money away.Also a shorter time limit may bring in too many transactions under the scheme and cause too much computational work.Therefore a time limit of three months has been suggested for both deposits and advances.All accounts above this line will be maintained in gold-equivalents and all others in normal currency.

The analysis in this book has shown that the action necessary to counteract the effects of inflation is limited to only three areas: time deposits, medium- and long-term loans, and government bonds.All the other areas of commercial banking operations can continue as at present.The latter involve the bulk of the work at a commercial bank, and the introduction of gold-equivalent scheme does not add to this load.Therefore introducing this effective method against inflation is much simpler than would appear at first.Furthermore, it is a general method and can be applied equally well in conventional banking as in interest-free banking.

How does it work?In theory, all deposits will be accepted and returned in terms of gold units, and all loans will be granted and collected in terms of gold units.In other words, all capital transactions will be in gold.In practice, however, one has to deal in normal currency.This is where the gold price comes in — to compute the currency equivalent of the same amount of gold at the beginning and end of the term.

Using the rate of inflation on capital given by the gold price, one can compute the loss suffered by capital in currency units.For example, if the capital (deposit or loan) was 5000, and the rate of inflation (on capital) was 15 percent per annum, then the loss due to inflation in one year is 750 (= 0.15*5000).Thus, after one year, the inflation-compensated capital is 5750, in currency units.This is the amount the bank will return to the depositor, if the capital was a deposit.If it was a loan, the bank will collect this amount plus the other four components of the cost of borrowing from the borrower.

The important point to note here is that the compensation for inflation is computed at the time of withdrawal or repayment.Therefore, the prices used are *actually realised prices*.They are not predicted or expected future prices.Hence, there is *no uncertainly* in the computed values.What is computed is only what the capital really *did lose* due to inflation *while it was away* from the lender (depositor or bank).

When capital is so protected against inflation there is little sense in holding one's wealth in cash, or indeed in many other forms of property.Therefore, the opportunity this approach affords to bringing out idle capital into the banking system, and thus making it available for national development, is great.It deserves serious consideration by banks and governments, especially of the developing world.

Application to Participatory Financing

In the second book, a whole chapter has been devoted to the study of the effect of inflation on participatory financing.It has been recommended that, "... considering the [value] erosion of investor capital as part of project expenses, and reimbursing the amount to the investor (or rather to the project) before distributing the resulting profit/loss to the partners will form a better and more equitable approach."This amount was to be computed using the rate of inflation.But what that rate was and how it was to be estimated had been left unanswered.The inflation rate on capital developed in this volume can now be used as the rate of inflation required in participatory financing.

Government Bonds

Governments issue bonds to obtain long-term loans from the public.The face value of the bond is guaranteed on maturity, and, since the bonds are bought on issue at less than the face value, there is a return on them.Because they can be bought and sold easily, these are good liquid assets, especially for the banks.However, there is a problem when the economy is interest-free.The return is interest, and if one wished to avoid interest then he should buy the bond today at its face.But the face value realised on maturity would have lost part of its purchasing power due to inflation!Some have suggested that these bonds be issued on a profit-and-loss-sharing basis.But then such funds are invested by governments in non-profit projects (such as infrastructure, schools and hospitals) or in long-term projects (such as power or irrigation).The dilemma and the debate continue.The book suggests that the bonds be denominated in terms of gold-units.Then there will be no *riba*, for what is given and what is returned will be the same, in kind and amount; and the lender will not suffer the inroads made by inflation.

There is an interesting aside to the suggestion:"... many Muslim individuals and institutions will buy government bonds without any qualms about being involved in *riba*.The government too stands to gain, because they will now be paying less for the funds than before.But the other side of the coin is that the money now comes in with a moral string attached —with a patriotic or *fi-sabilillah* (for-God) motive— unlike in the conventional case where the motive is private gain — guaranteed positive return on capital.This puts the government under a moral pressure to use the funds properly and for good causes."

MODULAR IMPLEMENTATION

The system proposed in the three books can be considered as consisting of a number of modules.Each module is practically independent of the other.Therefore, one can tailor a system, consisting of one or more modules, depending on the specific circumstances of what is required, where it is required and who wants to implement it.The implementation can also be staggered over time.A few examples are considered in the next paragraphs.

The major modules are: (1) the full commercial bank module, (2) the participatory financing module, (3) the compensation for inflation module, and (4) the government bonds module.Within the first module there is a savings-and-loans sub-module, and within the second there are several options ranging from pure two-person *mudaraba* and small investment companies to large investment banks.Except the last module others do not need explicit changes in the laws of the country or of the banking business. Modules 1 and 2 can be implemented under existing banking and business laws.Module 3 will need new laws and Central Bank co-operation for strictly legal enforcement.However, it is possible to implement it by mutual agreement between the bank and its clients.Module 4 needs government action. In the oil-rich Middle-eastern countries, and in many developed countries, inflation is negligible.Therefore the third and fourth modules are not of immediate importance.Module 1 can be implemented to provide a complete commercial banking system that is free of *riba*.These banks will offer all current accounts, savings and loan facilities.Loan facilities will include short-term financing, temporary overdrafts, bills of exchange, treasury bills and letters of credit.All that an existing conventional bank has to do to convert to an interest-free one is to adopt the accounting system proposed in the first book and delete the pure interest component.This would also make all its dealings transparent.

Countries like Pakistan, Iran and the Sudan (where interest is prohibited by law and where inflation is also high) will have to implement all four modules to fully benefit from the proposed system.But the implementation can be done in stages, module by module.

Muslim communities living in non-Muslim countries, such as North America, Europe and India, may consider implementing the savings and loans sub-module of module 1 and some options of module 2.Where the population is large, such as in India, they may even implement all the modules except the last (government bonds). Modules 3 and 4 concern inflation.And inflation is no respecter of religious convictions or prohibitions — it affects all capital equally.As such these modules are of general applicability.Therefore they can be implemented, independently of other modules, by any country afflicted with inflation.That includes practically all developing countries.

Module 2 is a responsible form of financing.It is not the sole property of Muslims.Therefore it can be implemented (in any form of its several options) by any group of people concerned with where their money is invested and how their income is earned.

CONCLUSIONS

The three books under consideration have put forward a comprehensive banking and financing system.It has been developed to address primarily the needs and concerns of Muslims today in all parts of the world.Yet many of its components are of general applicability.It *avoids* almost all the pitfalls encountered by Islamic banking as practised today and successfully addresses many issues currently being debated.It offers sufficient flexibility to be tailored to suit a variety of situations.It is compatible with the conventional system, and uses many of the latter's tried and proved methods and procedures; thus avoiding any clash with the existing systems, and escaping re-inventing the wheel.Above all it is easy to understand, to explain, and to implement.As such it deserves serious consideration by the Muslim community as a whole, as well as by others interested in a transparent system of banking and a responsible form of financing.

9

Meeting the Financial Needs of Muslims: A Comprehensive Scheme

INTRODUCTION

Today, a fixed deposit in a bank is considered an investment because it earns a return, and a loan is considered an asset by the bank for the same reason. But they are both interest-earning loans. Whatever the purpose, money is available only as a loan at interest. The lenders (both the depositors and the bank) are not really concerned about whether the money was invested in a productive activity or consumed; neither is their return related to the result of any productive activity in which their capital was used. Even when the loan was intended for consumption, or the investment resulted in loss, the pre-determined interest must be paid. In contrast to this, in the Islamic tradition, the distinction between investment and lending had been clearly recognised and provided for, but unfortunately, in modern times, its importance does not seem to have been fully appreciated and acted upon.

The Qur'an recognises two different sets of purposes for which money is needed, and notes the two techniques used by capital-owners to cater for these needs. But the techniques must match the purposes. The need of entrepreneurs for capital is recognised, and in order to cater to this need investment of capital in productive employment is encouraged, but it must be done on a profit and loss sharing basis. Borrowing and lending (for productive or non-productive purposes) are also recognised as legitimate need and technique, but they should be done on the basis of mutual help — without loss or profit to either party. The need of entrepreneurs for short-term (couple of weeks to couple of months) advances and loans (to overcome cash flow difficulties, for unspecified purchases, miscellaneous expenses, bridging loans, import/export credit, letters of credit, etc, etc.) fall within the latter category. This is a very important type of financing need for all running enterprises, but especially critical for small businesses, which are the backbone of all developing economies, to which category most of the populous Muslim countries belong. Conventional banking deals with it very effectively by advancing short-term loans, at interest. But Islamic banking and finance as practised today has great difficulty in dealing with this need; in fact, it is one of its major shortcomings.

The Qur'an also recognises a set of circumstances in which one may find himself/herself — circumstances which warranted leniency or pure charity. A borrower, who borrowed with the intention of repaying the loan, hoping on better future circumstances, may find that hope remaining unrealised within the expected timeframe. He needs leniency until better times return. Others may find themselves in circumstances where they could not even promise to repay. They deserve charity. The Qur'an encourages leniency on the part of lenders, and recommends voluntary charity to those who posses the means.

By recognising the different types of needs and circumstances which naturally occur in any human society and dealing with them using suitably different techniques, the Qur'an seeks to prevent unpleasant consequences, rather than seeking to find solutions after the damage is done. In this essay we propose to explore the specifics of this comprehensive approach in the context of the present-day world.

The circumstances in which man lives changes in time and space. But there seem to be also some inherent characteristics that remain constant. It is necessary to distinguish the latter from the former, and to devise new methods and institutions that address the needs of these inherent characteristics when circumstances change. The inherent characteristics that remain constant are: 1) the need of capital-holders to earn an income using their capital; the need of traders, merchants and entrepreneurs for such capital; the latter's ability to use that capital to earn a profit doing their business; and hence their ability to reward the capital-providers for their contribution, 2) the need for loans (for business and personal use), and 3) the need for charity.

How do we address the above needs and characteristics in the circumstances of our day? Many of the verses of the Qur'an were revealed to address specific questions or situations that arose during the lifetime of the Prophet (peace be upon him) but the general guidance contained therein is independent of time and place. The messages should be understood in the context in which they were revealed but the resulting guidance is for all time and place. The Qur'an is no cookery book; it leaves the details to the humans, giving them enough latitude to devise their own solutions according the circumstances in which they happen to live in time and location. In our present-day circumstances, we need to realise that there are subdivisions within these major categories and that these need be dealt with appropriately.

Investment and Finance

This falls under the first category. To illustrate the position of the Qur'an in this case, let us take an example. Suppose a person at the time of the Prophet (peace be upon him) in Mecca had some capital. He could earn an income from it in one of two ways: by engaging in trade (buying and selling) or by lending at interest. The Qur'an said: do the former and avoid the latter, for they are not the same though some do argue so.

At this point, it is necessary to note that trade was the main occupation of the Meccans at the time. But the principles involved are applicable to all enterprises. Trade was practised either individually or in partnership. Partnership was on the basis of either *musharaka* or *mudaraba. Musharaka* is where both partners invested capital in a business (trade) and jointly ran the business, and shared the resulting profit or loss. A capital-holder who did not wish to engage himself directly in the business opted for *mudaraba,* where he teamed up with an entrepreneur (trader), provided him with all the necessary capital, and shared in the profit of the enterprise at a pre-agreed ratio (or absorbed the full loss if and when that occurred). In effect, a sleeping partnership. So a capital-owner who wished to earn an income using his capital but without directly engaging himself in an enterprise was given only one option: go into partnership with an entrepreneur on the basis of *mudaraba* (profit sharing and loss absorbing).

It is remarkable that the same choices exist even today: a) put your money in a partnership company (with you as the sleeping partner) or buy shares in a shareholder company; b) deposit in a bank or buy bonds and securities. In the former you share in the profit and loss, and in the latter you receive an interest income.

In the circumstances of the present-day world, investment and finance can be dealt with efficiently by recognising the subcategories within this main head and adopting appropriate techniques.

Shareholder Companies

The first need is easily addressed in the form of sleeping partners and shareholders in modern companies. Unfortunately, this type of modern company is rather rare in the Muslim world, though it is actually the modern version of the ancient practice of *mudaraba.* On the contrary, they play a major role in the economies of the developed countries. Large-scale industries and trading concerns, contributing to the real economy, were established using such investment and finance. What exist in the Muslim world are the one-person-owned-and-operated businesses and enterprises. These are, of course, necessary but they have their limitations. To advance, Muslims will have to follow the example of others. The idea of sleeping partner and shareholder companies should be promoted among Muslim financiers and entrepreneurs and such enterprises should be set up and professionally run in all sectors of the real economy. There is no choice, even though, in doing so, they will be only regaining their lost heritage of 1400 years ago.

Participatory Financing

Another complementary form of investment option, also based on the *mudaraba* principle, which caters to small capital-holders who would otherwise resort to bank deposits and/or bonds, is presented in Gafoor (1996). This can be operated by investment companies and investment banks, and provides the investors with a unit-trust/unit-share type of investment and will finance enterprises that are currently financed by bank loans. This is a new concept and a comprehensive project proposal is available at the author's website. This was developed as a *riba*-free alternative to fixed deposit accounts and medium- and long-term loans in order to address the concerns of Muslims. But the resulting product does not require the participants to be Muslims. It is simply a responsible form of financing, operating under conventional business laws. Hence it can be practised by anyone in any country. This should go a long way in preventing businesses and enterprises going bankrupt due to their inability to service bank loans. And thereby provide stability to all economies.

Mudaraba Partnerships

Pure *mudaraba* partnerships between known parties at the local level also should be promoted and popularised. This will help both the small capital-holders and budding entrepreneurs, and will contribute to the development of the local economy. This is another lost heritage that Muslims should revive at the earliest opportunity. It requires trust, honesty, integrity and professionalism. But advice and intermediation by independent accounting professionals and bookkeepers should be used to substantiate such trust by verifiable documentation.

Banking and loans

This falls under category of lending and borrowing. Here too, by recognising the subcategories within this head and adopting appropriate techniques, we can deal with the needs very efficiently.

COMMERCIAL (RETAIL) BANKING

The first thing that comes to mind when one thinks of a bank is bank loans. But the bulk of the work that goes on within a commercial bank (retail bank, deposit bank) is transfer of funds, from one account to another — within the same branch, between branches of the same bank, between different banks, between different countries, etc. Individuals use their demand deposit (current) accounts to pay their bills and receive their salaries/wages/pensions; businesses use current accounts to make and receive payments for the goods and services supplied; government and other entities use them to pay and receive their dues. This has become a basic necessity in practically all countries, a backbone of all modern economies and societies — the more advanced a country the more essential this service. It saves tremendous amounts of time and effort for individuals and organisations in travelling and carrying the necessary cash to and from *each* of their creditors and debtors. Thus its contribution to the national economy and its efficient running is immeasurable.

Yet, this important service is provided by the banks, in large measure, free of charge. Why free, and how is the operational costs of this services met by the bank? For, on the one hand, this transfer of funds from account to account without actual movement of funds makes possible what is called bank credit creation (that is, the act of lending more money than that available in the vaults of the bank). Therefore, the bank encourages the public to use its services to transfer funds by providing the service free. On the other hand, the costs of the operation is recovered from the borrowers as part of the interest. Thus, in conventional banking this essential service has become intertwined with *riba*, in the form of interest charged on bank loans and interest paid on bank deposits (which is the major source of funds for the loans). This is unacceptable to the Muslims, yet they too need the banking services (transfer of funds as well as loans) just like everyone else.

Islamic banking theory sought to resolve the problem by offering the loans completely free of interest (or grudgingly with some service charge) and meeting the costs of the services from earnings made elsewhere (profits made from buying and selling, and other forms of trade) using funds in the investment accounts.

This has led to several complications. A major problem is that this form of banking is not workable under conventional banking laws and therefore cannot be implemented, except in a few Muslim countries where special laws have been enacted. In all other countries, banking services and loans have been left to the conventional banks and Islamic banking has limited itself to financing, tacitly calling itself Islamic Finance. Thus a *riba*-free (retail) banking system is still to be designed and implemented.

The question of providing loans and all other banking services without involving in *riba* is addressed in Gafoor (1995). This uses a general model of the cost of borrowing and a courier-bank concept. A detailed discussion of this is available as an article at the author's website. A comprehensive project proposal is also available at the author's website.

The proposed banks will provide all banking services and are designed to operate under the conventional banking laws and regulations. They will accept demand deposits and ordinary savings deposits, and will use the funds in these deposits to provide short-term and (some) medium-term loans and advances. To be sure, this is only "half" of a modern bank, the other "half"— consisting of the fixed deposits and the long- and medium-term loans — being given over to the participatory financing companies and banks mentioned earlier. The need for and the advantages of such a division and separation are given in the project proposal referred to above.

Again, though the system was developed in order to address the *riba* concern of Muslims, the resulting product does not require the clientele to be Muslims. It has been shown that when the bank is constituted as envisaged here, the *riba* involvement becomes insignificant and its removal will be hardly noticed by the clients. It becomes simply a transparent form of banking that can be implemented in any country, without any changes to the present banking laws. This should be of special interest to Muslim communities living in non-Muslim countries.

SAVINGS AND LOANS AT COMMUNITY LEVEL

Historically, all banks have generally served governments, businesses, and the well-to do. For good collateral and guaranteed revenue to service the loan are essential considerations in granting a loan.

As time passed on, the banking business expanded into the newly developing middle class that had gradually acquired savings, properties and stable incomes. Their savings made them welcome, and their properties and stable (mainly wage) income made some of them eligible for small loans.

Legislation has been passed to safeguard the interests of both parties, though by now the banks have emerged as the stronger of the two. This is the case in the developed countries. In the developing countries, with their low levels of literacy and economic development, participation of the majority in the banking sector is very limited.

They have a long way to go. Yet, they too have need for credit, *albeit* in small measure. But the conventional banks are not designed to cater to them. Neither will the *riba*-free commercial bank we have presented above be able to act differently. One little appreciated reason is that the modern banks are not like their forerunners, the moneylenders of old who lent their own funds. The modern banks handle, borrow and lend other peoples' money and are managed by professional executives who are governed and constrained by legally binding rules and regulations. They have very little personal discretion.

That leaves a large section of the population in the developing countries, and many small communities in the developed countries, outside the banking system. This is where the private moneylenders come in.

They are still alive and well, and ready to pounce. They usually know their clients, live in the same locality, are very reasonable as to collateral, and are quite accommodating — no lengthy approval procedures either — provided the "risk premium" is set suitably high. It is difficult to beat them — they have survived many attempts — but a try is still worth it. Massive efforts at education and economic development at grassroots level are still necessary to keep the unfortunate out of their clutches.

In the meantime and beyond, there is a need for institutions between the type of commercial banks described above and the others to be described below. It is possible to set up savings and loans societies at the local community level to serve the needs of those not served by the commercial banks. They can be organised and run along the lines of the non-profit community lending discussed in the article, "*Interest, Usury, Riba and the Operational Costs of a Bank*", mentioned earlier. Community leaders can play a major role in this project, and religious leaders should promote and support it, because, being an alternative to private *riba*-based money lending, it is an effective preventive strategy.

Grameen Bank

There is still another section of the population — the un-bankable, who are either fully avoided by the moneylenders or mercilessly exploited. These are the ones living on the fringes of the society; their concern is daily subsistence. They are not beggars, neither are they unwilling or unable to work. They often have a useful locally marketable skill. They simply lack that very small capital which can enable them to own the tools and the small stock of raw materials necessary for their trade. In dollar terms, the capital they need is often less than the cost of a meal in New York or London.

The Grameen bank movement in Bangladesh has proved that such people are bankable, and that with very little help they can be put on their own two feet and enabled to regain their place in society with dignity. It has a twenty-five year successful history, and its methodology has been adopted in many countries around the world. So the tools are already there. What is necessary in any community is to examine whether the concerned community needs such a bank, and then to set about it. It needs dedicated workers, but the results can be very satisfying. See Gibbons and Sukor (1994) for its theory and practice.

Private Lending

Private person-to-person lending at interest is, and has always been, the primary focus of all religious and social prohibitions. But the need for such personal lending has always been there and will continue to be there for all times. Often it is mutual (borrower today, lender tomorrow, etc.) between known persons — friends, family, colleagues, etc. Sometimes, one may need to go outside this small circle, to wealthier persons who are in no need of the supplicant's help in money matters. It is in these cases that the lender tries to derive some benefit from the borrower's need, by charging interest. The ill effects of interest in this transaction can be removed only by personal refrain by the lender. This can be attained only by personal enlightenment or the fear of accounting on the Day of Judgement. The revulsion of society to such an act is also an effective restrainer. The work is cut out in this area for the religious leaders and teachers of morality.

The leniency and charity recommended in the Qur'an, when the borrower is in straitened circumstances, can be practised only in the case of private lending. For a person can exercise such personal judgement and authority only on his/her own possessions. All other cases considered above relate to people handling other people's property.

The fact that private money lenders were the forerunners of conventional banks, and that no banking institutions comparable to the modern ones existed in Muslim history, seem to have led today's Muslims to apply the *Shari'a* rules relating to private lending to bank lending as well. However, not recognising the difference between a private lender lending his own funds and a bank lending other peoples' money, has created much confusion, false expectations and some misuse by borrowers. Islamic scholars and banking institutions could spare a lot of trouble by recognising this difference, declaring it and advising the borrowers and the general public *beforehand* that no leniency or charity of this kind is to be expected from banking institutions.

Charity

The money-related needs discussed in the previous section (Banking and loans) concern a section of the population that is able and expects to repay their debts, as well as any expenses incurred in the process.

But there is always, in any society, another section of the population which simply cannot even expect to pay their debts. They are poor, unemployed or unemployable and have no or small and uncertain income; most often they will not be given any loans and therefore will not even dare to ask for one, small as it may be.

They are the ones the society as a whole, and the able in particular, are obliged to look after by means of charity. But this is the area of private individuals and not of banking institutions. Conventional banking wisely kept out of it; but Islamic banking, in its enthusiasm to solve all problems with one tool, tried to deal with it too and got itself into trouble. Like personal lending, charity too should be left to individuals. They only have full authority over their own funds to use it as they see fit.

Charity is the third category of needs, and here too we find subcategories that need be dealt with using different techniques.

Personal Charity

The third need is recognised and charity is recommended in several places in the Qur'an. (Here we are not talking of the obligatory alms-giving called *zakaat* but of optional charity, which is called *sadaqa*.)

This is a personal affair. Those who have extra funds may give any amount they wish to whomever they wish. This does exist and will continue to exist, but people must be continuously reminded of its necessity and merit. Personal charity should be encouraged at all levels. This is a task especially of social and religious workers at the personal and community levels.

Institutional Charity

However, in the present crowded world where fewer and fewer people know others at a personal level, there is also a need for organised charity. Therefore, charity organisations catering to specific needs, purposes, places or communities should be set up and run, perhaps on the lines of modern Western ones.

The Qur'an talks of two types among the poor, the needy and the beggar — *miskin* and *fakir*. The needy are generally not known to the others because they do not ask, but they may be in more straightened circumstances than the beggar. This is one area where an organised charity may be of great relevance on account of the (donor and receiver) anonymity it can provide. Social and religious workers along with like-minded professionals should give some thought to this.

CONCLUSION

In the above paragraphs, we saw the Qur'an guiding us to recognise the existence of three different needs in any society — investment and finance, banking and loans, and charity — and pointing to the proper techniques for dealing with each of them. The guidance is applicable to our present-day world too and the techniques are already available. We need not re-invent the wheel. We need to only recognise them and make use of them. It is hoped that our small exercise in the foregoing pages has enabled us to identify the necessary components of a comprehensive financial system for an Islamic economy in today's context, and has placed them in perspective.

10

Lending and Borrowing: An Overview

Lending and borrowing between humans has taken place since time immemorial. People borrowed and returned implements, animals, foodstuff, etc from their friends, neighbors and relations. They returned the same after use or in the case of foodstuff consumed and returned the equivalent when they came into possession of similar stuff. When money came into being people borrowed that too and returned. It was all on the basis of mutual help — the borrower today may be the lender tomorrow and vice versa. As time progressed professional moneylenders appeared on the scene, and they demanded a "fee" for the use of their money. This fee is now called interest, but till a few centuries ago it was called usury. In Islam, interest or usury, which in Arabic is called *riba*, is prohibited. Demanding, receiving, paying, witnessing, and anything connected with these activities are all equally prohibited. There is no controversy over this. Similar prohibitions exist also in the religious laws of Judaism and Christianity. Although other religions may not have written laws explicitly prohibiting usury, their followers do eschew the practice of usury.

LENDING AND BORROWING: THEN AND NOW

In earlier times, lending and borrowing was mainly between individuals, and what was meant by usury in these transactions was commonly known and understood. In money matters, any amount over and above the lent sum was defined as usury or *riba*. The ill consequences of usurious lending — the ruination of individuals and families — were witnessed at the local level and therefore the community held the practitioners in contempt. But the need for capital and loans existed and, in the absence of alternative solutions, the usurious lenders became an indispensable component of the society. They also exercised invisible power over their clients' resources. If the clients happened to be in authority, the power extended to other areas as well; the greater the client's authority the extensive the power of the lender.

Kings and nobles needed money to wage war or to live extravagantly. Moneylenders were happy to oblige, not only for the profit it brought them but also for the privileges and concessions they could extract from their royal clients. Mining concessions, special trading licenses, tax exemptions, lucrative contracts for public projects, land grants, and personal privileges such as royal titles and appointments to influential positions are just a few examples. These dealings were carried out discretely and the public was generally ignorant of them. But the citizens paid the price, one way or another.

The most important concession so extracted was the passing of the Usury Law. This law introduced an innocuous term called interest and usury was defined as high rate of interest. Usury was still prohibited, in deference to the Church, but "reasonable" interest was made permissible. What is reasonable and what is high was to be determined by the parliament! Now that interest is legal, kings may lose their thrones, soldiers may lose their lives, families may lose their livelihoods, but the country must pay its debts with interest. Moneylenders extracted their pound of flesh.

In recent times, presidents and ministers have replaced kings and nobles, and corporate and international financial institutions the individual moneylenders. The same game, only new names and wider settings. It is now global, the suffering is universal, and the statistics are in the public domain. Yet, hardly anyone dares to point the finger at the real culprit — usury, whatever the legal name it may assume. Neither are the real needs objectively looked at. Consequently, no meaningful alternatives are offered.

LENDER, BORROWER AND THE CHURCH: DIFFERENT GOALS

Governments, businesses and individuals need money for various purposes. The methods of catering for these needs must match the purpose for which the money was needed. A mismatch can lead to disastrous consequences, but this requires much thought and effort. Borrowing is an attractively easy solution, and this is what the moneylender would recommend for all situations, for it is the most profitable one from his point of view. When the borrower is impatient or desperate and the only game in town is the moneylender, borrowing from him is the only option and the consequences are inevitable.

To avoid disasters, then, we have to first study the different purposes for which money is needed and then devise methods most appropriate to each purpose. We have to provide more alternatives. The moneylender has only one purpose and concern: his profits and benefits. But the society has more and larger concerns, for it is its responsibility to cater for and protect all its members, individually and as a whole, those living now and those still to come. In this connection, it is well to remember that all the basic rules, methods, procedures and laws relating to banking and finance were either formulated by the moneylenders themselves or they had a hand in their design and/or execution.

When the usury law was proposed, it was argued that the merchants needed financing, they made profit using the borrowed funds and, therefore, they had the ability to pay the financiers a portion of that profit. Very reasonable. The trouble was, once the law was passed, it was applied to all situations — whether the borrowed funds brought about a profit or not. The Church had become too weak but still dogmatic, and the merchants and moneylenders too strong. The Church could not grasp the new need, brought about by the increased trade in Europe, and failed to provide an appropriate solution. Nor could it argue successfully to limit the application of the new law to trade financing only. Neither did it demand that the law should not be applied to non-profit-creating loans intended for basic consumption needs. It seems that the Church granted the moneylenders a blank cheque on a platter, by default — by its all or nothing insistence on a complete prohibition and by failing in this dogmatic stance.

ISLAMIC APPROACH: DIFFERENT CONSEQUENCES

In Islam, the situation was different. First, from the beginning of the history of Islam in the seventh century, the (large-scale) merchants' need for (additional) funds was fully recognized and provided for. There were two ways in which a merchant could finance his trade. One: two or more merchants could pool their funds together and conduct the business together and share the profit or loss according to their (financial) contribution. This was called *musharaka,* similar to the present-day partnership company. Two: a merchant could obtain his funds from one or more financiers and share the profit with his financiers in an agreed proportion. But he has full freedom in the conduct of his business, and any genuine financial loss must be borne entirely by the financiers. This was called *mudaraba*, similar to the present-day shareholder companies.

Consequently, while the *riba*-prohibition of Islam related to all lending and borrowing operations, it took special note of the financing needs of traders and businessmen as well as the investment and income generation needs of those who possessed extra funds. It does not mean that *riba* is acceptable in these cases; it is prohibited here too. But a *different and equitable* solution was already available in Arabia when the Qur'an was revealed; so it approved of it and went onto prohibit *riba* in all cases. Therefore, the merchant-need-based and return-on-investment-based arguments of Europe were not relevant or valid in the case of Islam and Muslim lands. It is necessary to recognise this fact. That is, the all-embracing usury-prohibition law of the Church and the *riba*-prohibition law of Islam are not exactly equivalent, despite the similarity of appearances.

Second, throughout the long history of Islam, Muslim caliphs, kings and nobles have, by and large, kept away from borrowing at interest. Even though many of them had their share of shortcomings — in common with their counterparts elsewhere — their belief in after-life and the strong words used by the Holy Book against the dealers in *riba* kept them away from it. The same applied to all would-be moneylenders as well. This saved the Muslim masses and the society from many of the ills experienced by other societies, even though this blessing goes generally unrecognised and unappreciated. Even under colonialism they have enjoyed this benefit. However, it would be naïve to believe that there existed absolutely no *riba*-based lending and borrowing, but it certainly was personal, local, small, isolated, discrete and unorganised.

Only in the second half of the twentieth century, especially after many countries became independent, established their own governments, and had to run the affairs of the country on their own, that they began to experience the claws of interest through the banking system. They needed the banking system because it provided the various services needed by the different sectors of modern society. But the moneylenders had developed it for their own benefit, based on the all-embracing usury law. It did not make the differentiation the Qur'an had made. Muslims had slumbered through the formative years of the modern world, and failed to build on the head start they had and shape a business and banking model to suit modern needs. Yet their desire to comply with the commandments of their Creator did not die. Their leaders and intellectuals have awoken to the demands of their constituents, experiments with Islamic banking have begun, but there is still a long road to travel.

LENDING WITH AND WITHOUT INTEREST

Before we travel further, let us state clearly what we mean by interest and *riba* and then note the difference between lending/borrowing with and without interest, usury or *riba*. Limiting ourselves to monetary dealings only, any benefit demanded or received by a lender in addition to the sum he lent is termed *riba*. This would, however, include both monetary and non-monetary benefits. Interest, on the other hand, would legally limit itself to monetary benefits only. It is useful not to forget this difference and its significance.

When a person lends without any benefits to himself, he is bound to assess the ability of the borrower to pay back the capital as well as to ensure that the capital is to be used for a purpose that he approves of. It is also a condition of such borrowing that the lender and the borrower are known to each other or that a reliable mutual friend/relative/acquaintance has introduced them. In such a situation, there is an unspoken moral/ethical responsibility (and a sense of shame and reluctance, otherwise) in asking, recommending or granting such a loan.

All these restraints are absent when the lending is done at interest. The lender assesses only the borrower's ability to (or the means to) repay the capital and the interest. A collateral is usually demanded, and by the very nature of interest — its dependence on time — the lender expects that he would eventually be able to acquire the collateral at a favourable price. Both the interest and the possibility of acquiring property at very low cost drive the moneylender to readily accede to request for loans, as well as to encourage such requests. Thus, when *riba* or interest enters the picture, the attitudes of both the lender and the borrower head in a direction directly opposed to the one prevalent in its absence. This *riba*-induced change of attitude is remarkable, as are the opposing characteristics of the two attitudes. One discourages debt, and the other encourages it. One restrains expenditure on morally or ethically unacceptable items and purposes; the other places no such restrains. One is open to social control, the other not. One limits both the size of borrowing and its frequency; the other encourages increase in both. One encourages short-term loans; the other thrives on long-term arrangements.

The last two are very interesting. For since more and larger loans would bring more profit to the lender he would try to acquire more funds. This eventually led the moneylender to borrow from others at low rates of interest and use the same funds to lend at higher rates, as if it were his own. The bank's credit-creation technique was also developed for the same end. Furthermore, long-term loans provide a stable and steady source of income to the moneylender. This and the availability of increased funds led the banks to widen their reach and, in recent times, to enter previously untapped areas such as housing finance and student loans.

NEED FOR MONEY

Let us now examine the need for money in some detail. To begin with, there are purposes that bring profit, and others that do not. Within these two categories there are necessary, unnecessary and harmful purposes. In the modern world one has to also make a difference between the needs of individuals, business organisations and governments. Let us take them in turn.

Extravaganza and Vanity

When the borrowing is for extravaganza or vanity, the borrowed fund produces no profit. Therefore, if the borrower is unable to repay the loan and interest from his other income sources, the interest would keep on mounting and the moneylender would eventually confiscate the collateral. All religions and sages throughout the ages have condemned extravaganza and vanity, and have advised against it. The Qur'an has specifically prohibited spending in vanity. Here the reference is to one's spending from his own resources, and the onus is on the individual. As such, if one engages in such spending using borrowed money, he is seeking his own doom. Yet, by making the *riba*-prohibition applicable to *both* the lender and the borrower, Islam seeks to protect people against their own selves. If there is no borrower there will be no lender; if there is no lender there will be no borrower. This closes all doors to doom. Thus there is no need to find any other solutions to the apparent need of the extravagant.

Housing and Education Loans

Housing and education are real needs, and therefore their financing deserves close attention. Building or purchasing a house is obviously a capital acquisition. So is education, though it does not seem that obvious. Capital acquisition has always been done using one's own savings or wealth. *It should continue to be so.* House-owning leads to individual and collective independence. In turn they add to national wealth and well-being. This fact is recognised by wise governments and they actively encourage private initiatives. Free education has produced wonderful results in the twentieth century.

However, the modern trend, especially in the developed world, is to have them financed by long-term bank loans. But unlike the loans for commercial purposes these loans produce no immediate profit to the borrower. Yet, to a moneylender a loan is a loan, and from his point of view these have some attractive advantages, including a secured regular return guaranteed for a long period. In many developed countries the fiscal laws encourage borrowing and discourage saving/investment/capital acquisition by taxing the interest/dividend received from the latter and granting tax exemption to the interest paid on loans. These laws enable the banks to price the products very attractively and encourage mortgages, but the subsequent experience of the borrower and the effect on the nation are different.

For example, a house-owner who bought it on mortgage remains a debtor for practically the rest of his working life and ends up paying several times the original price. On the other hand, if he fails to pay his instalments on time, he is kicked out as if he were only a tenant. A student forced to take a loan for his education leaves college/university with a certificate and a millstone round his neck. He may become a government administrator, business executive, politician or any other, but he is still a bonded man. And a bonded person cannot think or act independently. Anyone whose parents are too poor or unwilling to pay for his education, and himself refuses to be bonded, is denied higher education. It is a national tragedy. These characteristics of housing and education set them apart from other needs. Therefore these require special treatment.

War

Wars, in general, bring only death and destruction to people and property — never any profit. The winner and the loser are both losers in the end. If a war is fought by borrowing money at interest, win or lose the country will have to pay the debt with interest, and borrow again to rebuild. Whether the war was an offensive one or a defensive one, in the end, only the moneylenders celebrate — on both sides. Consequently, in history as well as in the present time moneylenders have played an important behind-the-scenes role in both beginning and prolonging wars. Only a total prohibition of *riba* on both the lenders and borrowers and its adherence at all levels, especially at the highest levels, could eliminate this factor in the war equation. Since everyone is a loser in a war, it is in everybody's interest to avoid any war; eliminating its financing by funds borrowed at interest will go a long way in this effort. Therefore we need not seek any other solution to this contingency.

Government Expenditure

Government expenditure consists of two types: capital and current. The funds for both are expected to come from taxation. So a government's ability to acquire capital goods — to buy equipment and material and to build roads, bridges, schools, hospitals, communication infrastructure, etc — are dependent on, and limited by, the tax revenue. However, the current expenditure, such as salaries of government officers, supplies and maintenance, has priority over capital expenditure. Often, like in the case of an individual, little is left over from the tax revenue for capital expenditure. Consequently, since all capital expenditure cannot be postponed indefinitely, there arises a budget deficit. A budget deficit is financed by printing money, borrowing, or both. Printing money leads to inflation, which is a tacit form of taxing the population. Borrowing increases national debt and interest payment. Credit creation by banks based on the new money (printed or borrowed) increases inflation even further.

Government bonds

Government bonds is one of the instruments used for borrowing money. Since capital expenditure on infrastructure does not produce any profit, borrowing at interest leads to additional current expenditure in the form of interest payments. This in turn requires curtailment of other current expenditure or further borrowing. Government bond is big business, it provides those who have money to spare with a great source of guaranteed return. But the public debt it creates keeps mounting. So does the interest on it. And the inflation generated by money-printing and credit creation add onto the interest rate and lead to further increase of the public debt.

Thus once a government begins to spend more than its tax income, or fails to tax sufficiently to cover its essential expenditures, it gets into a vicious cycle of borrowing to spend and spending to borrow. To tax sufficiently the country must produce enough, and taxes are always unpopular. Borrowing is the easy way out and the country finally ends up in the grip of the moneylenders — national and international — no matter which party or person runs the government. The debt is open and legally binding but the grip — do this or return the loan, do that or no more loans — is unseen, undeclared and least understood, and hence more hideous. It is a great mystery, though, that developed countries with very large national debts keep on prospering, while underdeveloped countries with much smaller debt burdens crumble under it. However, this is no place to probe into that mystery.

Treasury bills

It is a time-honoured practice of any individual to spend on his needs from what he has earned. If there is no more money left, he either curtails his spending or postpones it till he comes into sufficient funds. If his income is fixed and regular, such as that of a salaried employee, and he finds himself short of money at the end of the month, he must curtail his expenditure. Otherwise he will find himself at a worse position next month because his income is not going to increase next month, but the gap would have doubled. If, instead, he borrows to bridge the gap he will have to borrow the next month and the following month too — an increasing amount every subsequent month. Eventually he will have to borrow to eat, and pay the loan as soon as he receives the salary and then borrow again for the expenses of the next month. Suppose he borrows at interest, then he will be bankrupt very soon on account of the interest payments, even though he continued to work and earn. One could get out of this situation only by earning more or selling some property and paying off all the debts and begin to live within the income and spend only from already earned income. Or by severely curtailing his expenditure, save and pay off the debts, and by living within one's means from then on.

In the case of government current expenditure too, somewhere along the line, they threw away the time-honoured practice of spending from realised earning (collected tax) and began to borrow and spend, expecting to repay when the tax revenue came in. This committed them to an interest payment cycle. An instrument called the Treasury Bill was developed for this purpose. This, in effect, is a three-month loan, interest paid in advance. The funds are used to pay the current expenditure for the next three months and the loan is paid from the taxes collected at the end of the quarter. New treasury bills are issued every quarter, month or week. The cycle goes on. An elaborate set of financial tools and markets are built around this. So elaborate that no one remembers when, how or why it started in the first place, or how it keeps perpetuating itself. It is a given in Finance and Government, and theory and practice have canonised it. Moneylenders (private individuals, banks, financial institutions, insurance companies, pension funds, etc) thrive on it, and a whole army of professionals service it. But the general public pays for it, suffers the consequences, and is blissfully unaware of what is happening to it. Enlightening the public further on this point is not within the purview of this essay.

ISLAMIC BANKING CONFUSION

Islamic banking is rooted in the facts that *riba* is prohibited and trade is permitted, and the profit resulting from trade is permissible income. By extension, it was argued that interest, which is equated to *riba*, must be replaced by profit. To achieve this, lending transactions must be replaced by trading transactions. This simple concept is religiously applied to all situations. Where the difference was not clear, legal devices were adopted to dress it up as trade and profit. One may cheat himself, but can you fool God? He may be amused by our poor attempts, but does He approve of it? Whatever God does or does not, others are laughing at us. Sincerity is supposed to be the bedrock of our relationship with God. If we are sincere in our efforts to obey His commands, He will certainly show us the right way.

When the commands were issued 1400 years ago, they were directly understood in the context of the social and economic environment then prevailing, and their application was easily achieved. Today, the environment has changed and that makes the application seem difficult. But the solution is not through legal devices, but through our studying and understanding the new environment and sincerely seeking to apply the commands without any adulteration. Trade and profit have their place, but it is not appropriate for all occasions. We have to explore other options. If our intention is sincere, He will certainly guide us to the right solution.

SOLUTIONS

By looking at the needs of society, we can identify three different kinds of needs — investment and finance, banking and loans, and charity — and they each need be handled using a different technique. Moneylenders offered one solution for all three needs because it was to their advantage, but the society has to cater for larger concerns and therefore must offer more appropriate solutions. The Qur'an points out these different needs and presents us with different techniques to suit each need. It is for us to translate them into present-day "language" and set up appropriate institutions. Outlines of such institutions are presented in another essay (see Meeting the Financial Needs of Muslims: A comprehensive scheme). Other essays elsewhere expand on these outlines. Properly dealing with lending and borrowing transactions requires an understanding of the meaning of modern bank interests in relation to usury and *riba*. In an essay entitled, Interest, Usury, Riba, and the Operational Costs of a Bank, the history of interest, its relation to usury and *riba*, the origins of dogmas and theories that prohibit or justify its practice, and the meaning of interest in the modern setting of banking are explored. It also presents a general model of interest in which several scenarios — from person-to-person lending to modern commercial bank lending — become sub-models. This enables one to separate *riba* from the operational costs of a bank and thus to devise a *riba*-free system of commercial banking that is both viable and compatible with the conventional one.

Inflation has become a fact of life, it erodes the value of capital — depositors' savings, banks' loans, cash-in-hand. It has also been offered as an excuse for charging and accepting interest. But the main cause of modern-day inflation is not in the short-term supply-demand pull-push tensions, but in the long-term effects of increased money supply. The basic cause of this increase is the de-linking of the currency-gold relationship. It occurred gradually over time, but the final blow was dealt in 1971 when the US dollar was de-linked from gold and the promise to redeem every dollar for $1/35^{th}$ of an ounce of fine gold was withdrawn, reneging on the Bretton Woods Agreement of 1945. US dollar was allowed to float (meaning more dollars were printed without the constraint of the 35 dollars per ounce of gold ratio), and the other currencies, which were all linked to gold through the dollar, also started their free-floats, each in its own pace. Today, at 350 dollars an ounce, gold is ten times more costly. It is said that the price of gold has gone up; but the reality is that the currency has depreciated that much. Re-linking all currencies directly to gold, and strictly adhering to the agreed currency-gold ratio, is the proper solution to this problem. But a global agreement on this is not going to occur anytime soon. In the meantime savings, loans and cash-in-hand are going to lose their purchasing power. To neutralise the effect of inflation (due to currency depreciation) on capital, without recourse to increasing the interest rate, a new mechanism is necessary. Such a mechanism is presented in a book entitled, Commercial Banking in the presence of Inflation. This mechanism is applicable in person-to-person lending-borrowing transactions as well. It is straightforward and not difficult to implement.

11

Interest, Usury, Riba and the Operational Costs of a Bank

In conventional banking, the bank charges the borrowers interest on their loans and pays the depositors interest on their deposits. Both are called interest, though the former is always larger than the latter. Interest is also called usury. The Arabic word *riba* is often translated as both usury and interest. This begs an interesting question: are they all the same? If they are different, what does each mean? Muslims claim that charging interest on loans is prohibited. If so, how does a bank meet its operational costs? These questions bother many Muslims. In the following pages we attempt to find some answers.

LENDING AND BORROWING

Money lending is one of the oldest professions in the world. It had been, and it continues to be, practised everywhere in the world in various forms. Before the sophisticated arguments emerged, it was also universally despised. All the major religions and cultures explicitly or implicitly prohibited it. Documented and regulated bank lending is a recent (within the last two centuries) manifestation; it grew out of documented lending by private moneylenders at organised and individual levels. Much of this documented lending involved borrowing by businesses and governments for productive or public (often war) purposes. Recorded history is largely confined to this period, and the economic theory and arguments are mainly based on this history. It should also be noted that both the above — history and theory — largely concern and emanate from Europe. It is easily forgotten that money lending is a universal phenomenon and that much of it goes unrecorded and invisible in most parts of the world even today.

The invisible lending has two important characteristics: it is a private transaction between two persons, and the purpose of the borrowing is mainly unproductive (useful or not). The purposes include really urgent and necessary consumption needs (brought about by calamities, illnesses, unemployment due to unexpected causes or longstanding disability, etc.), avoidable consumption needs brought about by vanity and extravagance, and necessary and/or adventurous risky undertakings. The borrowers' expectation to repay is based on uncertain future good fortune, but the lenders generally take a dim view of that expectation. Some lenders are motivated by pity and trust, some ensure the safety of their capital by obtaining collateral, and others are positively sure of the borrowers inability to repay and redeem the collateral and look forward to confiscating it. These are the realities of life in many societies, given the nature of man and his environment. Most of the religious and cultural exhortations and prohibitions of money-lending relate to the experience of this reality.

Lending and borrowing also takes place at different levels. There is mutual lending and borrowing where colleagues, friends and relations help each other, usually for short periods, and it is a two-way traffic. There are the more fortunate ones helping out the less fortunate in their difficulties by lending, out of compassion; the latter repaying the loans with gratitude when good times return. There are the private moneylenders who lend money at interest, but discreetly. Others are professional lenders who lend their money openly at interest, whatever the circumstances of the borrower. And there is the modern bank that provides various other services in addition to money lending.

In studying and understanding the nature of lending and borrowing in today's context, it is necessary to keep in mind the different backgrounds against which economic theories, financial tools and religious/ethical guidelines evolved. Hopefully such an understanding will allow modern man's legitimate needs to be catered for more effectively and efficiently, without causing personal or social hardships and disasters.

ARGUMENTS FOR AND AGAINST INTEREST

In order to understand the arguments, it is pertinent to examine the purposes of lending and borrowing. When the purpose of borrowing is to invest in a venture and make a profit, it seems reasonable for the lender to ask for a share in the bounty. For practical convenience, the reward (interest) is fixed in advance; and for the safety of the capital a collateral is demanded. Therefore, charging of a reasonable interest, agreed upon by both sides, is seen by many to be perfectly logical. On the other hand, where the purpose is for consumption when one has for some reason or other lost his income, to demand a fixed return where no return is produced is often regarded as unfair. Especially so if the collateral demanded is the house in which the borrower lives or land from the future produce of which he expects to pay back the loan. Thus, depending on the assumptions made at the beginning, opposite conclusions can be arrived at. There is nothing wrong with that, but the problem begins when the resulting conclusion is applied universally.

All through the ages, moneylenders have used the first type of argument to justify their profession. Ironically it is their application of it to the second set of circumstances that created the ground for the second type of argument. Western economic theories are mainly based on the first type of argument. Religious and social objections to interest are often based on the second. At different times in history different circumstances and needs were predominant, and different groups wielded political, economic or religious power. Earlier, when the Church was in power and the misery of the poor and the unfortunate who borrowed for consumption was in focus, religious dogma and prohibition held sway. The needs of the traders and merchants for short-term credit, their use of it to earn a profit and hence their ability to reward the lenders, were practically ignored. But the need existed and the lenders operated underground. Since the fourteenth century, however, trade expanded and merchants became important in Europe. The big moneylenders catered for this group and prospered. Their voice grew strong, and their arguments came to be seen as reasonable. And they, in turn, ignored the existence and needs of those who needed money for non-productive purposes. Small moneylenders continued to service, the less well off, using the arguments of the former to justify the profession but charging much more heavily and thus causing more misery. Over time, the voice of the Church became weak, their arguments lost force, and the poor were forgotten.

But never did the different circumstances cease to exist; perhaps they would never, for they are rooted in human nature and the environment in which man is fated to live in. It is unfortunate that this reality is not taken into consideration in devising modern institutions. Banking operations are based on economic theories, and they apply the resulting system to all situations; while the social institutions have largely failed to take into consideration any situations other than those that deserved charity. The particular aims and objectives of the two groups (profit and greed *versus* pity and service) have also contributed to this state of affairs.

USURY AND INTEREST

Until a few hundred years ago any extra amount demanded by the lender in addition to his capital was called usury. Early European philosophers such as Plato (427-347 BC) and Aristotle (384-322 BC) condemned the practice of taking usury. Aristotle compared money to a barren hen which laid no eggs — a piece of money cannot beget another piece of money, he held. The Roman Empire, in its early stages, prohibited charging of usury. The Christian Church prohibited all usurious transactions. The famous incident in Jerusalem where Jesus Christ chased away the moneylenders from the Temple was kept alive in Church preaching. Though usury was practised all over the Christendom and elsewhere the Church was consistent and vehement in its condemnation of usury.

However, by the end of the thirteenth century several factors appeared which considerably undermined the influence of the orthodox Church. Eventually, the reformist group, led by Luther

(1483-1546) and Zwingli (1484-1531), agreed to the charging of interest on the plea of human weakness. According to Encyclopaedia Britannica,

"In Old English law, the taking of any compensation whatsoever was termed usury. With the expansion of trade in the 13th century, however, the demand for credit increased, necessitating a modification in the definition of the term. Usury then was applied to exorbitant or unconscionable interest rates. In 1545 England fixed a legal maximum interest; any amount in excess of the maximum was usury. The practice of setting a legal maximum on interest rates was later followed by most states of the United States and most other Western nations."

Thus, beginning in the mid-sixteenth century, the prohibition on usury (in the old sense) was legally removed in all Western countries. The environment in which it took place, as evidenced by the above quote, is noteworthy — expansion of trade and demand for credit. Borrowers were mainly the rich merchants, and they used the short-term credit for buying and selling goods. And the moneylenders were lending their own money and/or that of their wealthy clients. The borrowers knew how much they could make using a given amount of credit, and they paid the lenders a portion of this profit. This supplied the justification for demanding the extra amount.

But this justification for "limited interest" under a particular circumstance was, in the course of time, stretched out and applied in general. Support was forthcoming on other grounds too. For example, Sir Francis Bacon (1561-1626) advocated, "Since of necessity men must give and take money on loan and since they are so hard of heart that they will not lend it, otherwise there is nothing for it, but that interest should be permitted."

Now that the new "moderate" form of usury — interest — was legal and "moral", economic theories were developed with this limit and justification as the base. Theories found their way into textbooks, more theories were developed, and interest became an integral part of economic theory. In practice, the theory was applied universally whether the original conditions that justified the extra payment existed or not. Practice reinforced theory and, once incorporated into the foundations of economics, it is now difficult to think of any economic theory or activity without interest being an integral part of it.

In 1545, the "legal maximum interest" rate in England was fixed at ten percent per annum, but it did not remain fixed for long. It varied from time to time and from place to place, depending on the economic and political circumstances. Eventually, the concept of "maximum interest" ceased to exist, and usury as a word even went into disuse. Today, practically everywhere, charging and paying interest is legal, no matter how much, and it is acceptable both in theory and practice.

THEORIES OF INTEREST

Shaikh Mahmud Ahmed, in his interesting book, *Towards Interest-free Banking*, presents and disputes many of the theories of interest.

"... leaving out some notable exceptions, like Bohm Bawerk's Capital and Interest, significant parts of Keynes' General Theory and parts of Harrod, Hawtey and Kurihara, questioning the validity of interest, bulk of the effort of economics has been to justify it, yet not a single argument advanced in favour of this institution has a leg to stand on. All theories of interest evolved till the time of Bohm Bawerk, including those resting on productivity, abstinence and demand and supply concepts, were unanswerably repudiated by him. Yet economics continues whipping these dead horses, without evolving any persuasive answers to his criticism."

He takes some more theories, including time preference, liquidity preference, deposit mobilisation, scarcity of capital, and rationing capability of interest, and proves them untenable. We will take up here only two most popular ones.

Opportunity Cost of Money

If one possessed some capital and had it at hand in liquid form (i.e. readily available for use), he can make use of any opportunity that may come his way to make some profit, using that capital. If that capital was held up elsewhere, he loses the opportunity to make that profit. If someone else had borrowed that capital and could not make it available to the owner when the opportunity came his way, the borrower is expected to compensate the owner for the profit he would otherwise have made. This is the opportunity cost of money.

This argument is valid, if the owner of the capital is a person who is always on the look out for opportunities to make money — and prepared to take the risk of making or losing money on his adventures — and the only thing that would prevent him from doing so is the lack of liquid capital at his disposal. This applies to many businessmen. But moneylenders are generally not businessmen on the lookout for business opportunities that involve risk — they lend only when a good positive return is assured. Therefore this argument of opportunity cost does not apply to them.

As for the modern capital-holder, who has his capital deposited in a bank — whether in a fixed or ordinary savings account — his money is available to him anytime he wants. So, where is this lost opportunity, asks Sheikh Mahmud. Not only did he *not* lose any opportunity, his money was earning interest even when he had no opportunity!

Thus, once again, we have a theory developed assuming a specific set of circumstances and then applied to situations where the assumptions do not hold.

Time Value of Money

"Time is money" is the present-day business slogan. It is so in the case of loans from a moneylender too since interest on a loan is calculated in terms of time — the longer the loan remains unpaid the larger the interest to be paid. But how does the simple passage of time add value to capital? Suppose there is a shopkeeper. He has a stock of goods, and he sells them to anyone who asks for any item and pays for it. He uses the collection to purchase the replenishment as soon as possible because another customer may drop in anytime and ask for the same product. If he does not have it in stock when demanded he may lose the opportunity to make a profit. Since the demand may occur at anytime, the longer the absence of an item the greater the chance of a loss. Therefore a shopkeeper would rather hold stocks of goods than cash. Now, suppose an item is sold on credit. The money due is now not available to the shopkeeper to replenish his stock. Consequently he may be unable to serve some of his customers' demands and thereby lose income and profit. In this case the longer the credit remains unpaid the greater the loss the shopkeeper suffers. Here is a case for "time value of money", and if the shopkeeper has two prices for the sale of the same good — one for cash sale and another (greater one) for credit sale — there is some justification for it.

But when the argument is taken out of context and applied to money in general it loses its justification. A moneylender does not operate like a shopkeeper. He holds onto his money, earning no income and enjoying no "time value" nor "lost opportunity" until a borrower turns up promising to pay a positive interest. His money begins to enjoy "time value of money" the moment it leaves his hands — but not until then! "Time value of money" is not an intrinsic characteristic of money; it is dependent on the context.

BANK INTERESTS

It is interesting and instructive to note that all the above theories were developed in Europe before the invention of modern commercial banks. But it is also necessary to note the circumstances in which loan transactions of the merchants of Europe took place. Here the borrowers often had equal (or even greater) clout with their lenders. This is noteworthy. Furthermore, lenders lent their *own* money, and the transactions took place mainly in a *person-to-person* context. Borrowing and lending was mainly for the short term, and the parties were known to each other. The risk of default was minimal. So was the risk of failure of the project for which the money was being borrowed, for in general credit was requested only when a trading proposition was at hand, and the gains were roughly known. Paper currency had not yet been invented, and inflation, as currency depreciation, was still in the future.

Economic theories of interest evolved against this background. One consequence was that interest was a single entity — the extra amount paid by the borrower to the lender. All economic theories treated interest as a single entity. Though the environment has changed over time, and several new factors have come into play, even new formulations treat interest as a *single entity.*

With the invention of the modern commercial banks, as an intermediary between the depositor (the fund-provider) and the borrower, two types of interests emerged. One, the interest the bank paid its depositors, and two, the interest it charged the borrowers. The latter is always larger in magnitude than the former. To illustrate, keeping it simple, the depositors may be paid

5 percent while the borrowers are charged 15 percent, and the difference is the due of the bank. That due to the bank consists of components such as the real costs it incurs in providing the service, a risk premium against possible defaults, compensation for inflation and its own profits. Economic textbooks rarely refer to the existence of the two types of interests. Nor does any theory of interest treat it as consisting of several components.

When these facts are taken into consideration in devising a theory of interest, a way opens for greater understanding of the working of banking and economics, and provides transparent solutions to some knotty problems. We will return to this later in this essay.

THE ISLAMIC POSITION ON INTEREST

Today, a fixed deposit in a bank is considered an investment because it earns a return, and a loan is considered an asset by the bank for the same reason. But they are both interest-earning loans. Whatever the purpose, money is available only as a loan at interest. The lenders (both the depositors and the bank) are not really concerned about whether the money was invested in any productive activity or consumed; neither is their return related to the result of any productive activity in which their capital was used. Even when the loan was intended for consumption or the investment resulted in loss, the pre-determined interest must be paid. In contrast to this, in the Islamic tradition, the distinction between investment and lending had been clearly recognised and provided for, but unfortunately, in modern times, its importance does not seem to have been fully appreciated and acted upon.

The Qur'an recognised two different sets of purposes for which money was needed, and noted the two techniques used by capital-owners to cater to these needs. But the techniques must match the purposes. The need of entrepreneurs for capital was recognised, and in order to cater to this need investment of capital in productive employment was encouraged, but it must be done on a profit and loss sharing basis. Borrowing and lending (for productive or non-productive purposes) were also recognised as legitimate need and technique, but they should be done on the basis of mutual help — without loss or profit to either party.

Besides these two, the Qur'an also recognised another set of circumstances in which one may find himself/herself — circumstances which warranted leniency or pure charity. A borrower, who borrowed with the intention of repaying the loan, hoping on better future circumstances, may find that hope remaining unrealised within the expected timeframe. He needs leniency until better times return. Others may find themselves in circumstances where they could not even promise to repay. They deserve charity. The Qur'an encourages leniency on the part of lenders, and recommends voluntary charity to those who posses the means.

To illustrate the position of the Qur'an, let us take an example. Suppose a person at the time of the Prophet (peace be upon him) in Mecca had some capital. He could earn an income from it in one of two ways: by engaging in trade (buying and selling) or by lending at interest.

The Qur'an said: do the former and avoid the latter, for they are not the same though some do argue so. At this point, it is necessary to note that trade was the main occupation of the Meccans at the time. But the principles involved are applicable to all enterprises. Trade was practised either individually or in partnership. Partnership was on the basis of either *musharaka* or *mudaraba*. *Musharaka* is where both partners invested capital in a business (trade) and jointly ran the business, and shared the resulting profit or loss. A capital-holder who did not wish to engage himself directly in the business opted for *mudaraba*, where he teamed up with an entrepreneur (trader), provided him with all the necessary capital, and shared in the profit of the enterprise at a pre-agreed ratio (or absorbed the full loss if and when that occurred). In effect, a sleeping partnership. So a capital-owner who wished to earn an income using his capital but without directly engaging himself in an enterprise was given only one option: go into partnership with an entrepreneur on the basis of *mudaraba* (profit sharing and loss absorbing).

It is remarkable that the same choices exist even today: a) put your money in a partnership company (with you as the sleeping partner) or buy shares in a shareholder company; b) deposit in a bank or buy bonds and securities. In the former you share in the profit and loss, and in the latter you receive an interest income.

By recognising the different types of needs and circumstances which naturally occur in any human society and dealing with them using suitably different techniques, the Qur'an seeks to prevent unpleasant consequences, rather than seeking to find solutions after the damage is done.

RIBA

The Holy Book of Islam, the Qur'an, prohibits the demanding and receiving of interest in the following terms:

O ye who believe! Devour not usury, doubling and quadrupling (the sum lent). Observe your duty to Allah that you may be successful. (Qur'an, 3:130)

Again,

O ye who believe! Observe your duty to Allah, and give up what remaineth (due to you) from usury, if ye are (in truth) believers.

And, if you do not, then be warned of war (against you) from Allah and His Messenger. And, if ye repent, then ye have your principal (without interest). Wrong not, and you shall not be wronged. (Qur'an, 2:278-279)

The Holy Prophet (pbuh) has prohibited accepting of *riba*, paying of *riba*, and recording and witnessing it in the following terms:

Jabir (ra) said that Allah's Messenger (pbuh) cursed the acceptor of interest, its payer, and the one who records it; and the two witnesses; and he said: They are all equal. (Sahih Muslim, Hadith no.3881)

The prohibition of *riba* is clear from the above statements in the original sources. However, the Qur'an did not define it — the same way it had not defined gambling, theft or adultery. What was meant was assumed understood. And the Prophet (pbuh) did not explain every possible aspect of *riba.* Later on, *Ulama* have attempted to define the word *riba* based on the practices obtaining at the time of the Prophet (pbuh). But unanimity of opinion had not been reached on all aspects. Furthermore, since the reasons for the prohibition have not been given in either of the two original sources, it is impossible to give a new all encompassing definition of *riba* under any present or future conditions.

Yusuf Ali, in his Commentary of the Qur'an, says:

> *Usury is condemned and prohibited in the strongest possible terms. There can be no question about the prohibition. When we come to the definition of usury there is room for difference of opinion. Umar, according to Ibn Kathir, felt some difficulty in the matter, as the Prophet left this world before the details of the question were settled. This was one of the three questions on which he wished he had had more light from the Prophet, ... Our* Ulama, *ancient and modern, have worked out a great body of literature on usury, based mainly on economic conditions as they existed at the rise of Islam.*

The difficulty arises mainly because of the existence of two kinds of *riba.* One is called *riba al-Nasiah* and the other *riba al-Fadl.* The former relates to money-loans and credit transactions using money, and was well known and widely practised by the Arabs since long before the advent of Islam (hence it is also called *riba al-Jahiliyya*). *Riba al-Jahiliyya* is very similar to the present day interest on loans and credit sales. The core concept is a loan at a pre-agreed rate of interest. The variations include a grace period during which there is no interest (similar to today's credit cards), regular interest payments till the loan is fully paid (simple interest), and interest on interest and/or punitive additions beyond the pre-agreed period. That this practice was prohibited by the Qur'anic injunctions there is no disagreement.

Riba al-Fadl relates to commodity transactions and has been mentioned only in the prophetic traditions. Here *riba* may enter when barter-exchanging two different commodities, or due to differences in quality and/or quantity in the exchange of the same species. Umar's difficulty is said to be related to only some details of this *riba.* According to the recent (23 December 1999) historic judgment of the Supreme Court of Pakistan (section written by Justice Taqi Usmani):

> *These narrations [given earlier] of the statement of Sayyidina Umar,* Radi-Allahu anhu, *clearly reveal two points: firstly, that all his concerns in the issues of* riba *related to* riba al-Fadl *and not to* riba al-Nasiah *which was prohibited by the Holy Qur'an, and secondly, that even in the issue of* riba al-Fadl *he did not feel difficulty in many transactions which were clearly prohibited, however, he was doubtful only with regard to some transactions which were not expressly mentioned in the relevant* Hadith *or in any other saying of the Prophet,* Sall-Allahu Alayhi wa sallam.

In banking and finance, our concern is with money and money-loans. Therefore what is relevant to our discussion here is only *riba al-Nasiah,* and there has never been any doubts or differences of opinion as to what it meant. The Qur'an has prohibited the taking of this kind of *riba* in the strongest possible terms. Its authorised interpreter — the Prophet (pbuh) — has said that accepting, paying, recording and witnessing it are all equally prohibited. On the other hand, the Qur'an also says, "... then ye have your principal (without interest)," thus entitling the lender to the full return of his capital. Therefore, in order to comply with the prohibition fully and without a shade of doubt, and in order not to infringe on the right of the lender, a simple but comprehensive definition is popularly adopted: that in money matters, *any* addition to the principal sum is *riba*. This also accords with the definition of usury in other faiths.

THE COST OF BORROWING

According to the above definition the additional amount paid to the lender is *riba* and is prohibited in Islam. Does borrowing involve any other costs besides *riba*? If so, who is to pay these costs, and is it *riba*? We propose to answer both the questions by analogy, using a scene that is played out all over the world, every day — one equally true today as in the time of the Prophet (pbuh).

Suppose a man (or woman) asked a friend of his (or hers) to lend him (her) some money. The friend agreed. But the friend (now the lender) lived in a distant place. So our man (now the borrower) has to travel (say, by train) to the lender's place. It is necessary to pay the train fare and it is the traveller who must pay it. The traveller in this case is the borrower, and it is neither customary nor fair to ask the lender to lend money as well as to pay for the train; nor would one ask him to bring the money to the borrower. In fact the borrower has to travel again to return the loan. It is obvious that the borrower had to spend some money to obtain the loan, but that was not *riba* by any stretch of imagination because the lender did not ask for or receive any amount besides his principal. The borrower did spend some extra money to obtain the loan, but that was paid to the train operator, not to the lender. It is clear then that borrowers sometimes do incur expenses in obtaining loans and they are not necessarily *riba*.

On the other hand, if the borrower and the lender lived in the same city or village and met each other in the course of their daily activities, such as in the market, the mosque, the work-place, the bath-house, the eating house, etc., the question of travel and extra expense would not arise. Similarly, if they lived close by and the borrower could reach the lender by foot or by using his own transport such as a horse, camel, donkey, bicycle, or car, the travel cost would be nil or negligible and hence goes unmentioned. This is a person-to-person transaction in a small geographical area. This occurs everyday in numerous locations all over the world, and will continue to take place for all time to come. These were also the situations in the small towns of Mecca and Medina 1400 years ago. It was against this background that the Qur'anic prohibition of *riba* was promulgated. Even then, if, for example, the lender lived in Mecca and the borrower in Medina, the earlier scenario would have come into play and the lender would have had to incur extra expenses, which were not *riba*.

Let us now take our scenario a step further. Suppose our borrower, instead of going himself to meet the lender, employed someone else to do the job for him. He has to pay the same train fare and, in addition, remuneration to the one he employed. The latter is an intermediary — a courier of money — and he is paid his costs and remuneration by the borrower. Again this has nothing to do with the lender. Therefore it is obvious that these cannot be regarded as *riba.*

Now, let us go another step further. Suppose the law of the land requires that for any money transaction beyond a certain amount to be valid an attorney should attest it. The attorney has to be paid. Who will pay the bill? Naturally it is the borrower. Similarly, if the collateral for the loan has to be evaluated or its title checked, a payment has to be made. Again it will be on the shoulders of the borrower. It is of course, obvious that these are not going to the lender, and are therefore nothing to do with *riba.*

From the above we have come to the point that there are at least three different kinds of costs incurred by the borrower that are not *riba.* Now, suppose the borrower asks the courier to go to the attorney as well to get the transaction attested and also to have the title checked by a notary or attorney, and the courier agrees. This will make the borrowing process easier and quicker, and the borrower need to deal with only the courier; and he could pay all the costs to, and through, the courier. Since none of the above costs are *riba,* and since the lender did not demand any *riba* and the borrower did not pay any *riba* and therefore the courier did not carry any, there is no *riba* involved in the entire transaction. Yet it did cost the borrower some extra money to obtain the loan. The loan was *riba*-free, but not cost-free.

THE COURIER BECOMES A BANK

Now, suppose this courier does a good job, the word spreads, and more borrowers retain him to do similar jobs for them. He grows, he no longer runs the errands himself but employs others, and as time passes and the business grows, he employs his own attorney and notary so that their work can be done in-house. Now he is an institution. His couriers travel to many towns and cities, his institution is well known and trusted. On account of the economies of scale his per-transaction cost is reduced, and the borrowers find his charges cheaper compared to employing a private courier; and more convenient too.

As time passes he discovers that there are borrowers and lenders in every location, and even though a borrower in a particular location may be borrowing from a lender in a distant location, since money is the same wherever it comes from, the courier could give the amount to the borrower in a particular place from the money obtained from the same location. This would reduce his costs, transaction time, and transport risks. His services become even cheaper.

In course of time, borrowers and lenders discover that they need not deal with each other directly, nor even know each other, and that they could approach this courier institution for their respective needs. Borrowers go to the courier to obtain loans, and they can get from this courier more funds than they can from any specific lender known to them, and trusting and willing. They are no longer obliged to any particular friend-lender. The lenders now deposit their funds with the courier, for safety and with the knowledge that their money will possibly be used by others, including their friends, while they are not in need of it. The courier assures the safe and full return of their funds whenever needed. The courier no longer sends his staff to the lenders and borrowers but they come to him. A bank is born!

But this bank has two distinguishing features. One, its progenitor is a courier of money rather than the moneylender of old as is the case with the conventional bank. It started as a courier of money and remains a courier of money — it is no moneylender. Two, this bank is not involved in any *riba* transaction, and the fee it charges the borrower is not *riba*.

THE OPERATIONAL COSTS OF A BANK

Our arguments that the bank may charge a fee for its services, and that it is not *riba* have been based on common sense and general knowledge. However, it is good to know if there are any other supporting voices. Iran is one country where *riba* is prohibited and which has a comprehensive law on usury. Pakistan is another country where *riba* is prohibited. Siddiqi is the most referred-to author on interest-free banking. Therefore, let us examine the provisions in the Iranian, Pakistani and the Siddiqi models. All three models provide for loans with a service charge. Though the specific rules are not identical, the principle is the same. Therefore we are not alone in our conclusions.

Current Approaches

Let us now look at the existing relevant rules in the three models.

The Iranian model

The Iranian model provides for *Gharz-al hasaneh* whose definition, purpose and operation are given in Articles 15, 16 and 17 of Regulations relating to the granting of banking facilities:

Article 15

Gharz-al-hasaneh is a contract in which one (the lender) of the two parties relinquishes a specific portion of his possessions to the other party (the borrower) which the borrower is obliged to return to the lender in kind or, where not possible, its cash value.

Article 16

.... the banks ... shall set aside a part of their resources and provide Gharz-al-hasaneh for the following purposes:

(a) to provide equipment, tools and other necessary resources so as to enable the creation of employment, in the form of co-operative bodies, for those who lack the necessary means;

(b) to enable expansion in production, with particular emphasis on agricultural, livestock and industrial products;

(c) to meet essential needs.

Article 17

The expenses incurred in the provision of Gharz-al-hasaneh shall be, in each case, calculated on the basis of the directives issued by Bank Markazi Jomhouri Islami Iran and collected from the borrower.

The Pakistani model

In Pakistan, permissible modes of financing include:

Financing by lending:

(i) Loans not carrying any interest on which the banks may recover a service charge not exceeding the proportionate cost of the operation, excluding the cost of funds and provisions for bad and doubtful debts. The maximum service charge permissible to each bank will be determined by the State Bank from time to time.

(ii) Qard-e-hasana loans given on compassionate grounds free of any interest or service charge and repayable if and when the borrower is able to pay.

The Siddiqi model

Siddiqi has suggested that 50 percent of the funds in the "loan" (i.e. current and savings) accounts be used to grant short-term loans. A fee is to be charged for providing these loans:

An appropriate way of levying such a fee would be to require prospective borrowers to pay a fixed amount on each application, regardless of the amount required, the term of the loan or whether the application is granted or rejected. Then the applicants to whom a loan is granted may be required to pay an additional prescribed fee for all the entries made in the bank's registers. The criterion for fixing the fees must be the actual expenditure, which the banks have incurred in scrutinizing the applications and making decisions, and in maintaining accounts until loans are repaid. These fees should not be made a source of income for the banks, but regarded solely as a means of maintaining and managing the interest-free loans.

It is clear from the above that all three models agree on the need for having cash loans as one mode of interest-free financing, and that this service should be paid for by the borrower.

Another Approach

A more comprehensive and direct approach has been employed in Gafoor (1995). Here, the usual interest charged by the conventional banks has been taken and split into six distinct components, the purpose of each component is determined, each is examined to see if it contained any element of the prohibited *riba,* and then a formula is developed with respect to each component in order to compute its value. It has been shown that, of the six components only one is *riba* and all the other five belong to the category of costs and remuneration. On account of this the usual interest charged by conventional banks is called the cost of borrowing. Its six components are: interest paid to the depositor, cost of overheads, cost of services, a risk premium, profit (or remuneration to the bank), and compensation for the value loss of capital due to inflation. The reader is best referred to the original for details, and for how this model of the cost of borrowing is used for many analyses. For the present we will examine the components of the model briefly with the above courier-bank in mind.

Interest

In normal commercial banking practice, the funds used for lending are mainly derived through the savings deposits. The bank pays a certain percentage as interest to the depositors and recovers it from the borrowers when it lends. This interest is the first component in our model of the cost of borrowing. Of all the six components of the cost of borrowing, only this component is received by (or paid to) the depositor, in addition to his capital (deposit). In the general case, this component is positive and is dependent on the interest rates the bank pays its depositors. In the case of a Muslim community, this component is *riba* because any addition to the capital has been defined to be *riba*. Therefore, a Muslim depositor will not demand or accept this component. Hence, this component will be zero in our version of the model. The implication is that the bank will not collect this component from the borrowers in order to pass it onto the depositors.

Services cost

This is the cost involved in processing the application. This may include legal and other charges paid by the bank for services such as the evaluation of the collateral and checking its title, preparation of loan documents, postage, etc. This cost is specific to the concerned loan, and therefore need be borne entirely by the concerned applicant. This is an actual cost incurred by the bank, and is independent of the size of the loan (except, perhaps charges such as stamp duty) or the period of repayment. Therefore there should be no objection to it on grounds of any resemblance to interest (or *riba*).

Overheads cost

This goes to the maintenance of the bank, including staff salaries and office expenses. This is unavoidable, but it is also difficult to determine the exact amount used up by any given loan. Therefore a method has to be found to charge an average rate. What has been suggested is to compute the bank's average total running expenses per annum (p.a.) and divide it by the average total assets of the bank p.a. to obtain a per dollar p.a. cost. Then this rate will be used to compute the overheads cost due from the borrower. For example, if this rate works out to be 1.5 cents per dollar per annum, a loan of 5000 dollars paid over two years will entail an overheads component of 0.015*5000*2 = 150 dollars. It may sound like the usual interest rate, but we know why and how we arrived at it, and we know that it is not *riba* but a cost necessary to maintain the bank whose services the community, the depositors and the borrowers need. For a more elaborate explanation see Gafoor (1995).

Profit

The proposed bank is a commercial concern providing a service — carrying money from the lender to the borrower and back, keeping it safe, receiving from and paying to both the depositors and the borrowers, keeping accounts, buying and selling services from third parties (e.g. hiring a lawyer for title checking), etc. The costs of these are taken into account in the two preceding components. But, how about remuneration to the courier-bank for arranging these services? Should it do it without any benefit to itself, investing its own money, time, expertise and effort? Is such remuneration *riba*? Obviously not. However, it may give rise to concerns depending on how it is computed. If it is computed as a percentage of the loan amount there may be some room for doubts. But, here it is proposed to be computed as a percentage of the costs of the services the bank provides (i.e. the services and overheads components, seen above). Thus it is a legitimate remuneration or profit.

Risk premium

The proposed approach has already introduced a radical change in the perception of a bank— from a moneylender to a money-courier. Now it introduces another radical innovation in guaranteeing the capital of the depositor by ensuring the full repayment of the loans — now the onus is on the borrower and not on the bank. Instead of the banks joining a deposit insurance scheme, here the borrowers join in a loan default insurance scheme. This is a collective insurance scheme designed to compensate the bank in case of defaults, and to discourage delays and encourage early settlements. The premium is proportional to the size of the loan. But good behaviour increases the credit rating of an individual borrower and decreases his premium rate, and *vice versa*. The scheme is to be run by a third party, and the unused part of the premium is to be returned to the borrowers *pro-rata*.

Compensation for inflation

Inflation comes into this model in two different forms: the general inflation affecting the costs (second and third components), and currency depreciation affecting the value of capital. The first is unavoidable, inseparable and legitimate. Therefore we need not do anything about it. But the second is value erosion of capital; in fact, an illegal and surreptitious tax on all cash holdings. In fairness to the capital holders this loss must be compensated, so that their capital is not eroded due to no fault of their own. This component is the amount (in terms of currency) that needs to be paid to the capital holders (depositors) in order to restore their capital to its original value. For the rationale and computational details please see Gafoor (1999). (This model provides for the reverse action too, in case of currency appreciation.)

A GENERAL THEORY OF INTEREST

The alternative approach presented above is a general model of the cost of borrowing (CoB). In fact, it is a general theory of interest. Here the interest charged by a bank is split into several components, which are all factors every bank takes into consideration in determining its interest rate. However, bringing them all into a comprehensive model is new. In addition, each component is estimated separately and independently of others. This too is new and innovative. In the process, each component of the bank interest is shown to be originating from different considerations. In economic parlance, each component is influenced by a different set of economic variables. In turn, each component influences another set of economic variables. This should lead to more meaningful economic and econometric modelling and to a deeper understanding of the working of interest in the economy. In this essay, however, we will limit ourselves to a few applications of this theory to situations that concern us. For the sake of simplicity we will assume zero inflation in what follows. The complications of inflation are dealt with in Gafoor (1999).

Person-to-person Lending

Person-to-person lending and borrowing is something that takes place everywhere in the world, millions of times every day, from time immemorial to the present. Its essential components are: 1) the lender and the borrower are generally known to each other (or are introduced and guaranteed by mutually trusted acquaintances), meet in person, the transaction is hand-to-hand, and any writing and witnessing is done without cost — hence the second component of the model is zero; 2) since the lender and borrower are generally from the same locality or live in close proximity the travel cost to the borrower is insignificant, and since such transactions are also infrequent there is no cost (such as employing an assistant on account of the large volume of transactions) to the lender — hence the third component is also zero; 3) since the second and third components are zero, the fourth component (profit) which is a percentage of the other two is automatically zero; 4) the lender lends only if he is satisfied that the borrower is able to and will repay the loan in full and in time (he is free to deny a loan if he is not sure) — hence the risk premium (fifth component) is also zero; 5) in the absence of inflation, the sixth component is also zero.

Therefore, in a person-to-person lending/borrowing as described above, all components except the first are zero. Hence, in such a transaction, if the borrower has to make any extra payment to the lender it can only be due to the first component being positive, and that is *riba*. This was the case dealt with in the original injunctions, and this had also been the case in all transactions till the advent of the banks, and even today in millions of transactions outside the banking system. Thus, in the case of a person-to-person lending, the cost of borrowing (CoB), interest, usury and *riba* all turn out to be the same and equal. The model helps us to see this clearly and directly.

"Low interest" lending

We will now use our model to examine two types of "low-interest" lending schemes to see if they involve *riba*.

Educational loans

Suppose, some philanthropist sets aside a certain sum to help needy students. He could proceed in several ways. Let us take three scenarios. 1) He could hand out a certain amount to every needy student who applies until his money is used up. This is an outright donation and a one-time operation. After that he would not be able to help any more students unless he brings in new funds. 2) He could do as before, but require the students to pay back when they are employed. From the money so recovered he can help more students. This is a loan scheme and a continuing operation. But this would require the employment of a person to disburse the funds, keep records, receive repayments and keep accounts, etc. He needs to be paid and his office expenses met. We are talking here about several years. Unless the philanthropist provides fresh funds every year for the upkeep of the office, the original funds would be used for this purpose as well and, eventually, the operation will shut down. 3) He could proceed as 2) above but require the students to pay for the upkeep of the office as well, in addition to repaying the full amount of the loan. This might be called a "low interest" loan scheme. Since the original fund will remain intact, this is a sustainable continuing operation.

What is common to all the above scenarios is that the philanthropist did not ask or receive any monetary benefit for himself. In Islamic parlance, no *riba* was involved in any of these operations. However, of the three schemes, only the third is sustainable. In terms of the above theory, in the absence of inflation, all components of the CoB except the overheads component are zero. Accordingly, though the cost of borrowing is positive, it is not *riba.* In customary language, however, it is called interest, *albeit* low.

Unfortunately, Muslims take the word interest literally and equate it to *riba.* In the process they lose out on the benefits of a useful and sustainable system devised by a sympathetic and well-meaning philanthropist. This is not being true to the faith or is the strict practice of its rules, but refusing a helping hand due to ignorance. This is not to say that the ordinary Muslim who wishes to be faithful to his creed is wrong, but that he had not been given the knowledge about what is meant by *riba* and what is meant by interest as understood today, and that there is a difference. Showing this difference, however, is not possible if interest is treated as one single item. Neither the bankers, nor the economists, nor the Islamic scholars have been of help here. Hence the need and relevance of the above model which sees present-day interest as consisting of several components, only one of which is the prohibited *riba.*

The theory should help explain to the believing Muslims that all that is called interest is not necessarily *riba* and provide them with a tool to examine any interest to see if it contained *riba* or not. Its practical application will enable to them to set up sustainable endowments for useful purposes. Such an understanding and use of the tool will also help them to examine and benefit from several so-called low-interest loan schemes (which many currently reject out of hand), without any qualms about getting involved in *riba* dealings.

Housing loans

One such low-interest scheme which many good Muslims reject and deny themselves an important basic necessity is the housing loans organized by some well-meaning governments. Essentially they act exactly like the philanthropist in the above example, and use the third option in order to have a sustainable and continuing system. However, on account of the large size of the loans, its long term nature (20 to 30 years to recover the capital in monthly installments) and the geographical spread of the coverage, the Government will prefer to make use of the well established infrastructure of the banking system. It is cheaper, more convenient and reliable than setting up one for this single purpose. The Government simply deposits a certain amount of money with a bank, gives the specifications as to who qualifies etc, and leaves the rest to the bank. The Government does not require any interest on its deposit but the bank must make sure that the original capital remains in tact (and is used again and again to give fresh loans) by ensuring proper loan recovery. The bank may also recover from the borrowers all its own processing costs. This arrangement brings about the low-interest on the loan and ensures the continuation of the scheme.

The fact that it is called interest and, more importantly, that it is (seemingly) coming from a bank frightens off Muslims. If we apply our model to this scheme we will see that no *riba* is involved in this loan, since the real lender (the government) does not demand or receive any amount in addition to its capital. What is recovered from the borrower is the operational costs of the bank. In this case too, both the CoB and "interest" are positive and equal but they are not *riba.*

Non-profit Community Lending

In addition to the individual person-to-person lending and the philanthropic long-term lending by individuals or Governments as seen above, one could also think of the members of a small community helping each other in a collective manner. Suppose the members of a small community decide to set up a savings and loans society. Members deposit their savings with the society in order that other members who need some loan for a short period could be helped from this fund. This is a mutual fund; a depositor at one time may become a borrower at another time and vice versa. Members are free to withdraw some or all of their deposits if and when they want (or at short notice). No depositor demands or receives any amount in addition to his/her capital. Assume that this society is a non-profit organization, and that the members are known to each other and trustworthy and therefore there is no room for default on loans. Assume also no inflation. In this case all the components of the cost of borrowing, except the services and overheads costs, will be zero. Even if the operations of the society are run by volunteers, using some free office space, there may still be some costs for stamps, stationery, transport, communication and so on. Who pays these costs? Cannot ask the depositors for it! They already do a favour by making their savings available to the borrowers free of interest. Naturally the borrowers have to pay the costs. Here too we see that even where the capital is cost-free the loan is not. It is *riba*-free but not cost-free. Again, the model enables us to see the difference clearly. In this case too the CoB and what some might prefer to call "interest" are positive and equal, but they are not *riba*. This should help small communities to set up their own savings and loans societies and serve their members in their needs, with clear conscience about not getting involved in *riba*.

Bank Interests

As we mentioned earlier in this essay, banks pay the depositors interest on their deposits and charge the borrowers interest on their loans. Both are called interest, but they are not equal — the latter is always greater than the former. Let us examine them in turn more closely, using our model of the cost of borrowing and the definition of *riba*. Again, inflation is assumed zero.

Deposit interest

In the first case, depositors are the lenders to the bank and the bank is the borrower. The depositors receive an extra amount from the bank as interest on their capital. According to our definition of *riba*, this is *riba*. Let us call it the deposit interest. This is what the bank pays the depositors to get their funds. Therefore, from the bank's point of view it is the cost of funds or its CoB. According to our definition of *riba*, this too is *riba*. Hence, in this case, deposit interest, bank's CoB and *riba* are all the same and equal. As far as Muslims are concerned this falls within the category of the prohibited, and there is no doubt about it.

Loan interest

In the second case, the bank is the lender and its client is the borrower. The bank demands and receives interest from the borrower. Call it the bank's loan interest. But this "interest" consists of the deposit interest the bank pays the depositors (whose money it lends to its clients), and other components (which are costs incurred by the bank, and the remuneration for its services). The bank collects both the deposit interest and the other components from its borrowers, passes on the former to the depositors, and keeps the rest for itself. While the deposit interest is *riba* the other components have been shown to be no *riba*. According to our model, then, the bank's loan interest and the borrower's CoB are both the same and equal. Both of them *contain* the prohibited *riba*, but not all of either is *riba*. Consequently, when deposit interest is zero both of them are free of *riba*, and neither the bank nor the borrower is involved in any *riba* dealing.

Present-day banks' loan interest might also contain, besides the six components discussed above, an additional component arbitrarily introduced by the bank which will then qualify as *riba*. It may even turn out to be directly proportional to the size and period of the loan. If present this component too should be eliminated to make the transaction truly *riba*-free.

CONCLUSIONS

In the foregoing paragraphs we began with explaining the meanings of interest, usury and *riba*. We traced their historical development, examined the arguments for and against their practice, and worked out their relationship to each other. And, we examined the Western and Islamic views on interest, and the consequences of the separate attitudes. We also looked at a new theory of interest that helped us to understand the meaning of bank interests in some detail. This in turn helped us to realise that while bank's deposit interest was the same as *riba*, its loan interest consisted of both *riba* and the operational costs of the bank. This enabled us to devise viable lending systems without becoming involved in *riba*.

A note of caution is necessary at this point. The conclusions about deposit interest and loan interest should not be interpreted to mean that if the bank does not pay any interest to the depositors its loan interest becomes *riba*-free and therefore automatically acceptable, whatever its size. No, for it is subject to an important condition. How each component of the cost of borrowing came into existence was fully explained when formulating the theory and therefore its implementation is based on the assumption that each component will be separately estimated as explained earlier, and that this will be done transparently. That is, the data necessary for that estimation is routinely collected, the estimated coefficients (this includes the bank's profit/remuneration rate) are made available for public scrutiny (and monitored by the Central Bank), and that each customer is routinely given the value of each component making up his total CoB. Unless this transparency condition is appreciated and strictly adhered to the theory is vulnerable to misunderstanding and misuse.

The transparency condition ensures that the profit rate is known, and any hidden *riba* component is revealed. If a *riba* component is present it will violate the *riba*-free assumption and will be illegal and morally reprehensible. If the profit rate turns out very high (as will be the case if this theory is applied to estimate it using present-day banking data) market forces will step in to correct it, provided there are several independent banks competing in a genuinely free market environment, to the benefit of the borrowers. Thus eliminating another two important aspects of *riba* – exploitation and injustice. The benefits will trickle down to the society through reduced costs, prices and, eventually, help curb inflation. Reduced cost of borrowing will also help on-the-brink enterprises to stand on firmer feet.

Bibliography

Abdeen, A.M. and Shook, D.N., 1984. *The Saudi Financial System*, J. Wiley and Sons, Chichester.

Ali, M. 1982. *Islamic Banks and Strategies of Economic Cooperation*, New Century Publishers, London.

Choudhury, Masul Alam, 1986. *Contributions to Islamic Economic Theory: A Study in Social Economics*, St Martin Press, New York.

DiVanna, Joseph, A., *Understanding Islamic Banking: The Value Proposition that Transcends Cultures*, Cambridge: Leonardo and Francis Press, 2006.

El-Asker, A.A.F., 1987. *The Islamic Business Enterprise*, Croom Helm, London.

Homoud, S.H., 1985. *Islamic Banking*, Arabian Information, London.

Iqbal, Zubair and Mirakhor, Abbas, 1987. *Islamic Banking, International Monetary Fund*, Occasional Paper 49, Washington D.C.

Irshad, S.A., 1964. *Interest-Free Banking*, Orient Press of Pakistan, Karachi.

Khan, W.M., 1985. *Towards an Interest-Free Islamic Economic System*, The Islamic Foundation, Leicester.

Mayfield, James, 1971, *'The Rural Politics of Nasser's Egypt'*, University of Texas Press.

Naqvi, S.N.H., 1981. *Ethics and Economics: An Islamic Synthesis*, The Islamic Foundation, Leicester.

Partadireja, Ace, 1974. *'Rural credit: the Ijon system'*, Bulletin of Indonesian Economic Studies.

Qureshi, Anwar Iqbal, 1946. *Islam and the Theory of Interest*, Lahore.

Scharf, T.W., 1983. *Arab and Islamic Banks*, OECD, Paris.

Udovitch, Abraham L., 1970. *Partnership and Profit in Medieval Islam*, Princeton University Press, Princeton, N.J..

Index

□□□